ASTROLOGY IS REAL

ASTROLOGY
IS
REAL

Revelations from My Life as an Oracle

Rob Brezsny

Televisionary Publishing

Astrology Is Real: Revelations from My Life as an Oracle
Copyright © 2023 by Rob Brezsny

Televisionary Publishing
PO Box 4400
San Rafael, CA 94913
Newsletter.FreeWillAstrology.com
FreeWillAstrology.com
fluxmojo@gmail.com

Library of Congress Control Number 2023911264
ISBN 978-0-9723452-0-0
ISBN 978-0-9723452-1-7 (ebook)

Cover art by Elena Ray
Book design by Paul Hersh and Rob Brezsny

Contents

Introduction   xi

Chapter 1

Your Wounds Healed   16
Origin Story   17
Divinations for You #1   33
Astrology Is a Mythopoetic Language   39
Cultivating Holy Desires   44
I Don't Want You to Be Like Me   46
Accidental Bonanza   47
Go with What Flow?   51
Poet in Disguise   52
You Need Magic   60

Chapter 2

Thanks for Making My Life Better   62
I² <–> Thou   63
Love Cues and Clues: Taking a Love Inventory   67
Slam Book   68
Divinatory Homework #101   71
The Astrologer's Curse   73
My Prayers for You   77
Oracular Homework #102   78
Love Cues and Clues: 'I'll Cavern You'   80

Chapter 3

Love Cues and Clues: Truth Loves Beauty   82
The Art of Prediction   83
Theory of Divination   88
Love Cues and Clues: You Have Always Been in Love   91
Astrology for the Soul   92
Oracles for You #2   99
Loving The Catalytic Abyss   115

Oracular Homework #103   116

Chapter 4

The Spiritual Power of Pleasure   118
To Honor the Dazzling Muses   119
Where Does Help Come From?   125
You Are a Prophet   127
Divinatory Homework #104   130
Syndication   131
Up All Night   135
Enchantments for You #3   138

Chapter 5

Be Alert for the Subtle Miracles   140
Feed Your Imagination with Beauty   142
Taking a Break from the Collective's Monkey Mind   144
Auguries for You #4   145
Fear Versus Intuition   151
Relationship with Intuition   155
Disappear Fear   157
Arguments with Goddess   158
Telepathics Anonymous   159
How to Not Be a Know-It-All   161

Chapter 6

Sacred Trails   166
The Surprising Truth   167
What Are Your Liberating Thoughts?   169
Thanks to My Adversaries!   171
Reader Mail   175
Oracular Homework #105   181
Redemption Story   183
The Greatest Gift You Can Give Yourself   185
Love Cues and Clues: Write a Love Letter to Yourself   186

Chapter 7

Be Tastefully Gonzo   188

When I Do Personal Horoscope Readings 189
Divinatory Homework #106 192
Losing What's No Good for You 193
Training Our Imaginations to Do Magic 194
Tips to Promote Self-Management 198
Divinations for You #5 199

Chapter 8

Interpret All Omens Favorably 208
The Blessings of Saturn 209
Impossible Dreams 213
Pluto Demoted? 216
Revelatory Homework #107 219
Mercury Retrograde 220
Love Cues and Clues: How to Be with Each Sign 226
Mars within Us 228
Oracles for You #6 230

Chapter 9

Wishes for You 238
The Horoscope-Writing Process 239
Effects of the Moon on Earth 243
Lunar Eclipse 245
Uranus 246
Divinatory Homework #108 248
Do It Now 249
As Above, So Below 250

Chapter 10

Utter Pragmatism 252
What Nourishes You Emotionally and Spiritually? 253
Love Everything about Life? 254
Love Cues and Clues: Golden Repair 255
Oracular Homework #109 256
Love Cues and Clues: So Much to Love 258
Unfuck the World 262

Love Cues and Clues: Clues to Your Loved Ones' Mysteries   263
Fortunes for You #7   264

Chapter 11

Holy Attention   280
Sublime Feminine Intelligence   281
Intimacy with All Things   283
Enlightenment and Individuation   286
It's a Free Country   290
Empathy Is a Superpower   291
Emotional Intelligence   292
Real Compassion   293
Can We Love a Nazi?   294
Divinatory Homework #111   295

Chapter 12

Love Cues and Clues: Deciphering Love   298
Loving Our Bodies   299
Spells for You #8   301
Your Primal Longings   307
Oracular Homework #112   308

Chapter 13

Dear Beloved Ego   312
Do These Titles Suit You?   314
Decrease Your Connection   315
Salutations   317
You Have Educated Me   318
Oracles for You #9   319

Chapter 14

Retool Your Amazement   332
Astrology Is a Gnostic Art   333
Love Cues and Clues: The Guardian Angel of Your Relationship   340
Transparency   341
A Reader Protests   345
Why Do People Believe in God but Not in Fairies?   347

True Skepticism   352

The 80 Percent Rule   355

You Must Earn Your Right to Criticize and Debunk   358

Carl Sagan and Me and Ayahuasca   360

Fairy Tales and Richard Dawkins   361

Supernatural Communion and the Scientific Method   362

Dreamwork as a Foundation for Activism   364

Portents for You #10   366

Chapter 15

Is Love Always Courteous?   376

Three Percent Mastery   377

The Perfect Sometimes Undermines the Good   379

Perfectionism Sux   384

Maestro of the Obvious   385

Love Our Imperfections   386

The Art of Changing Our Minds   387

Divinations for You #11   391

Chapter 16

Pick Your Battles   398

Not Sticking to Astrology   399

Wish List   402

Love Cues and Clues: How to Cultivate a Vibrant Relationship with Me   404

Auguries for You #12   405

New Language   412

New Words   416

Revelatory Homework #113   421

Chapter 17

Invitation to Love the Riddles   424

Thanks for Your Hard Work!   425

Creating a Golden Age   426

Who We Are   427

Your Specific Goals   428

Mission Statement   429
Romancing the Paradox   432
Oracles for You #13   433

Chapter 18

Long Live You and Me   450
Fortunes for You #14   454
Useful and Soulful Secrets   460
Love Cues and Clues: Being Only Who You Are   462
Divinations for You #15   463
Secret Methods   469
How to Increase Intelligence   470

Chapter 19

Your Prime Objective   472
Karmic Credit Card   473
What Color and Smell and Animal Are 'Free Will Astrology'?   477
Cities Where 'Free Will Astrology' and 'Real Astrology' Have
Been Published   482
The Entrepreneur and I   486
Further Connections   488
'Free Will Astrology' in Translation   491
Frequently Asked Questions   492
Oracular Homework #114   495

Coda

Blurb Jubilee   498
Limitless Gratitude   514

Introduction ✳

Is astrology real? Of course! Yes! Astrology is very real—although not in the same sense that the orange vermillion steel towers of the Golden Gate Bridge are real, or the lavender soap you used for your last shower, or the great horned owl you saw roosting in a juniper tree.

Astrology is real in the way that an Emily Dickinson poem is real, and psychology's theory of the unconscious mind, and the dream of your dead ancestor you had last night, and the myths of Gilgamesh and Inanna, and the story Toni Morrison told in her novel *Beloved*.

Is astrology true? Of course! Though it's not true in the same sense that the binomial theorem is true. Not true like the speed of light is 186,282.39 miles per second or like every molecule of water is composed of two hydrogen atoms and one oxygen atom. Astrology is not true in the same way as the fact that over 50 big American corporations pay no federal taxes.

But astrology is intensely and intimately true in a trillion other ways. It's as true as the epiphany you had when you realized you wanted to move to a new location or get married to a person you loved.

Astrology is true like the mix of delight and melancholy that seeps into you as summer turns to autumn. True in the same way that you feel cheerful and frisky when the first spring leaves appear on oak and elm and maple trees. As true as the fact that you are sleepier in the depths of winter than at other times of the year.

Astrology is very much true, deeply and gloriously true, in

the sense that Patti Smith is true as she sings her song "Radio Ethiopia." True like the inspiration Georgia O'Keeffe tapped into as she painted *Flowers of Fire*. True like the wrathful hope that motivated Martin Luther King Jr. to write his "I Have a Dream" speech. True like the Indigenous Anishinaabe trickster spirit Nanabozho, an unruly, gender-changing hero whose job it is to learn the names of all creatures.

Astrology is as real and as true as your imagination. As real and as true as the story you tell yourself about your life. As real and as true as your never-ending cavalcade of yearnings.

Instructions for Reading This Book ≡

Start at the beginning of this book and read sequentially straight through to the end;

OR

start anywhere in the book and read here and there, trusting your intuition to find exactly what you need, exactly when you need it;

OR

when you feel the need for inspiration, open the book at random and regard the first thing you see as an oracle;

OR

ignore the above suggestions and improvise your own approach.

Element 1

*If we don't give birth to the genius
within us, it will undermine us.*

If we give birth to the genius within us, it will liberate us.

—my adaptation of a message in the Coptic Gospel of Thomas

Chapter 1

Your Liberated Educated Fascinated Genius

+

My Liberated Educated Fascinated Genius

=

Our Liberated Educated Fascinated Genius

Your Wounds Healed

your wounds healed

your apologies accepted

your generosity expanded

your love educated

your desires clarified

your untold stories heard

your insight heightened

your wildness rejuvenated

your leaks plugged

your courage stoked

your fears dissolved

your imagination stoked

Origin Story

Every week, I write 12 horoscopes for readers who find my offerings in newspapers and on the internet. That has been my main gig for most of my adult life. I love it! The task of creating crisp new oracles always renews me.

I enjoy doing other jobs, too: musician, singer, poet, monologist, philosopher, political pundit, and author of books.

If you and I were sitting across a table from each other in a cafe, and you asked me, "What consistently incites your lust for life and joie de vivre?", I'd say, "Making stuff." I'd tell you I was born to be a begetter, a composer, a generator.

Creative zeal infuses everything I do. I regard every moment, whether it's conversing with the clerk at the 7-Eleven or riding my mountain bike up a steep dirt path or meditating in my sanctuary adjoining a wetland, as a novel opportunity to add to the playful work of art that encompasses all the rest: the performance art ritual that is my life.

Many of the people who know me don't care about any of that, though. There's one thing I do that defines my identity in their eyes: the internationally syndicated astrology column I have written for years.

Since the mid-1990s, my weekly collection of 12 oracles, "Free Will Astrology," has appeared in over 100 newspapers, including translated versions in France, Italy, Japan, the Netherlands, Venezuela, and Finland. "Real Astrology" was the name of the column for over a decade before I crossed the threshold into fame.

The combined readerships of all the publications carrying my divinations are over 7 million. Hundreds of thousands of additional viewers come to my website weekly and subscribe to my newsletter.

But I'm aware of the modesty of my accomplishment. Of all the literary genres in the world, the astrology column gets the least respect. Reputable critics don't even bother to revile it because they're too busy ignoring it. Romance novels may rival its disrepute, but in that field, there are professional organizations that confer prestige and award prizes to the top practitioners.

Both scientists and religious fundamentalists regard the astrology column as an abomination that deserves to be consigned to a fiery abyss. That's understandable. But what's unexpected is that many professional astrologers think the same. They dismiss "sun sign" horoscopes like mine as debasements of their ancient art—and not "real" astrology.

In light of these facts, you may be amused and wondrous to hear me say that I feel "Free Will Astrology" expresses the best of me. It's an excellent use of my talents and intelligence.

I'm proud of my vigorous writing and interesting ideas. I'm pleased I don't dribble out banal pellets of generic and cliché-ridden advice like "This could be the moment to ask for a raise at work" or "Romance is in the offing if you play your cards right."

Trained as a poet as well as an astrologer, I treat every horoscope as an opportunity to craft a pithy oracular burst or a comic lyrical riff or an epigram packed with quirky wisdom. My single most driving aspiration is to deliver soul food to my readers' imaginations.

I would rather work as a bagger at a grocery store than whip up their narcissism, aggravate their fears, or encourage their superstition.

Is there anyone alive who is not one of my potential teachers and muses? Wherever I go and whatever I do, even in my dreams, I am alert for seeds that might sprout into oracles I can offer to my beloved readers.

If it's possible to tell a good story in 150 words or less, I will. If I can apply the perennial themes in myths and fairy tales to the issues affecting people here and now, I'll seize the chance.

I enjoy exposing the corruption of American foreign policy and referencing iconoclasts like psychologist James Hillman and citing fantastic but verifiable facts like this one: It takes a river a million years to move a grain of sand one mile.

Writers like Octavio Paz, bell hooks, Emily Dickinson, and Rainer Maria Rilke make frequent appearances in my work, as do data culled from *Scientific American* and *National Geographic*.

On the other hand, I also exult in drawing lessons from less polished sources, like the tabloid report on the homesick New York supermodel who claimed she got jetlagged from making regular out-of-body jaunts to her native Siberia. On one occasion, I derived a metaphorical lesson from the *Weekly World News* report that Hell has a special pain-free section for masochists.

Nothing can stop me from calling on anything that has ever happened! It was so much fun to whip up an oracle citing Steve Jobs's scandalous statement that "doing LSD was one of the two or three most important things I have done in my life." I loved quoting painter Diego Rivera's testimony that he didn't believe in God, but he believed in Picasso.

Has any other astrologer in the history of reality critiqued the faulty idiom of "low man on the totem pole"? It wrongly refers to a person who has the worst job or the least status. But here are the facts, ma'am, which I reported in a horoscope in 2013: The creators of the original totem poles were Indigenous Native American tribes of the Pacific Northwest, and for them the figure at the bottom of the pole was the most important one.

In 2012, I composed a horoscope based on iconic novelist James Joyce's meetings with iconic psychologist Carl Jung. Joyce was worried about his daughter and asked Jung to analyze her. After a few sessions, Jung told her father she had a mental health challenge. A telltale sign was her obsessive tendency to make puns, many of which were quite clever. Joyce reported that he, too, enjoyed the art of punning. "You are a deep-sea diver," Jung replied. "She is drowning."

My column is popular in part because it appeals to people who might not normally read horoscopes. "'Free Will Astrology' is to other horoscope columns what James Joyce is to Danielle Steele," wrote a reviewer in the *Sacramento News & Review*. "This well-crafted compendium of poetry, anecdotes, aphorisms, and wit is a literate 'love letter' that has no precedents in the media."

The New York Times said: "Brezsny's horoscopes are like Valentines, buoyant and spilling over with mischievousness. They're a soul prognosis."

A psychotherapist once told me that he believed just 5 percent of the population is conversant with metaphorical thinking. So I risk alienating the other 95 percent as I indulge in metaphors, allegories, parables, and metonymies.

That still leaves me with a potential audience of 75 million English speakers all over the world, as well as 2 million Italians, 15 million French, 1 million Dutch, and 6 million Japanese.

Here's a sample horoscope I once wrote for Aries:

The ancient Greek god Dionysus did not, in fact, encourage people to get sloppy drunk, lose control, and commit stupid mayhem. His preference was that they free themselves from their inhibitions by imbibing moderate amounts of alcohol. With this medicinal spur, they might get unstuck from their worn-out behavior patterns and invite refreshing doses of wildness into their lives. Healing was the intention, not craziness and frenzy.

It is true that if someone was not willing to escape their rigidity—if they clung to their hidebound attitudes and refused to open up to the call of self-transformation—Dionysus might lure them into reckless inebriation. I have a strong suspicion that you would benefit from meditating on these themes right now.

As the writer of a horoscope column that rebels against horoscope columns, I don't predict the future. If anything, I predict the present. My entire practice—*free will* astrology—is based on the hypothesis that your destiny is not set in stone, is not held hostage by planetary fiat.

Rather, the future is at least partly subject, in mysterious ways, to the influences of your discerning analysis and disciplined imagination and fired-up willpower. That's especially true if you can uncover the unconscious patterns and hidden agendas that come to bear on you. It's my joy and privilege to assist you in that noble work.

I aspire to be your guide and companion as you learn more and more about the art of liberation: liberation from suffering, from habit, from lazy thinking and bad ideas.

As I've developed this ethical esthetic over the years, my innate insurrectionary urges have ripened. From age 16, I have been a progressive activist who satirizes institutionalized hypocrisy, rails against the delusional insanity of conventional wisdom, and crusades against the haters who perpetrate idiotic injustices.

I still draw from that high-octane fuel, but I've expanded my targets. Now my dissidence is also directed toward educated fools who act as if cynicism is an inherent sign of high intelligence. I fight for the right to proclaim that life is good, that it's a privilege to be a human being on this planet. I am a prophet of convulsive goodness, of reverent insurgency, of guerrilla splendor.

Not long ago, a person who has never liked me, a guy named Jonas who was a fellow student in my poetry classes at Duke University, wrote me an email in which he delivered what he imagined was the ultimate putdown.

"You worked for years perfecting your mountain-climbing skills," he crowed, "and then you climbed to the top of a mountain so puny and insignificant that no one else has ever bothered to conquer it. So now you are in a position to gaze skyward and howl triumphantly, 'I am the best climber ever of the puniest mountain in the world!'"

Though Jonas looks down on me, I don't look down on myself. On the contrary. I'm pleased about the ways I have tweaked and twisted the genre of the horoscope column to serve my own tricky but noble ends.

Because it gets meager honor and is accorded feeble legitimacy, no one cares if I mess with its conventions. So I have done that. Because I have zero investment in impressing my fellow astrologers or being known as an astrology superstar, I'm free to play around like a subversive poet and maverick philosopher and renegade performance artist.

I'm excited to celebrate and stimulate the freedom and power of our single most important asset—the imagination.

That leads me to the main reason why I am thrilled by the role that life has given me to play: I love my readers. I'm always working to love them stronger and wilder.

And my astrology column is the best vehicle I can imagine for practicing that righteous art. Week after week, year after year, I serve up short oracular bursts in an intimate and empathetic voice that's rooted in the tender, lyrical style of love letters.

Not every reader greets my oracles in the spirit in which they are offered. Some don't want my love. They may even dislike me for advising them to engage in introspection or alter their behavior. They might heartily disagree with my assessment of their current mood and needs.

From them, I receive criticism or rejection or anger. They inform me how mistaken and foolish I am. Much of that feedback is valuable, though. It helps me learn about the effects my words have. It compels me to become smarter and more sensitive.

Most of the responses I get from readers match the tone with which I address them, however: kind, appreciative, helpful, and affectionate. Even that has the power to transform me, though. It's full of perspectives I've never considered.

Day by day, week by week, year by year, my readers have taught me and ripened me. Some of their influence arrives telepathically, in my dreams and altered states. Some comes through their letters and emails and social media messages and public encounters.

Thanks to the gifts they've blessed me with, I have overcome and outwitted myself. I have become far more of a multi-faceted creation than I could ever have on my own.

I love creating a collection of 12 horoscopes each week, and I hope to keep writing them until at least January of 2048—longer if I'm still alive.

To live up to that challenge with integrity, I must continue what I have been doing since the beginning: relentlessly reinventing the way I create them.

When I look back at the horoscopes I've composed over the years, I am amazed at how different they are from each other. My writing and thinking styles have dramatically evolved. I swear it's a different person dreaming them up these days than the character working in 2015 or 2009 or 2001.

That's how it should be. It's good evidence that I'm living up to my ideal of how to be a creative artist. Experimenting with endless revision. Being willing to dispense with old formulas, even those that have worked well, so as to welcome the surprises life offers. Deleting the old modes and models so new ones can emerge.

That's a sound strategy for me to pursue as a creative writer. It's also a cornerstone of my plan to excel at the art of being a soulful person. The unambiguous fact is that life has an extreme fondness for change. The Creator likes to keep things moving right along.

So if I hope to cooperate and even collaborate with the Primal Flux, I must be adept at dying and killing, metaphorically speaking. I have to celebrate the central formula of Western Hermetic magick: "Dissolution is the secret of the Great Work."

According to the wisdom of the ages, breaking down psychological fixations is an indispensable spiritual discipline.

So I write an astrology column for a lot of folks who normally wouldn't read astrology columns. It may be a puny mountain I've conquered, but it's exactly right for me.

Meanwhile, I've been climbing other mountains, too. Playing music has at times been a full-time job. I've spent years singing and composing songs with rock bands or in solo projects.

Nine books have appeared with my name as the author. Five are in Italian, Spanish, and Greek.

I've also performed my solo theatrical piece, a pagan revival show I call *Sacred Uproar*, at numerous theaters, festivals, and other venues.

Rock musician, author, performance artist: These other mountains I've climbed are higher than the horoscope columnist mountain—but my ascent has been lower.

My most successful band, World Entertainment War, was under contract to a major record label, MCA, and managed by one of rock's famous impresarios, Bill Graham. But Bill died in a helicopter crash before he could carry out his ambitious plan for our world domination. I'll say more about that tale later.

One of my books, *Pronoia Is the Antidote for Paranoia,* has sold a respectable but modest 90,000-plus copies. Among a small but feisty segment of the "cultural creatives," I'm renowned as the Godfather of Crafty Optimism and the progenitor of the rowdy think tank known as The Beauty and Truth Lab.

Another one of my books has sold fewer copies than *Pronoia,* but is equally beloved by me. It's *The Televisionary Oracle,* a docu-fiction memoir about my life as a radical feminist and my education in the arts of intimate relationship. For years, I have been working on two sequels, *Lucky Storms* and *The Other Real World: Reports from the Secret Frontier*. These love bombs will appear in print within a year after the publication of *Astrology Is Real*.

My solo show *Sacred Uproar* is a pagan revival extravaganza drawn from material in *Pronoia*. It attracts sizable crowds. I have performed it at nightclubs in New York, theaters in San Francisco, auditoriums in Seattle, bookstores in Milwaukee, cafes in Baltimore, and summer festivals like the Oregon Country Fair and the Symbiosis Gathering at Woodward Reservoir in California.

It's marvelous, if I do say so myself! Impeccably scripted, acted, sung, paced, and danced. I'm still perplexed why no enterprising producer has seen the wisdom of making it into an HBO special.

The planet Mars is prominent in my natal horoscope. At the moment I was born, the symbol of ambition and animal energy was directly overhead in the sky. As the highest heavenly body in my cosmos, it has been a key player in my life story. Astrology says that its position there brands me with the motto, "I fervently seek the highest."

Note the difference between "I fervently seek the highest" and "I achieve the highest." I may be a zealous quester, but my questing has brought less than spectacular results, at least according to the definitions of success that prevail in the profane world. Of the mountains I've described, I've climbed to the top of a puny one and made it to the middle levels of the tall ones.

Here's the rest of the story: other mountains I've been semi-secretly climbing.

First, some context. Mt. Everest is not the highest mountain on planet Earth. Surpassing it by about 4,000 feet is Hawaii's Mauna Kea, a volcanic mass that composes part of the Big Island. Only a portion of it is visible, though. Two-thirds of it is underwater, rising from the floor of the Pacific Ocean.

All over the globe, there are mountains even more hidden than Mauna Kea. Their roots lie at the bottom of the sea, but their peaks don't reach the surface. My favorite is Atlantis Massif, a 14,000-foot prodigy in the middle of the Atlantic. Its highest point is almost 2,300 feet beneath the waves.

My own inner landscape has three mountains that are as secret as Atlantis Massif. Most people who have enjoyed my music or writing or performances don't know about them—even though they are indispensable sources of inspiration for all I create. My visible work would be meager without the luxuriant gifts of these covert treasures.

The first hidden mountain is my love and practice of poetry. As a teenager, I discovered the brilliant, bratty poet Arthur Rimbaud and instantly shape-shifted into his imitator.

Soon, I was also gobbling up the lyrical, rowdy work of Allen Ginsberg, Anne Waldman, Diane di Prima, Lawrence Ferlinghetti, and others. At night, after my high school homework was finished, I composed screeds and rants and rhapsodies in hope of mutating myself into a smart beast with a crazy true understanding of the world.

Thousands of pages of that stuff remain unpublished to this day. In 1984, a small press published *Images Are Dangerous*, a sampling of my total output. But mostly I have been a covert practitioner, content to funnel my poetic sensibilities into my music lyrics and horoscope column.

But wow, yes, I have done that a whole lot. I once did an interview with a journalist at the *Boulder Weekly*, a newspaper that has published my column for many years. I told her I am a poet in disguise, carrying out what poets ideally do: fomenting liberation and creative action through the use of surprising, disciplined language.

My second hidden mountain is my Lushbuddy, also known as my Jellyroll, Freestyle Accomplice, Soul Velvet, TrixxxHoncho, and most of all, Freaky Consort.

Our bond is a holy grail and a work of art. It's arduous, exhilarating, exacting, and transformative.

As we collaborate to create our synergy's ever-surprising plot twists, we honor the poet Rilke's First Commandment: "For one human being to love another; that is the most difficult of all our tasks, the ultimate, the last test and proof, the work for which all other work is but preparation." (Translation by Stephen Mitchell.)

The influence of our ongoing collaboration permeates everything I do: my horoscope column, my books, my music, and my performances.

Luckily for me, she is a superbly skillful astrologer with robust psychological wisdom. Her original insights have regularly rubbed off on my practice of creating horoscopes.

My third mountain is my work and play in The Other Real World—the realm that other cultures and eras have called the

Dreamtime, the realm of the archetypes, the astral plane, the Qabalistic sephira Yesod, the *Alam al Mithal*, the Anima Mundi, fairyland, and the collective unconscious.

Since I wrote down a dream for the first time when I was six years old, I have amassed heaps of dream journals. Morning after morning for decades, I have doggedly recorded the adventures I've had while asleep.

Along the way, by apprenticing myself to dream experts, studying dream books, and analyzing my own dreams, I have earned the right to call myself a dreamworker, dreamquester, and dream alchemist.

All I have become in The Overt Real World, including my role as a syndicated horoscope columnist, has been made possible by my thousands of hours of exploration in The Other Real World, some while asleep and some while awake.

I'll tell you one of my favorite early dreams. I was young— not yet nine years old. Just before I woke up to get ready for school, I traveled to Mars on a giant pencil that functioned as a rocket ship. Once on the red planet, I attended Raucous Red Reason School, where I studied how to be a professional writer and dream interpreter.

I worked hard but rarely carried out my teachers' assignments precisely as they wanted me to. That made them mad, but they gave me good grades, anyway. The school building was always in flames and yet never burned down. Apparently, that's normal for Martian schools.

I can't imagine any other dream that could have been more prophetic about my life in the decades to come. Everything that I have become was foreshadowed there.

Through the years, many readers of my column have praised me for being tenacious and inexhaustible. "You never repeat yourself" and "You always surprise me" are typical comments. "You're so consistent and reliable and tireless" is another.

But I wouldn't dream of pretending that these talents are generated by heroic personal efforts. I am by no means a paragon of rugged individualism and self-sufficiency. The truth is, I am a creation of a vast array of helpers, informants, and consultants, both in The Overt Real World and The Other Real World.

In The Overt Real World, I am in constant communion with all the great thinkers and feelers who have ever written books and created art.

Here's a message I periodically send out to my readers:

> I am grateful that you are with me as I create the horoscopes. In a sense, you are my assistants. The magick happens two ways: first, through the emails and messages you deliver to me. And second, via the communiqués you offer me over the astral airwaves.
>
> Our telepathic connections are palpable and practical. The hopes and questions you project my way stream into my higher mind, coloring my psychic environment and enriching my desire to give you what you need, as well as some extra blessings.

Just as I commune with great thinkers and feelers who have left their legacies for me in The Overt Real World, I benefit from their input in The Other Real World—as well as from my conversations with the spirits of the dead, deities, daimons, devas, angels, animal spirits, and other non-material entities. Many of these are unknown or unrecognized by historical records.

For example, you won't get any results from a Google search for the wisdom of Serafima, a nurse-priestess of the Asclepieion healing center at Epidaurus in Greece of the third century BCE. But in her spirit form, she has been a fount of good ideas and interesting language for me. For example, she helped me create the horoscope below for Pisces in 2003.

> One of the most enduring stories from ancient Greece has been the set of events that legend says occurred at Troy, on the coast of Asia Minor. Yet this epic place, site of Homer's *The Iliad*, was a village covering only seven acres.
>
> Keep that factoid in mind, Pisces. I believe it serves as an apt metaphor for events that are unfolding in your own life. A humble patch of ground may become the scene of a mythic turning point. An experience that begins small may be the seed for a story that will achieve monumental importance for you in the years to come.

So here's my official testimonial:

I want to be transparent about the fact that I am in a very real sense, not just metaphorically, a compendium of creators who have forged me into their translator and mouthpiece. "I" am "we." There are many of us here within the confines of my body. Together we carry out the "Rob Brezsny" project

I apologize that I have mostly hidden this fact for the duration of my career. In my defense, I used to fear that revealing it would alienate some people who liked and benefited from my work. It was more important to keep providing them with nourishment than pushing them to know the total truth about who I am.

The book you're reading, *Astrology Is Real*, is in part a full acknowledgment and celebration of my life as a horoscope writer. It requires me to reveal the forces and sources that are behind and beneath and above my work.

Divinations for You #1

Here's a collection of divinations for you, dear reader. There are more batches later in the book.

Read your sun sign or your rising sign or both. Experiment with what works best for you.

★

ARIES: A martial arts competition on ESPN TV featured a macho dance-off, in which rivals took turns brandishing their high-octane warrior choreography. At one point the announcer waxed poetic as the eventual winner pulled off a seemingly impossible move: "And that was a corkscrew illusion twist rodeo spin!"

I invite you to use that phrase as an incantatory invocation in the regular pep talks you give yourself. Ask yourself every now and then, "What will be my next version of the Corkscrew Illusion Twist Rodeo Spin?"

TAURUS: Your body is holy and magical and precious. I advise you not to sell it or rent it or compromise it in any way.

I invite you to attend to your sweet flesh and blood and nerves with consummate care. Find out exactly what your amazing organism needs to feel its best. Lavish it with pleasure and healing. Treat it as you would a beloved child or animal.

I also hope you will have intimate conversations with the cells that compose your body. Let them know you love and appreciate them. Tell them you want to collaborate with them to create maximum well-being. Ask them for their counsel.

GEMINI: Of all the people in the world, you Geminis are the best at skipping, scampering, springing, capering, hustling, and hippety-hopping.

You are also incomparable when it comes to twirling, pivoting, undulating, gyrating, and rub-a-dub-dubbing. Bonus! No other sign of the zodiac has such an extravagant capacity to rumble, romp, rollick, cavort, and zip-a-dap-doodle. Congratulations!

On the other hand, few of you Twins ever develop an expertise in shuffling, drooping, mumbling, and wallowing. You're most likely unskilled at the low arts of dawdling, sniveling, pigeonholing, or pussyfooting.

But that's a good thing! Congratulations again!

CANCERIAN: Why are Australian sand wasps so skilled at finding their way back home after being out all day?

Here's their trick: When they first leave the nest each morning, they fly backwards, imprinting on their memory banks the sights they will look for when they return later.

In addition, their exiting flight path is a slow and systematic zigzag pattern that orients them from multiple directions.

The sand wasps remind me of you Cancerians. One of your key lifelong tasks—and potential talents!—is to keep finding your way back to your spiritual home, over and over again.

LEO: You are destined to become a genius of controlled burning. It's your birthright to be skilled in the fiery arts: to kindle and illuminate and energize and warm.

With each passing month, you know more about when it's smart to turn the heat up high and when it's right to simmer with a slow, steady glow.

You're a student of luminosity: learning to wield your flames with discernment and compassion rather than with pride or rage. You practice and refine your talent for the creative destruction that burns rot and dross.

VIRGO: By the time my Virgo acquaintance Cal was seven years old, he was lit up with a desire to know how things work.

Sometimes that caused problems. When he dismantled the toaster to examine its innards, for instance, his parents reprimanded him. In a working-class family of 12 kids, losing a valued appliance caused a financial crunch.

But Cal kept taking things apart to understand them better. In time his research led him to develop a skill for putting things back together again, often in better shape than they were before he got a hold of them. That is the mark of an evolved Virgo.

PS: As an adult, Cal creates interactive robots that perform in shows all over the world. He's a skillful builder.

LIBRA: You're like an estuary, where the salt water of the sea mingles with the freshwater of a river.

Your power spots are the boundaries where cumulus cloud and blue sky join; where the gray-brown oak trunk joins the brown-gray earth; where your shadow overlaps your companion's shadow in the rich double darkness.

Rejoice twice! Life authorizes you to brandish and celebrate potent dualities. You thrive on being two-toned and bicultural. You're a synergized fusion of the yes and the no, the give and the take, the lyrical and the well ordered.

In the description of poet Robert Frost, you're not confused, you're well mixed. In the words of the midwife muse in my dream of your rebirth, you're both the reflection of the white rose in the mirror and the rose itself.

Do you agree but also disagree? Excellent! That's you being true to yourself.

Your assignment is to be a humming juxtaposition, not a jagged contradiction. If you do your sacred duty, you'll never get crushed by the squeeze of opposites because you'll be faithfully massaged by oscillating complements.

SCORPIO: In the TV science fiction show *Doctor Who*, the title character lives in a Tardis, a time machine that is also a spaceship.

From the outside, it appears to be barely bigger than an old-fashioned phone booth. But once you venture inside, you find it's a spacious chateau with numerous rooms, including a greenhouse, library, observatory, swimming pool, and karaoke bar.

This is an excellent metaphor for you Scorpios. Anyone who wants your love or friendship must realize how much you resemble a Tardis.

They've got to understand that you're far bigger on the inside than you seem on the outside. If they don't, it's unlikely the two of you can have a productive relationship.

As a public service, I invite you to make sure everyone you're involved with knows this fact.

SAGITTARIUS: Walk your wisdom walk, Sagittarius. Talk your wisdom talk. Dream your wisdom schemes and stream your wisdom memes.

Excite us with your wisdom uproars and your wisdom surprises. Gaze out at our broken world with your wisdom eyes. Play your wisdom tricks and risk your wisdom jokes and erupt with your wisdom cures.

We need you to be a radiant cascade of irresistible wisdom. We ask you to conjure a restless flow of wisdom exploits and wisdom interventions. What are your wisdom mistakes? Your wisdom aches? We want those, too.

And please note: You don't have to wait until the wisdom is perfect. You shouldn't worry about whether it's eminently practical. Your job is to trust your wisdom body, to unleash your wisdom wails, to revel in your wisdom resurrections.

CAPRICORN: "Most humans have an absolute and infinite capacity for taking things for granted," declared author Aldous Huxley.

That's the bad news. The good news is that you Capricorns are the least likely sign of the zodiac to fall under that bad spell.

If you choose to develop your natural potential, you can make it a habit to regularly renew your passion for and commitment to all your familiar pleasures and fundamental supports.

You will be consistently aware of the everyday miracles that allow you to thrive. You will express your appreciation for the sources that nourish you so reliably.

AQUARIUS: More than any other sign of the zodiac you

have a knack for collecting and making savvy use of ah-ha! moments. Why?

I think it's because you have an extra willingness to periodically drop your fixed beliefs about how everything works. You're more likely to respond to surprises as welcome catalysts rather than annoying inconveniences.

No one else has a greater inclination to say, "I love to get my curiosity spiked, my hair mussed, my awe struck, my goose bumps roused, my dogmas exploded, and my mind blown."

PISCES: The Japanese term *wabi-sabi* refers to an interesting or evocative imperfection in a work of art that makes it more beautiful than if it were merely perfect.

Duende is a Spanish word referring to a work of art that astonishes and thrills its viewers because it's so emotionally rich and unpredictably soulful.

One of your special potentials as a Pisces is to be a work of art exuding an abundance of *wabi-sabi* and *duende*. Notice that in the last sentence I suggested that your life itself might be a tour de force masterpiece.

Your *wabi-sabi* gives you the *je ne sais quoi* to free yourself from hyper sleekness and excessive refinement in the quest for unruly beauty.

Your *duende* provides you with the lyrical ingenuity to be a maestro of surprise and creative flair.

Astrology Is a Mythopoetic Language 💎

Should I engage in conversations with people who long ago decided that astrology is nonsense? It's not a good use of my time. Their minds are as irrevocably and self-satisfyingly closed as an evangelical Christian Republican who already knows forever there's no such thing as human-caused climate change.

But if an open-minded person agrees to consider my rational discourse, I begin with the thoughts below.

The majority of those who deride astrology with kneejerk derision don't know that four of history's greatest astronomers were practicing astrologers: Johannes Kepler, Galileo Galilei, Tycho Brahe, and Pierre Gassendi.

Most of the deriders haven't read smart astrological philosophers like Dane Rudhyar, Alice O. Howell, Clare Martin, Steven Arroyo, Richard Tarnas, Antero Alli, Keiron Le Grice, Liz Greene, Bernadette Brady, Marsilio Ficino, Sue Tompkins, William Lilly, and many others. They aren't aware that trailblazing psychologist Carl Jung cast horoscopes for all his patients and believed that "astrology represents the summation of all the psychological knowledge of antiquity."

The deriders don't know about astronomer Martha Maiden. She was a program executive at NASA for years and achieved such prominence that she now has an award named after her (https://tinyurl.com/MarthaMaiden). Martha is also an excellent astrologer. I know because she and I were friends who attended Duke University at the same time. We lived next door to each other in Durham and carried on an astrology study group with two other friends.

The closest approach that fraudulent "skeptics" often make to studying the ancient art of astrology is to glance at a tabloid or internet horoscope column. To match their carelessness, I might make a drive-by of a strip mall and declare that the profession of architecture is shallow and debased.

That's one reason why the ill-informed "skeptics" spread ignorant lies about the subject. For example, every few years, there's an uproar in the press when an astronomer falsely declares that there is a 13th astrological sign, not just 12, and that therefore all our personal horoscopes are different from what we think they are.

Those astronomers haven't bothered to do the most basic research about how astrology works. Their "rationality" is profoundly irrational. I've compiled more information about this subject here: https://tinyurl.com/IgnoreTheHoax.

Here's another gross misunderstanding by "skeptics" who have eschewed basic research. They say that all astrologers think the stars and planets emit invisible beams of energy that shape people's lives. The truth is, some Western astrologers believe that, but many don't.

Science popularizer Carl Sagan provided an egregious example of this ignorance. In his TV series *Cosmos*, he portentously dismissed the straw-man notion that planets might impact a newborn baby.

He said, "How could the rising of Mars at the moment of my birth affect me, then or now? I was born in a closed room. Light from Mars couldn't get in. The only influence of Mars which could affect me was its gravity. The gravitational pull of the obstetrician was much larger than the gravitational influence of Mars. Mars is a lot more massive, but the obstetrician was much closer."

I'm still aghast that a scientist of Sagan's caliber could have been so poorly informed.

Every single one of the many astrologers I respect agrees with what expert astrologer Richard Tarnas says in his book *Cosmos and Psyche*: The planets don't emit invisible forces that shape our destinies as if we were puppets. Rather, they are symbols of the unfolding evolutionary pattern. Just as clocks tell time but don't create it, the heavenly bodies show us the big picture but don't cause it.

I don't want to provide space for every spurious argument made by unscientific scientists. But here's one more howler. Several self-described rational skeptics have assured me that astrology is nonsense because it believes "our behavior depends on the positions of the stars."

I laugh out loud when I hear such comically ignorant drivel. The fact is that most Western astrologers disregard all the stars except one: our sun. The rest of their practice is about planets.

The "rational skeptics" make another fundamental error. The truth is that smart astrologers are not determinists, not dogmatists, not superstitious manipulators. They don't believe that our behavior is dependent on or controlled by heavenly bodies.

Many scientists deride astrology as being a "pseudoscience." In making such a fallacious claim, they reveal they have shunned the most basic principle of science, which is to actually investigate the subject they aspire to understand.

If these incompetents took the trouble to do research, they would have discovered that Western astrology's best practitioners don't claim that astrology is a science—which means that it can't be a pseudoscience!

The lyrical and practical truth is that astrology is a blend of psychology, storytelling, and mythology. As Carl Jung said, it's an aid in understanding and articulating how the psyche works. Like any language, it's both logical and messy; it's useful in making sense of the world, yet full of crazy-making ambiguities.

Astrology is a symbol system that, when used with integrity, engenders soulful approaches for deepening our connection to life's great mysteries—not predictions of literal events. It liberates and fertilizes our imaginations and encourages us to think less literally. It teaches us to visualize our destinies as mythic quests and deepens our connection to life's gorgeous mysteries.

Psychologist James Hillman spoke of the joyous work of learning our soul's code—the blueprint of our destiny. That's what astrology does best. To imagine that this can be done in a scientific way is irrelevant and delusional.

ASTROLOGY IS NOT A SCIENCE! Nor is storytelling, depth psychology, mythology, dream interpretation, or poetry.

It makes as much sense to criticize astrology for not being scientific as it does to deride Joseph Campbell treatises on the world's mythic traditions or Ursula K. Le Guin's science fiction novels because they don't explicate and illustrate the quantum field theory of physics.

The scientific method is a wonderful method for achieving some understanding of the world. But we can't use it to analyze the Indigenous Bororo people's myth, "The Bird-Nester's Aria." It's not a reliable strategy for uncovering deep truths about how a Beethoven symphony might alter the way we think about a problem we're having at work.

We profoundly need the scientific method and logical deduction and objective perceptions. They are crucial to being human. But we also need mythopoetic storytelling and art that move us emotionally in mysterious ways, as well as playful fun that frees us from our fixations.

Does it make sense to say that analyzing and working on dreams is "pseudoscience"? Of course not. You can't design a repeatable experiment to test your hypothesis about those slippery marvels. And yet, working with one's dreams, analyzing them to find subconscious patterns that affect our behavior, can be intensely practical.

Astrology is not designed to compete with scientists' logical analyses of why things are the way they are. Rather, it's meant to open our minds to the mythic elements that underlie the surface-level interpretations of what we're all about.

I can't imagine any intelligent person who would believe that the scientific way of knowing is better and more important than the mythopoetic—or vice versa.

Last word: The question "Do you believe in astrology?" is like asking us if we believe in storytelling or art.

Picture a no-nonsense physicist exploring a Wes Anderson film or Octavia Butler novel or Leonard Cohen psalm and dismissing it as an unscientific distortion of objective reality.

Imagine a chemical engineer gazing at a Kandinsky painting, with its teeming blobs of mad color and exuberant shapes, and declaring it to be a superstitious eruption of delusion that's not based on a logical understanding of the world.

Cultivating Holy Desires

Some traditions preach the value of banishing or renouncing or eluding our desires. I don't subscribe to that view.

I prefer to encourage us to cultivate excellent, holy desires. Here are a few I recommend:

◈ A desire for beguiling riddles and enchanting challenges that excite both our minds and our hearts

◈ A desire for allies who enjoy our distinctive idiosyncrasies and eccentricities

◈ A desire to attract ongoing encounters with evocative, nonstandard beauty so as to always ensure a part of us remains untamed

◈ A desire to help create a world in which everyone gets the food, housing, and health care they need

◈ A desire for energizing surprises and unpredictable fun

◈ A desire to engage in group collaborations that enhance the intelligence of everyone in the group

◈ A desire to keep outgrowing what has worked for us in the past and a desire to ceaselessly explore renewed approaches to being ourselves

◈ A desire to be playful and imaginative with our libidinous energy

◈ A desire to foster and protect the health and beauty of the natural world

◈ A desire for revelations and experiences that steer us away from thinking and behaving like the machines we interact with so much

◈ A desire to keep recreating and reinvigorating our relationships with those we love

◈ A desire to steadily refine and expand our ability to learn
from nonhuman intelligences

◈ A desire to regularly refresh our quest for freedom and
deepen our capacity to be free

◈ A desire to move our bodies in ways that delight our souls

◈ A desire to extinguish bigotry, misogyny, plutocracy,
racism, and militarism

I Don't Want You to Be Like Me

Someone paid me a high compliment. She said, "I want you to know how often your process of being yourself has helped me in my process of being me."

Yes! I don't want her to be like me, and I don't want YOU to be like me.

I want you to be like you—to the fullest, deepest, most magnificent and sacred and idiosyncratic extent.

And another thing: I love it when you create your own fantastic, unprecedented reality. It inspires me to make my own.

Accidental Bonanza

In my early twenties, before I began writing my horoscope column, I lived in a moldy basement with nothing but a temperamental space heater to warm my fingers as I composed rebellious anthems on a dinky electric piano with three broken keys.

I received food stamps from the US government, but the $70 per month often ran out after two weeks. Sometimes I'd stretch it to three. And no, that didn't happen because I loaded up on caviar and grilled lobster with wine sauce. My main dishes were rice and beans and veggies.

How did I round up enough calories after I exhausted my paltry subsidy? I will spare you the thorny details of my resourceful quest to obtain meals. Suffice to say that my heroic efforts guaranteed that I would forever after be poignantly sympathetic toward anyone who goes to bed hungry.

My wardrobe? Both my street clothes and stage costumes were garnered from a thrift warehouse called the Bargain Barn, which charged a reasonable one dollar per five pounds of recycled garments.

I am not bragging, simply stating factual evidence, when I say that I also acquired three pairs of eyeglasses there. They weren't my exact prescription, of course, but they were close enough for an impoverished person who couldn't afford to buy new glasses, even with the assistance of California's Medi-Cal health insurance program for indigents.

Given my hardship, I was very receptive when I chanced across an opportunity to make money through creative writing.

Here's how it unfolded. A crook had recently stolen my rickety, one-speed bicycle, which was my only means of transportation besides my legs. Riding on public buses cost money!

On a cold, rainy day in January, I began my search for a cheap replacement. My first stop: the classified ads of the *Good Times*, Santa Cruz's largest weekly newspaper. As I scanned the "Misc. for Sale" section, my eye tripped across an intriguing invitation one column over:

> *Good Times* is looking for an astrology columnist. Submit sample column for the week of January 26. Address to Editor, *GT*, 1100 Pacific Avenue, Santa Cruz 95060.

I was at first confused. *Good Times* already had an astrology column, didn't it? I leafed through the paper to find it, but it was gone. Had the author quit? Not that I'd be sorry to see him go. My impression of his writing, from the few times I had read it, was that it covered the whole range between mawkish New Age clichés and unfunny silliness.

I had always despised horoscope columns in the newspapers, like those of Jeane Dixon and Sydney Omarr. Though I was a diligent student of astrology, not a teacher, I had high standards about how the ancient art form should be used.

And I considered newspaper horoscopes to be an abomination. Without exception, they were poorly written and dull. They encouraged people to be superstitious and often made the spurious implication that astrology preaches predetermination and annuls free will.

It was bad enough that their blather fed gullible readers inane advice that pandered to the least interesting forms of egotism.

Worst of all, they were based in only the most tenuous way on real astrological understanding.

Any reputable practitioner would have told you, for instance, that in order to assess the cosmic energies with authenticity, you'd have to meditate on the movements and relationships of all the major heavenly bodies of our solar system, not just the sun.

But newspaper horoscopes based their ersatz "predictions" solely on the sun's position. They made the absurd proposition that the lives of millions of people who share any particular "sun sign" are all headed in the same direction.

In full awareness of these truths, I struggled to drum up a rationalization for pursuing the gig in the *Good Times*. The prospect of being paid to write something—anything—was thrilling. Even more exciting was the fantasy of receiving a *regular* paycheck. This was a weekly column, not a one-shot deal.

Besides that, it was a gig I had the skills and motivation to do well—unlike the other tasks I had done to earn money: janitor, ditchdigger, taxi driver, dishwasher, apple-picker, grounds crew gardener, newspaper deliverer, and ice cream truck driver, to name a few. I was inept at performing all those services.

"It's a dirty job, but someone's got to do it," was my opening gambit in the campaign to convince myself that the pros of penning the astrology column outweighed the cons.

My next strategy was figuring out how I could write the column in ways that would not feel fraudulent.

Before I began writing my horoscope column, I lived in squalor and deprivation. For a long time after I launched the column, I did the same. *Good Times* paid me $15 a week. So my total guaranteed resources per month, including food stamps, totaled less than $150.

If I didn't want to be a starving homeless person, I would have to pick up extra cash in other ways. Fortunately, there was an employment agency called Manpower which sent me out on temporary jobs like digging ditches, weeding senior citizens' gardens, and volunteering for medical experiments.

The main reason I was as destitute as a refugee was that I hated to work at jobs I had no skills at or interest in, and I avoided doing so unless I had reached the cusp of starvation and homelessness.

Being a poor person with an abundance of leisure time was a tremendous perk. It enabled me to hone my techniques for becoming who I really wanted to be: remembering my dreams and doing dreamwork, singing homemade songs and composing poetry, reading as many books as possible, dancing alone at home or in music halls packed with intoxicated revelers, ingesting placebos I pretended were psychedelic drugs, and engaging in luxurious meditative sex.

In upcoming narratives, I will say more about this pivotal chapter of my life and the novel ventures it unleashed.

This current installment will conclude with a message from the older version of me sent back through time to the indigent but buoyant neophyte: Would you have done anything differently if you knew that you were about to hatch a calling you would tend to with love and devotion for decades to come?

Go with What Flow?

When they say, "Go with the flow," what "flow" are they talking about?

Do they mean the flow of our early childhood conditioning? The flow of our friends' opinions? The latest cultural trends? Our immediate instinctual needs?

When they say, "Go with the flow," are they urging us to keep doing what's easiest to do and what will win us the most ego points, even if it hinders us from being faithful to our soul's code?

Consider the possibility that there are many flows to go with, but only one or some are righteous.

Do you know which?

Maybe it's the one streaming through an underground cavern, far from the frantic crowd.

Poet in Disguise ✋

What were my justifications for taking on the shabby risk of writing a horoscope column? How did I rationalize the fact that as a serious astrologer, I had always shunned sun sign astrology?

Here's the main answer: I wanted to become a poet in disguise who got paid for writing poetry.

By the time I seized the horoscope gig, I had spent several years composing stuff that loosely qualified as poetry. From the declamatory rants I thunderstormed on audiences at my rock band's shows to the more disciplined stanzas I produced for creative writing classes at UC Santa Cruz, I worked diligently at the craft.

True, I couldn't help but notice that the culture at large regarded poetry as a stuffy irrelevancy; people I considered huge talents, like Diane di Prima, W. S. Merwin, Gwendolyn Brooks, and Galway Kinnell, were not getting rich selling their lyrical creations.

To a degree, I sympathized with the hoi polloi's underwhelming appreciation of the art form I loved. Many poets were humorless academics. They seemed to have studied at the feet of constipated celibates who overvalued thinking at the expense of feeling. It was shocking how little rowdy kundalini and sacred entertainment burst from the caste that I thought should be in charge of mining the frontiers of the imagination.

I was perfectly willing for poetry to be demanding, complex, subtle, and even maddeningly mysterious. The whole point was to dynamite the ruts established by ordinary waking consciousness, to sabotage cliché and common sense, to reinvent and replenish the language. But why did so much of this noble effort have to be uniformly listless, desiccated, pretentious, and inaccessible?

And then there was my secret agenda. I was peeved that so few of "the antennae of the race" had enough courage to blow their own minds with psychedelics. How could you explode the consensual trance unless you poked your head over onto the other side of the veil now and then? Allen Ginsberg, Jack Kerouac, Diane di Prima, Anne Waldman, and Charles Olson, at least, had the chutzpah to go where shamans go. John Berryman seemed to have accomplished the feat with the help of alcohol.

As for myself, I had been drawn to and in contact with the other side of the veil long before resorting to psychedelic technology. I had regularly remembered and treasured my dreams since childhood. My immersion in the realm of the dreamtime imbued me early on with the understanding that there are other realities besides the narrow niche that most everyone habitually focused on. My psychedelic experiments confirmed and extended that certainty.

As I gained confidence in the suspicion that my formal education had concealed nine-tenths of reality, I tuned in to the paper trail documenting the existence of the missing parts. It had been mapped by shamans, alchemists, magicians, and a few poets for millennia. So my readings of Carl Jung, Joseph Campbell, Mircea Eliade, Robert Graves, and Marie-Louise von Franz revealed. Their work in turn magnetized me to the literature of Western occultism, whose rich material was written not by academics but by experimenters who actually traveled to the places in question.

The myriad reports were not in complete agreement, but many of their descriptions overlapped. The consensus was that the other side of the veil is not a single territory, but teems with a variety of realms, some relatively hellish and some heavenly. Its names are many: Dreamtime, fourth dimension, underworld, astral plane, collective unconscious, afterdeath state, eternity, bardo, and Hades—among others.

There was another issue on which all the explorers agreed: Conditions and events in those "invisible" realms are the root cause of everything that happens here.

Even modern psychotherapists believe in a materialistic version of the ancient idea: How we behave today is shaped by events that happened in distant times and places. Furthermore, the imprints that affect us so intimately reside in an invisible realm that's hard to access—the deep psyche or soul.

As I researched the testimonials about the treasure land, I registered the fact that dreams and drugs were not the only points of entry. Meditation could give access, as could specialized forms of drumming and chanting and singing and dancing. The tantric tradition taught that certain kinds of sexual communion can lead there. As does, of course, physical death.

I wanted to try all those other doors except the last one. Pot, hashish, and LSD were good to me (never a single bad trip), but their revelations were too hard to hold on to.

As I came down from a psychedelic high, I could barely translate the truths about the fourth dimension into a usable form back in normal waking awareness. At least in my work with dreams, I had seen a steady growth of both my unconscious mind's ability to generate meaningful stories and my conscious mind's skill at interpreting them. But my progress was sketchy in the work of retrieving booty from the exotic places where drugs took me.

The problem was that unlike the other techniques on the list, psychedelics bypassed my willpower. Their chemical battering ram simply smashed through the doors of perception. No adroitness or craft was involved on my part. One of my meditation teachers referred to drug use, no matter how responsible, as "storming the kingdom of heaven through violence."

At a young age, I drastically scaled down my relationship with the easy access to The Other Real World that drugs conferred. Instead, I affirmed my desire to build prowess through hard work. Dream interpretation, meditation, and tantric exploration became the cornerstones of my practice. In time, I learned to slip into the suburbs of the mysterium via song and dance as well.

I must confess, though, that my plans did not immediately bear the fruit I hoped. Even my most vivid lucid dreams and illuminated meditations did not bring me to dwell on the other side of the veil with the same heart-melting ecstasy provided by psychedelics. Even my deepest tantric lovemaking and music-induced trances failed to provide the same boost.

But then a loophole appeared, with the help of artist and visionary William Blake. My encounter with his work alerted me to the fact that there is another way into The Other Real World—in the form of a common, everyday human faculty that many of us take for granted.

Here's the special message Blake seemed to have written just for me in *A Vision of the Last Judgment*:

> This world of Imagination is the world of Eternity; it is the divine bosom into which we shall go after the death of the Vegetated body. This World of Imagina-

tion is Infinite and Eternal, whereas the world of Generation, or Vegetation, is Finite and Temporal. There exists
in that Eternal World the Permanent Realities of Every
Thing which we see reflected in this Vegetable Glass of
Nature. All Things are comprehended in their Eternal
Forms in the divine body of the Saviour, the True Vine
of Eternity, the Human Imagination.

In my interpretation, Blake suggested that the worlds I encounter in my imagination may be just as substantial as, or even more
substantial than, say, William Carlos Williams' red wheelbarrow
in his poem "The Red Wheelbarrow."

I exulted in this discovery. Blake became a secret weapon I could
use in my covert struggle against the poets who refused to be antennae of the race, against the poets who regarded the visible world as
the only one that deserved to have poetry written about it.

Now it's true that some of these poets, whom I called "materialists," inspired me. William Carlos Williams, for instance, taught
me much about the art of capturing concrete beauty.

I loved this Williams poem:

so much depends
upon

a red wheel
barrow

glazed with rain
water

beside the white
chickens

Williams was one of the best materialist poets. His work helped me hone my perceptions and employ vigorous language. But my pal William Blake gave me the doctrinal foundation with which I could rebel against Williams and rise to a higher calling. Blake suggested that scenes we dream up in our imaginations might be more real than a red wheelbarrow.

Might be is a key qualifier. Even at a young age, I was cautious about the indiscriminate use of this liberating proposition. I had read Russian occultists P. D. Ouspensky and George Gurdjieff, who made me aware that the indulgent, out-of-control imagination in service to the ego is the function by which most people lie to themselves constantly, thereby creating hell on earth. Obviously, this was not the kind of imagination Blake meant, and I vowed to keep that clear.

More real than a red wheelbarrow. Blake showed me there was another way to access The Other Real World: working as a creative artist, striving to discipline and supercharge the engine of the imagination. That was a rapturous realization. I saw that my delight in playing with language and images and stories might dovetail perfectly with my longing to hang around the Empyrean.

And what if it were true, as testified by Blake, the witches, shamans, occult magicians, Qabalists, and alchemists, that every event on earth originates in the spirit world? Then the skilled imaginer is potentially the Divine's co-creator—not just describing conditions here below, but also creating them.

I wanted to be like that. I yearned to regularly and reliably glide away into the fourth dimension, reconnoiter the source of the messed-up conditions on the material plane, and give them a healer's tweak.

Better yet, I fantasized myself being so at home and adroit in

The Other Real World that I could rummage around there look-ing for attractive but embryonic archetypes to capture and bring down to earth for ripening.

As I plied this strategy, my relationship with dreams blossomed.

All these thoughts became fodder as I tried to imagine ways I could write an astrology column without violating my integrity. I wanted the gig desperately. But I would feel so much better about myself if I could refute my conscience's accusations of "Fraud! Panderer!" with highfalutin bullshit about William Blake and the shamanic tradition.

"More Real Than a Red Wheelbarrow." Why not give my horo-scope column that title? Why not do whatever my imagination wanted to do and disguise it all under the rubric of an astrolog-ical oracle? There was certainly no International Committee on Standards for Horoscope Columns that I would have to answer to. For that matter, as long as I shaped my horoscopes to be love letters to my readers, it was unlikely they would complain about the Blakean, shamanic stuff I'd wrap it in.

Before spying the help wanted ad in the *Good Times*, I had hated astrology columns because I knew they had no basis in astrological data and could not possibly be an accurate interpre-tation of so many readers' lives at the same time.

Driven by what had become an unstoppable intent, I now argued from a different angle. What happens to people, I told myself, tends to be what they believe will happen to them; the world runs on the fuel of self-fulfilling prophecies.

Therefore, couldn't it be said that my oracles would be accurate by definition, since anyone who regarded them seriously would subconsciously head in the directions I named?

As long as I diligently maintained an optimistic and uplifting tone, no one could fault me for manipulating people in such a way.

My initial column took me an agonizing 43 hours to compose. It had some good moments:

> What you have at your command, Scorpio, is a magic we'll discreetly not call black. Let's say, instead, that it's a vivid, flagrant gray. At your best you'll be a charming *enfant terrible* playing with boring equilibriums, a necessary troublemaker bringing a messy vigor to all the overly cautious game plans. If you can manage to inject some mercy into your bad-ass attitude, no one will get stung, and everyone will be thoroughly entertained.

Still, the first offering and many after it fell short of my lofty formulations. My work was sufficiently yeasty, though, to win the favor of the *Good Times'* boss. Or maybe he saw I was adept in the arts of spelling and grammar and looked forward to an easy editing job. For all I know, I was the only applicant for the job.

It's not as if the financial rewards alone would have drawn a crowd of contenders. As I said before, the pay was so meager, I was able to keep drawing my food stamp allotment.

I regarded it as a fortune, though, considering that I was getting paid to be a poet in disguise. My secret long-term agenda, after all, was to build an imagination strong enough to gain regular access to the fourth dimension without the aid of psychedelics. What could be better training for that than a weekly assignment to dream up 12 oracular riffs and shape them into terse word-bombs?

You Need Magic

Every day, we must wade through relentless swarms of soul-less information. The experience tends to shut down our sense of wonder.

Every day, we are over-exposed to narratives that are drained of delight and mystery. We must make strenuous and ingenious efforts to ensure our world is enchanted.

I aspire to contribute to the sacred cause of feeding our sense of wonder and enchantment. That's one of my prime motivations for offering you (and me!) my creative work.

PS: Factual information and reasonable thinking alone are not sufficient to guide us through life's labyrinthine tests. We need and deserve regular deliveries of uncanny revelation.

One of our inalienable rights as human beings should be to receive mysteriously useful omens on a regular basis.

Element 1

If we don't use our power to purge outmoded ideas and decaying habits, it will slowly kill us.

If we use our power to purge outmoded ideas and decaying habits, it will regenerate and redeem us.

Chapter 2

Your Soul Metamorphosis Prowess
+
My Soul Metamorphosis Prowess
=
Our Soul Metamorphosis Prowess

Thanks for Making My Life Better

Proposed experiment: Once every three weeks or so, deliver the following paean to someone—but only if you really mean it:

"Thank you for making my life better. Thank you for helping and encouraging me to be my authentic self."

I² <-> Thou 🌀

My career as a horoscope columnist began accidentally when I responded to a help wanted ad in a newspaper. Although I initially had doubts about how to do the job with integrity, I learned the secret quickly. In time, my lucky fluke of a gig evolved into a career I loved and performed with joyous devotion.

Along the way, I added an unexpected nuance to my job description. Although the ideas I fed my readers were more unruly than soothing, more rousing and beguiling than strictly practical, many of them could be construed as being advice. So part of my work as a horoscope columnist has been as an advice columnist.

A key element in most advice columns is counsel about love and romance and intimate relationships. And even in the early days, that became a specialty of mine.

My suggestions didn't offer readers directions on how to proceed if their lovers had less than perfect hygiene or harbored sexual inhibitions or were showing signs of cheating.

I was more likely to encourage readers and their lovers to write poetry on each other's naked bodies with felt-tip markers or sing songs to each other in the dark with their clothes on inside-out or run along the beach in the rain exclaiming improvised prayers to the muse of ecstatic melancholy.

Over time, I added earthier recommendations, too, although usually with an undertone of playful lyricism. I imagined my role as that of a healing trickster who incited and inspired rather than as a clinician who tried to fix what was broken.

My approach was inflected with the rebel ethic I had developed while a teenager in response to the dehumanizing status quo of American culture. I was part-punk, part-Yippie, part-insurrectionary artist. But I always meant well. Compassion infused everything I did. My anarchist sympathies were rooted in strong moral convictions.

Furthermore, my urge to foment benevolent trouble was well grounded. Though I had no formal training as a psychologist, I had read widely in the literature and was conversant in the language of psychotherapy. Among my favorite authors were Carl Jung, founder of analytical psychology, and the brilliant author and teacher he mentored, Marie-Louise von Franz. I also loved James Hillman, Carl Rogers, Virginia Satir, Karen Horney, Abraham Maslow, and Carol Gilligan.

Was it midway through my second year of writing the column? I remember a twilight in mid-June. As I rode my bicycle up a steep hill toward the UC Santa Cruz campus, training my lungs and legs for an upcoming rock and roll performance, I had an epiphany. I realized my horoscopes were love letters. Short and pithy, yes, not snaky long and crammed with purple prose. But they were clearly love letters: intimate messages from me to my readers.

As I reached the top of the hill, where High Street meets Bay Drive, my heavy breathing and rapid heartbeat bloomed in an understanding that my readers were not merely YOU. They were THOU—the sacred, higher octave of YOU.

I saw that together, we were interwoven in an I <-> THOU relationship.

I wondered if there was also a sacred, higher octave of "I"? Perhaps "I!" or "I²"?

I² aspired to see the glad genius in every THOU as well as the suffering struggler trying to find their way home to deeply

felt meaning and purpose. I longed to give them personal, intimate, playful versions of loving care that maybe only a dreamy
stranger could provide.

And their gifts for me were equal to my gifts for them. They
awakened me to my own deeply felt meaning and purpose.
Because of their influences, my half-dormant talents ripened
into more elegant self-expression. They gave me the sacrosanct
privilege of welcoming my words into their psyches. I was honored and exultant to compose my very best oracles for them.

At the top of the hill, at the entrance to UCSC, was a motto
carved into a redwood log: *Fiat Lux*, Latin for "Let there be light."
According to the Book of Genesis, these were the first words God
spoke to create heaven and earth.

I set my bike down and dropped to my knees in the grass, overcome by the urge to deliver a prayer. My face and hands bowed
down to touch the ground in a rhythmic repetition, 10 times, all
the while slowly singing:

I^2... am in holy service... to THOU
and
THOU... are in holy service... to I^2

So yes, during the years I have been a horoscope columnist, I
have also been a love advisor.

On regular occasions, I have offered ideas about how my readers might craft their amorous quests and cherished relationships
with exquisite intelligence and inspiration.

Even when my oracles are not specifically designed to bally-
hoo the causes of synergy and symbiosis, they are always rooted

in affection and empathy and compassion. Through the decades, I have regularly renewed my vows to the numinous, luminous I^2 <-> THOU.

In the spirit of my ongoing devotion to the Great and Mysterious I^2 <-> THOU, I am seasoning this book with a series of messages called "Love Cues and Clues."

Love Cues and Clues: Taking a Love Inventory ◎

Survey the history of your love life, starting with your first love.

Stream the memories across your mind's eye as if you were watching a movie. Feel the feelings roused by each scene. Be affectionately compassionate toward yourself and your co-stars.

For each partner write about the following:

◈ Why were you attracted to the person?

◈ Why were they attracted to you?

◈ What aspects of your relationship worked?

◈ What aspects of your relationship didn't work?

◈ What qualities in you kept the link from continuing?

◈ What qualities in them kept the link from continuing?

◈ What lessons did you learn from the bond?

◈ What did you do then that you won't do again?

◈ Have there been any recurring patterns from relationship to relationship? Any mistakes you've made more than once?

This inventory may show you what you've been dense about. It may motivate you to graduate from self-sabotaging behavior and unconscious patterns that have diminished your ability to create optimal togetherness. It may also demonstrate how wise you have been. That's valuable information!

Slam Book

Did anything good happen to you in seventh grade? Or was your pubescent mind ravaged by a relentless series of worried fantasies about whether you were smart enough, cute enough, and cool enough?

For me, at Heritage Junior High School in Cherry Hill, New Jersey, there was an event that made life worth living: the arrival of the Slam Book.

The Slam Book was a thick spiral-bound notebook converted by my desk companion, Daria Karner, into a freewheeling questionnaire for anyone brave enough to sign up. She had dreamt up scores of sassy queries, one printed neatly at the top of each page.

"Which teacher would you most like to see in their pajamas?" was the first entry, followed by "What actor or actress would you get to play you in the movie version of your life story?"

Page three posed a double question: "What's the last thing you thought about before you fell asleep last night? What's the last thing you want to think about on your death bed?"

Page four asked "If you knew Russia or China was going to drop atom bombs and poison gas on us next week, what crazy and illegal stuff would you try in the next six days?"

One hundred sixty-eight questions later, beneath a drawing of a stick-figure person with skull and crossbones for a head, was the final question: "How do you feel now that you've made a complete fool of yourself?"

Here's how Daria's Slam Book worked. Every horizontal blue line on every page was assigned a number from 1 to 27. When you signed in on page 1, you picked the number that would be yours throughout the book. I picked 22, so I wrote my answers on the 22nd line of each page.

With a black felt-tip marker, Daria had articulated the main rule on the slick red cardboard cover: "Don't even start this Slam Book unless you're willing to answer every single question from the bottom of your twisted little heart."

I dived into the assignment with a passion I had not previously known I was capable of. Working feverishly, skipping meals and homework, I returned the text to Daria two days after she slipped it to me.

During the ecstatic blur of those 48 hours, I realized for the first time that when I grew up, I wanted to be a writer. The Slam Book's questions had freed the genie of my authorial imagination.

Another potential lit up, too. As I read the 13 evocative contributions of the other Slam Bookers who had preceded me, I was inspired to dream up ideas I had never before entertained. My fellow students proved to be a source of teaching and illumination.

Years later, when I launched my career as a horoscope writer, I hearkened back to the lessons I learned from the Slam Book. I realized I didn't have to try to be a solitary, inexhaustible source of creative expression. Rather, I could call on my readers to teach and illuminate me.

The Slam Book initiated me further into the understanding that relationships are crucial to my creativity. There was no need to pretend to be an all-knowing, self-sustaining authority delivering wisdom from on high! Hooray! I could regard my oracles as collaborations between my audience and me.

Over the years, I have received thousands of messages from my readers in the form of letters, emails, social media communications, in-person testimony, and telepathic transmissions. They have guided me, changed me, and yes, created me.

Here's one of the keys to my success in attracting reader feedback: At the bottom of each of each of my columns, I offer homework, exhorting readers to tell about their fantasies, complaints, promises, and insights.

I've asked them to send me homemade money and their recordings of singing in the shower and photos of them kissing their own lips in a mirror. For years, I sponsored the Dream of the Month Club. Readers sent me their most entertaining dreams, and each month I published my favorites.

Once a year for a decade, I invited readers to compose love notes to their Future Selves, including vows they swore to carry out in the next 12 months. If they sent the love note to me, I promised I'd mail it back to them in a year. And I always did.

One April, I told readers: "Mail me a symbol of your greatest pain. I will conduct a sacred ritual of purification during which I will burn that symbol to ash."

Over 900 suffering readers responded, cramming my mail drop with everything from paintings and sculptures to what looked like real owl wings and a Jack Daniel's bottle filled with marbles and rose petals. (The person who sent the wings said they represented how she always felt watched.)

I took the entire stash to a beach in Marin County, near where I lived. I built a bonfire and hurled the sad symbols into the flames. "Dear Goddess," I prayed, "please release my readers from the karmic tweaks that brought them their suffering."

Over the next six months, I received missives from 422 of the participants, testifying that my ritual had worked: Their pain had dramatically dissipated.

Divinatory Homework #101 ≡

In the spirit of the Slam Book, I present to you a recurring feature: Divinatory Homework. Send me your responses, or keep them to yourself and use them in future meditations.

Guidelines: 1. Be innocently truthful and playfully thoughtful. 2. Have fun evading your habits and dogmas. 3. Exult in the chance to be improvisational and improbable.

ARIES: "Genius is the ability to renew one's emotions in daily experience," wrote French painter Paul Cézanne. Do you express that kind of genius? If not, ruminate on how you might develop it.

TAURUS: What is still worth waiting for? What is no longer worth waiting for?

GEMINI: Make amends to a part of yourself you have neglected, insulted, or wounded.

CANCERIAN: What are five conditions you'd need in your world to feel you were living in paradise or utopia?

LEO: What's your secret beauty—some great thing about you that no one or hardly anyone knows about?

VIRGO: Explore the possibility that there are things you don't know about your deepest desires.

LIBRA: If your Future Self came to you and said, "You've must shed two beliefs that are holding you back," which ones might they be?

SCORPIO: What part of your life would most benefit from a burst of redemption and regeneration?

SAGITTARIUS: "That in a person which cannot be domesticated is not his evil but his goodness," said the writer Antonio Porchia. Do you agree? If so, describe your undomesticatable goodness.

CAPRICORN: What don't you like? What don't you want? Who do you not want to become and what life do you never want to live? Resolve these questions with crisp clarity.

AQUARIUS: You're pulling a red wagon down the street, headed home to enjoy a party that's being thrown for you. In the wagon is a treat you were deprived of when you were a kid. What is it?

PISCES: Two versions of yourself are holding hands as they gaze at the moon's reflection on a river. What do they talk about?

The Astrologer's Curse

Long ago and far away, I left my original family's home in New Jersey and enrolled in Duke University in North Carolina. After two years there, I transferred to Goddard College in Vermont, a hotbed of radical approaches to education.

The day I arrived at my new school, a mix of naked and clothed students lolled in the lounge listening as a dancing octogenarian read from Anaïs Nin's erotic works. I felt I had come home!

By then, I had read many astrology books, including all written by my favorite author, Dane Rudhyar. Other key teachers: Marc Edmund Jones, Isabel Hickey, John Lynch, Frances Sakoian, Louis Acker, Derek Parker, and Julia Parker.

I wanted to be practical, not just scholarly, so I had learned how to cast charts and do readings for friends and acquaintances. Rudhyar's book, *The Practice of Astrology*, was an essential guide. At Duke, my buddies Helen Hancock, Martha Maiden, and Catherine Williams and I had convened a regular study group to enhance our proficiency.

But Goddard enabled me to get even more serious. It offered accredited classes in astrology, taught by Peter Kubaska, who later became president of the Theosophical Society.

Kubaska was more interested in the philosophy and mythology of astrology than the psychology. His special area of knowledge was the arcane teachings of Alice Bailey, who had authored books including *Esoteric Astrology*, *A Treatise on White Magic*, and *The Consciousness of the Atom*. But Kubaska also had skills as an interpreter of personal destinies and deigned to teach them now and then.

Halfway through the trimester, I enlisted him to analyze my natal chart. Most of the stories he told me about my future self were flattering and uplifting—except for one. Looking at my Mars conjunct Moon and Neptune in my 10th house, he declared, and I quote, "You will never be seen and appreciated for who you really are." What. The. Hell.

"Did you just blast me with a shadow magic curse?" I asked him. "You're telling me that no matter what wonders I create, I will forever be underrated, undervalued, and misunderstood?"

Peter was shocked that I was shocked. He made an awkward effort to walk back his malediction.

"What I mean to say," he offered, "is that you will be too iconoclastic and complex for people to fully understand. Your real life story will always be somewhat of a secret."

When the reading was over, I departed in psychic disarray. The positive and encouraging themes Kubaska had articulated seemed less significant and true than the jolting jinx he had hurled.

Here's a key lesson I harvested: I vowed that in my practice of astrology, I would never lead with fear or fling hexes that trumped all other themes. I would scrupulously avoid activating people's superstitious tendencies, and I would dissuade them from worrying that bad things would eventually win out.

So I am grateful to Kubaska for helping to give me that gift. My horoscopes have been relentlessly encouraging to my readers. Without suppressing news of challenges, I have guided people to proceed as if they have the power, freedom, and creativity to create destinies characterized by power, freedom, and creativity.

But Kubaska's curse cast an enduring shadow. When my music career, after years of hard work, failed to rise to the next level of success, I interpreted the loss as a fulfillment of his prophecy.

It didn't make sense that my band World Entertainment War faded away. I was a skillful singer, songwriter, and dancer. Other band members were virtuosos on their instruments. Our manager was legendary rock promoter Bill Graham, who personally promised me that he would make us "the Grateful Dead of the 1990s."

Our executive producer was Sandy Pearlman, who helped make The Clash and Blue Oyster Cult world renowned. We had signed a recording contract with a major record label, MCA, whose other artists included Tom Petty, Alanis Morissette, The Who, Patti Labelle, Mary J. Blige, Genesis, and Steely Dan.

What catastrophic twist of fate led to our demise? The full story is told in my book *The Televisionary Oracle*.

Eventually, the currents shifted. My imagination reconsidered. As my Life After Music ripened and my horoscope column became widely distributed and earned me a good living, I meditated on the hypothesis that maybe Kubaska's malediction was at least in part a blessing.

This line of thought was rooted in the fact that my ego was not attached to being known as a famous astrologer. As much as I love astrology, my self-image revolves around being a skillful writer and musician. I am pleased to offer my readers inspiration and helpful advice, and I love being paid to secretly write poetry, but I'm not focused on the prestige afforded me by my column.

On an April afternoon in 2009, an epiphany struck as I hiked through the Santa Venetia Marsh Preserve in San Rafael, California. I saw that because I wasn't seen for who I truly am, I was largely free from the temptations of egotism, status-seeking, and careerism. My motivation to create horoscopes had noble roots. I loved my readers. I loved being a subversive pop writer who sneaked poetry into the mainstream media.

Kubaska's curse began to transmute into a blessing. I realized I had been offered the spectacular privilege of wandering free outside all systems. No definitions imprisoned me. I felt no duty or obligation to live up to anyone's expectations. I was anomalous, inscrutable, beyond the boundaries, permanently liminal, immune to the demands of authorities and the pressure of public opinion. Careerism was not a temptation.

I mused on the Emily Dickinson poem that begins, "I'm nobody! Who are you?" and ends like this: "How dreary — to be — Somebody! How public — like a Frog — To tell one's name — the livelong June — To an admiring Bog!"

In all of poetry, is there anyone who got away with as much idiosyncrasy and irregularity as Emily? No one sounds like her. Her majestic trickster gambits outwit and outflank all the norms.

That's why, in 1892, the influential *Atlantic Monthly* magazine dismissed her poetry as incoherent and grotesque, and declared that an "eccentric, dreamy, half-educated recluse" like her "cannot with impunity set at defiance the laws of gravitation and grammar."

Because yes, Emily even made up her own rules of grammar and punctuation! And as long as she was alive, no one saw and appreciated her for who she truly was.

I decided I was the Emily Dickinson of astrology writing.

My Prayers for You

An interviewer once asked me if I perform any special ritual before sitting down to compose my horoscopes.

I told her I say a prayer in which I affirm my desire to provide you, dear Beloved Champions, with these services:

∞ That what I offer will be of practical use to you

∞ That it will help you cultivate your relationship with your inner teacher—or rather, to borrow an Emily Dickinson gambit, with your Inner Teacher

∞ That it will inspire you to tap into and use the substantial freedom you have to create the life you want

∞ That it will stimulate you to feel joy at giving your best gifts to those who need them the most

∞ That it will help you understand that you always have more help at your disposal than you realize, and that knowing this will liberate you to ask uninhibitedly for such help

Oracular Homework #102 ≡

ARIES: "It is hard work and great art to make life not so serious," said John Irving. How are you doing with that, Aries?

TAURUS: Motivational author Sark has a suggestion: "Love imperfectly. Be a love idiot. Let yourself forget any love ideal." What might you do to experiment with that approach?

GEMINI: Tell about a time when an unexpected visitation cracked open a hole in your shrunken reality so as to let juicy eternity pour in.

CANCERIAN: Write a rant that proves you deserve all the beauty and truth you can handle.

LEO: What's a kind of joy or pleasure you're not getting enough of? How could you get more of it?

VIRGO: What image or symbol represents the fulfillment of your noblest desires?

LIBRA: Poet Muriel Rukeyser said, "The world is made of stories, not atoms." I'd add, "You are made of stories, too." What's your favorite story that you're made of?

SCORPIO: What is the best gift you could give your closest ally right now? What is a blessing you could gladly give a person you both love and hate?

SAGITTARIUS: Upon waking up for the next seven mornings, sing a song that fills you with feisty, glorious hope.

CAPRICORN: Imagine your future self—from, say, exactly five years from today—sends a message to you back through time. What is it?

AQUARIUS: Make a playful effort to change something you've always assumed you could never change.

PISCES: Compose an exciting prayer in which you ask for something you're not "supposed" to.

Love Cues and Clues: 'I'll Cavern You' ⊚

I'll cavern you,
and grotto you,
and waterfall you,
and wood you,
and water you,
and immense-rock you,
and tremendous-sound you,
and solitude you.

   —poet John Keats in a letter to his friend John Hamilton Reynolds

Element 1

If we don't play at our work and work at our play, we will take everything too personally, too seriously, and too literally.

If we play at our work and work at our play, we will cultivate a chronic, low-grade ecstasy that steadily forestalls fixations.

Chapter 3

Your Playful Work and Workful Play
+
My Playful Work and Workful Play
=
Our Playful Work and Workful Play

Love Cues and Clues: Truth Loves Beauty ﷼

TruthLovesBeauty

YourVictoriousLove

AlwaysCreatingYourself

SuperpowerEmpathy

YourLifeTreasure

CrazyGoodTruth

YourWildBlessings

HopeIsADiscipline

YourMagickStory

LoveEducatesYou

YourHolyPleasure

EverChangingBeauty

YourBlissfulFortitude

LoveCreatesFreedom

The Art of Prediction ☄

People who blindly despise and deride astrology may assert that consulting a horoscope column or getting a reading from a professional astrologer is an unsound approach to making judicious decisions about one's life.

The haters never follow up that assurance with a detailed revelation of what ARE valid ways to gather the data and insights and ideas for making judicious decisions about one's life.

Do they know of a Bureau of Acceptable Life Information that can help us determine what is and what is not worth considering as we chart the course of our destiny?

I don't mean to be glib. I am honestly puzzled by the apparent certainty that there are unambiguous methods.

Would the astrology haters approve of the guidance and inspiration we have gleaned from our teachers and coaches? From parents and relatives? From friends and colleagues? From psychotherapists and professional consultants? None of them are entirely reliable narrators. They are not to be trusted to deliver 100% accurate and wise counsel on how best to conduct our lives.

And how about the lyrics of Missy Elliott, and the poetry of Nobel Prize-winner Louise Glück, and the movies of Akira Kurosawa? Is it a brilliant move for us to eagerly take on influences from them, allowing their art to infiltrate our subconscious minds and skew and shift our attitudes? Or might we make foolish moves and bad decisions if we regard them as unfailing sources of smart guidance?

Or how about the philosophy of the Upanishads or Georg Wilhelm Friedrich Hegel or Susan Sontag? Or the psychological ideas of Carl Jung or Clarissa Pinkola Estés or Erik Erikson? Or the writing of Joan Didion or Pema Chödrön or Ta-Nehisi Coates? Or the social science of Malcolm Gladwell? Or the economic theories of Paul Krugman?

Are they all foolproof, unimpeachable sources of sage tutelage that we can unconditionally rely on to steer our personal lives in a righteous direction?

Or should we be ruthlessly careful to draw our direction and inspiration only from paragons of rationalism and science?

Should our night tables be stacked with books by Stephen Hawking and Charles Darwin and chess grandmaster Garry Kasparov and mathematician Terence Tao?

Should we read passages from their teachings every night in the expectation that they will shape us into paragons of reason and science? That they will unfailingly lead us to make prudent decisions about how to live?

I don't think so. It's fine if those tomes and others like it constitute a part of our own personal Bureau of Acceptable Life Information. But we need to get education from a variety of other sources, as well—each of which, like Hawking and Darwin and Kasparov and Tao, is imperfect and incomplete.

It's perfectly sensible to look to astrology as one of our sources, because astrology is a branch of psychology, as well as an art form—a mode of storytelling.

It's designed to stimulate our imaginations as we ruminate on what it means to be a human.

It's an evocative mythopoetic system that helps us identify and transform our subconscious patterns and have fun speculating about the big picture of our destinies.

Self-anointed "debunkers" rail against astrologers' predictions, acting as if speculating about the future is a crime against levelheaded thought.

Meanwhile, economists, meteorologists, sportscasters, trend analysts, and political pundits are out there regularly making bad prognostications based on dubious data.

They spread far more delusions and cost people more money than those of us who divine cosmic omens. In the case of errant weather forecasts, they can even be responsible for the deaths of people who are in the paths of extreme events.

Cliff Mass, a meteorologist and professor of atmospheric sciences, analyzed how badly the National Hurricane Center botched its forecasts for Hurricane Patricia in 2015 and Hurricane Matthew in 2016. Mass presented his critiques as evidence of a systemic pattern of incompetence by official sources.

Matthew killed 603 people. Has any astrological prognostication been as lethal?

On the other hand, there are documented examples of astrologers preventing lethal disasters. In 1226, Mongol astrologer Yelu Chucai saved over 100,000 lives. His boss, Genghis Khan, had ordered a massacre of the Tangut people, but the sage insisted that a heavenly sign—a colossal planetary conjunction in Capricorn—was a clear omen not to proceed with the plan. Amazingly, Khan agreed.

How about doctors? Are they skilled at offering forecasts? Systematic research addressing one aspect of this subject appeared in *PLOS One*, a peer-reviewed, open-access scientific journal.

The report studied the accuracy of physicians who give predictions to terminally ill patients about how long they will live. That information can be crucial for families as well as the patients. How will they spend their final days? How much time is there to do all they want to do before they die?

The research included 42 studies covering 30 years of research and over 12,000 prognostic estimates. Its conclusion: "Clinicians' predictions are frequently inaccurate." See the study: https://tinyurl.com/PhysicianPrognosis.

As for predicting financial futures, public finance journalist Liza Farmer wrote an article with a headline that sums up a consensus: "Why Economists' Predictions Are Usually Wrong." Read it here: https://tinyurl.com/WrongPredictions.

Writing in *The Guardian*, journalist Adam Shaw added another nuance, discussing "Why Economic Forecasting Has Always Been a Flawed Science": https://tinyurl.com/FlawedPrediction.

Macroeconomist Prakash Loungani of the International Monetary Fund found that his fellow economists whiffed on predicting 148 out of 150 recessions. "The record of failure to predict recessions is virtually unblemished," he said. See https://tinyurl.com/MostlyGetItWrong.

Why economists get so many of their predictions wrong: https://tinyurl.com/BadEconomics.

Why economists can't forecast: https://tinyurl.com/PoorProphecies.

Why economic models are always wrong: https://tinyurl.com/ErroneousPredictions.

Shall I hazard a guess about how many human lives have been misdirected and damaged, sometimes catastrophically, by the erroneous advice of financial forecasters?

Now excuse me while I go read Nobel Prize-winning James M. Buchanan's book, *Economics: Between Predictive Science and Moral Philosophy*. I have important decisions to make about the future of my family and the arc of my work, and I'm sure he will provide excellent counsel.

Theory of Divination ⟳

Quoting Greek philosopher Plotinus, astrologer Richard Tarnas writes, "The stars are like letters that inscribe themselves at every moment in the sky. Everything in the world is full of signs. All events are coordinated. All things depend on each other. Everything breathes together."

So it's not just the distant globes whose movements and relationships serve as divinatory clues. If we're sufficiently attuned to the gestalt of creation and pay close attention to its unfolding details, we can read the current mood of the universe in any and all phenomena. The theory of divination proposes that everything reflects everything else.

Let's say that when you're done drinking a cup of tea, you tear open your tea bag and randomly scatter the wet leaves on your saucer. The theory of divination says that their seemingly random arrangement tells a story. It's a microcosmic reflection of the entire macrocosm—a miniature symbol of the way the whole system is currently arrayed.

But it's unlikely you have developed experience or skill in collating analogies between tea leaf patterns and the rhythms of your personal life and world history. You wouldn't know how to discern macrocosmic meanings from this particular microcosmic event.

Likewise, you could theoretically learn to read the up-to-the-minute mood of the universe in the display of sandals sold at the drug store or the fluttering of sunlight and shadow on a mimosa tree or the scatter of soap suds in your sink after you've finished washing the dishes. But there is no collection of data from people who have studied such correlations in the past. You won't have useful information to draw on.

Using astrology as a divination tool is very different, though. There's a rich trove of data gathered by thoughtful, imaginative researchers for hundreds of years. They have worked to correlate the heavenly bodies' movements with patterns of world affairs and individual destinies.

Most Indigenous cultures study natural phenomena to discern illuminating clues about the rest of their world. Those include the movements of stars and planets but are not confined to them.

When acacia flowers start to bloom, for example, the Yanyuwa people of Australia know that sea turtles and dugongs (a marine mammal) are getting close to being as fat as they ever get, and are therefore ready to be hunted.

In the 17th century, prominent Italian astronomer Galileo asserted that the movements of the moon were unrelated to the ebb and flow of tides on the earth. But the Indigenous Yolngu of Australia knew better, even back then. They had acquired detailed knowledge of how the lunar phases were linked to the ever-changing tides. This wisdom enabled them to travel efficiently by water and predict the optimal availability of seasonal foods.

The Yanyuwa and Yolngu studied the signs of heaven and earth to make inexact but reliably approximate deductions with practical value.

Some modern people who spend a lot of time in the natural world have similar prowess. For instance, renowned outdoors person and author Tom Stienstra makes long-term weather forecasts by analyzing seemingly trivial details like the quality of red onion skins. He attests that he can tell what each spring will be like by observing the thickness of winter coats on coyotes.

Astrology works because it has resemblances to the divinatory practices of Stienstra, Yanyuwa, and Yolngu. The planets, the sun, and the moon are signatures in the sky that tell stories about everything else in the world.

Are there causal relationships between the thickness of coyotes' winter coats and the quality of red onion skins and upcoming spring weather? Do blooming acacia flowers somehow have a role in fattening the dugongs and sea turtles? Of course not. They are signifiers for each other, not influential agents.

The movements of the moon *are* causal in the behavior of the earth's tides. As far as we know, though, 17th-century Yolngu people had no theory about this relationship that would be accurate by the standards of modern science. They simply deciphered lunar behavior to gather useful information about their environment. They noticed connections.

The situation is comparable to astrology. The heavenly bodies provide correlative signs to understand individual lives and the patterns of history. But they don't cause events. They don't shape our personalities via long-distance magical vibes.

Plotinus again: "Everything in the world is full of signs. All events are coordinated. All things depend on each other. Everything breathes together."

Love Cues and Clues: You Have Always Been in Love

You have always been in love. You will always be in love.

In fact, it is impossible for you NOT to be in love. You would be unable to get out of bed each morning unless there was someone or something that roused your heart and stirred your imagination.

So please admit you are alive because of love. You are MADE of love.

★

Now I invite you to meditate on the relentlessness of your yearnings to give love and receive love.

Recognize the fact that your urge to merge will never leave you in peace, will never allow you to remain static, will always ask you to outgrow and transcend the current version of you.

Accept that your yearnings to blend your fate with the fates of others will forever torment you, delight you, bewilder you, and inspire you.

Understand that your desire for endearing connection will just keep coming and coming and coming, teaching you unpredictable secrets, and keeping you creatively off-balance, and stimulating you to constantly revise your ideas about who you are and what your purpose is.

Astrology for the Soul

As I compose horoscopes, I like to imagine how I might inspire you, my Beloved Champions, to know and fulfill your soul's code. I would love you to get a steady gaze at your life's blueprint.

My aspiration is to see you ripen into the most interesting and colorful version of your deep self.

Maybe it will take a year. Maybe it will require five years, even longer. But in a sense, it's irrelevant how long it will take. That's not your concern, or at least it's not under your control. What you can manage, and what is your concern, is to develop a vigorous, rigorous drive to live the life that best expresses your soul's code.

How do you do that? The most important thing is to know the destiny that your soul yearns to live.

Please note that the destiny your soul yearns to live may be at least somewhat different from the destiny your ego wants to live. It probably is at least somewhat different.

For example, in the case of my story, my ego longed to be a famous rock star, whereas my soul mostly just wanted to create and play and perform music. And I got what my soul wanted, but only got a part of what my ego wanted.

To be candid, I have come to believe that if my ego had gotten what it wanted—if I had become a famous rock star—it would have been harder for my soul to get what it wanted, which was simply to exult in making music.

When we talk about ambition and the drive for success and the pursuit of excellence, it is crucial to discriminate between the soul's ambitions and the ego's ambitions, between the soul's drive for success and the ego's drive, between the soul's pursuit of excellence and the ego's pursuit.

How does all that play out in you? Maybe your ego wants to own $10 million and have a stunningly attentive lover and win awards for the work you do.

Your soul, on the other hand, may be less interested in that stuff. Your soul might want to create elegant environments, or heal the wounds you suffered in childhood, or get into a dynamic relationship that teaches you how to love. Your soul might want to conquer your fears or travel widely or develop a close connection with nature.

So here's the thing: If you want to develop an indomitable drive to create the destiny you want, make sure it's the destiny your soul yearns for. As long as you are obsessed with your ego's goals, you may never be able to access the core fuel of your ambition.

There may, of course, be an overlap between the destiny your ego wants and the destiny your soul wants. If your soul wants to heal the wounds you suffered in childhood, such a longing could be compatible with your ego's desire to be rich and famous. Maybe you could write a bestselling book about how you healed the wounds you suffered in childhood.

But the soul's vision must be primary: your highest priority.

To derive the best inspiration from my horoscopes, I encourage you to emphasize your soul's ambition. Do everything you can to supercharge your soul's desire to succeed and strengthen your soul's drive for excellence.

Here's a problem: Many ultra-rationalists and fundamentalist materialists imagine "soul" to be imaginary and delusional.

Even to believers, it may be hard to define. Some regard it as a ghostly blob of magic stuff within us that keeps us connected to the world of dreams and the divine realms.

So what is the soul?

Is it an amorphous metaphor for the secret source of our spiritual power? Is it a myth that people entertain because they desperately want to believe there is more to them than just their physical bodies?

Here's what I suspect: The soul is a perspective that pushes us to go deeper and see further and live wilder. It's what stokes our imagination to flesh out our raw experience, transforming that chaotic stuff into rich storylines that animate our love of life.

With the gently propulsive force of the soul, we probe beyond the surface level of things, working to find the hidden meaning and truer feeling.

Just as astrology is real and true, but not real and true like the Golden Gate Bridge or the binomial theorem, so is the soul.

"If you need to visualize the soul," writes novelist Tom Robbins, "think of it as a cross between a wolf howl, a photon, and a dribble of dark molasses. But what it really is, as near as I can tell, is a packet of information.

"It's a program, a piece of hyperspatial software designed explicitly to interface with the Mystery. Not a mystery, mind you, the Mystery. The one that can never be solved."

As part of our ongoing crusade to wrestle the English language into a more formidable servant of the ecstatic impulse, I'm pleased to present alternate designations for "soul."

See if any of the following concoctions feel right coming out of your mouth:

- ∞ Undulating superconductor
- ∞ Nectar plasma
- ∞ Golden lather
- ∞ Smoldering crucible
- ∞ Luminous caduceus

PS: Here's Robbins's conclusion: "By waxing soulful you will have granted yourself the possibility of ecstatic participation in what the ancients considered a divinely animated universe."

I assert that "soul" is not a soggy buzzword owned and operated by lazy thinkers and superstitious supernaturalists.

As evidence this isn't the case, below I offer references to "soul" by great thinkers and feelers and creators. I will start with Walt Whitman:

> I am the poet of the body,
> And I am the poet of the soul.
> The pleasures of heaven are with me, and the pains of
> hell are with me,
> The first I graft and increase upon myself—the latter I
> translate into a new tongue.

How prompt we are to satisfy the hunger and thirst of our bodies; how slow to satisfy the hunger and thirst of our souls!
    —naturalist Henry David Thoreau

I cannot live without my life! I cannot live without my soul!
    —novelist Emily Bronte

The soul should always be ready for the possibility that the divine may come to call at any moment, wrote poet Emily Dickinson. It's not a good idea to risk ignoring sacred intervention.

This earth is honey for all beings, and all beings are honey for this earth. The intelligent, immortal being, the soul of the earth, and the intelligent, immortal being, the soul in the individual being—each is honey to the other.
    —Brihadaranyaka Upanishad

Movement never lies. It is a barometer telling the state of the soul's weather to all who can read it.
    —dancer Martha Graham

Nothing can cure the soul but the senses, just as nothing can cure the senses but the soul.
    —author Oscar Wilde

"There is a saying that when the student is ready, the teacher appears," writes Clarissa Pinkola Estés. But "the teacher comes when the soul, not the ego, is ready. The teacher comes when the soul calls, and thank goodness—for the ego is never fully ready."

Oracles for You #2 ॐ

ARIES: Below are hunches and guesses about the topic "How to Be an Aries." My readers provided some ideas, which are noted.

◈ Take big, strong steps whenever you move down the street, swagger through a building, or hike in nature. Walk loudly. Swing your arms forcefully. Imprint your intense presence on your surroundings.

◈ Five necessary things:
- Start lots of sentences with "I."
- Be adept at fulfilling your own hype.
- Avoid getting caught up in the boring fact that everyone takes everything too seriously.
- If you get upset about people taking things too seriously, forget why you're mad and run off to play.
- Now and then, be impossible.

◈ Always keep a jar of extra charisma under your bed. You may not need it; you usually wake up every morning dripping with it. But just in case. You have a mandate to radiate charm and magnetism. —Randy Eller

◈ Proceed on the hypothesis that you are always correct, even if you just changed your mind. —Ama Lessing

◈ Be confident of your ability to gather the energy to get unstuck, to bustle, to glide, to initiate—for yourself and others. —Norma Quesada

◈ Be rational and calm in unreasonable circumstances. Be non-rational and mischievous in reasonable circumstances. —Jason Thompson

◈ Be completely unable to understand how anyone can resist

you or not find you alluring.

◈ On a first date, offer to arm wrestle.

◈ Declare yourself monarch and president of absolutely everything, then stage a coup d'état. Overthrow yourself and install yourself as the new monarch and president. Do this on a regular basis.

TAURUS: Below are hunches and guesses about the topic "How to Be a Taurus." One of my readers provided some ideas, which are noted.

◈ Never stop building! Keep building and building and building: your joy, your security, your love, your beauty, your stamina, your sense of wonder.

◈ Trust and exult in the feel of velvet, the taste of crème brûlée, the sound of the cello in Dvořák's *Cello Concerto in B Minor*, the sight of the full moon rising out of a beloved lake, and the smell of the night-blooming jasmine.

◈ Have faith that your slow, gradual triumphs will work productive magic and last a long time.

◈ If I had to choose ancient deities to be your symbolic helpers, I would of course pick Venus. The planet Venus is ruler of your sign, and the goddess Venus is the maven of beauty and love, which are key to your happiness.

But I would also assign Hephaestus to your sign. He was the Greek god of the metalworking forge. He created Zeus's thunderbolts, Hermes's winged helmet, Aphrodite's magic bra, Achilles's armor, Eros's bow and arrows, and the thrones for all the gods and goddesses in Olympus.

The things he made were gorgeous and useful. I nominate him to be one of your spirit guides. May he inspire you to be a generous source of practical beauty.

◈ Taurus says, "If it's comfortable, sensuous, beautiful, or delicious, I made it or I own it." —Jennifer White

◈ You are a specialist in the art of body language. No one wields the power of gesture and posture with more articulate elegance than you.

◈ "If you don't love everybody," said the character Dicky Fox in the movie *Jerry Maguire*, "you can't sell anybody."

In other words, the most effective strategy for getting what you want is to feel tender affection for the world.

Taurus is the sign most likely to employ this advice with utmost integrity.

GEMINI: Below are hunches and guesses about the topic "How to Be a Gemini."

◈ Bounce up and down when you walk. Have 15 different kinds of laughs. Be impossible to pin down or figure out.

Relish the openings that your restlessness spawns. Keep changing the way you change.

Be easily swayed and sway others easily. Let the words that flow out of your mouth reveal to you what you think.

◈ Your worst times are when you lose contact with your other selves. Don't let that happen.

◈ Live a semi-dangerous life in your daydreams but not in real life.

◈ If you have turned out to be the kind of Gemini who is both saintly and satanic, remember that Goddess made you that way. So let Goddess worry about it.

◈ To be a true Gemini, you must yearn for knowledge—
whether it is about coral reefs, ancient maps of Sumer,
sex among jellyfish, mini-black holes, or celebrity gossip.
You need to be an eternal student who craves education.

   Are some things more important to discover than others?
Of course. But that gauge is not always apparent in the
present. A seemingly insignificant clue or trick you glean
today may become unexpectedly useful a month from now.

   With that perspective in mind, I encourage you to sometimes be quite promiscuous in your lust for new information and teachings.

◈ The key to genius is the ability to keep two contradictory
ideas in your head and maintain sanity. But it's sometimes
fun to omit the "sanity" part.

◈ Your mind is always aswarm with zesty mysteries. That's
good! It gives you an enhanced power to generate insight
and solve problems in daydreams.

◈ Your curiosity is your superpower but also potentially your
albatross. It entertains and educates you, but may get you
into tight spots and awkward transitions.

   That's why Goddess armed you with a razor-sharp silver
tongue. You can talk your way out of trouble.

CANCERIAN: Below are hunches and guesses about the topic
"How to Be a Cancerian." My readers provided some ideas,
which are noted.

◈ Be fluid and flexible while still being rooted and sturdy. Be
soft and sensitive even as you are also firm and resolute.

   Be mostly modest and adaptable, but become assertive

and outspoken as necessary. Be cautious about inviting and seeking out challenges, but be bold and brash when a golden challenge arrives.

Be your naturally generous self most of the time, but avoid giving too much.

Got all that, Cancerian?

Carrying out the multifaceted assignments I just described might be nearly impossible for most of the other signs of the zodiac, but they are in your wheelhouse. You are a specialist in fertile complexity.

◈ Gently and tenderly haunt people's dreams with your lyrical intimacy and generous mystery and inscrutable magic.

◈ Compare your everyday life to the narratives in storybooks and fairy tales and legends. Act as if you have the power to attract experiences that others believe are only true in fantasy. Really, truly believe in fantastic creatures. Whenever you need a vacation from reality, induce waking dreams to whisk you away.

◈ Listen attentively to your inner child, but don't spoil and overindulge your inner child.

◈ More than any other sign of the zodiac, you feel the sadness and suffering of the world. Is that a debility or asset? It all depends on how you choose to respond to the inflow. Compassionate action is most likely to make it an asset.

◈ When your cup of sensitivity runneth over, MAKE ART! —Sy Pfy

◈ To entice people to surrender, flood them with love. —Shiloh Manwaring

LEO: Below are hunches and guesses about the topic "How to Be a Leo." My readers provided some ideas, which are noted.

◈ Without apology or inhibition, be the STAR you are. Yes, people may want to use you for your radiance, your charisma, and your strength. But that doesn't have to interfere with your holy duty, which is MAXIMUM SELF-EXPRESSION. —Hassan Allen

◈ Never break your own heart. Never apologize for showering yourself with kindness and adoration. —Amy Clear

◈ Be alert for the intense shadows you may cast with your intense brightness. Consider the possibility that even if they seem iffy or dicey, they may have beauty and value of their own.

◈ At the moment of orgasm, scream out your own name. —Bethany Grace

◈ People should try to understand that you are only bossing them around for their benefit. —Harlow Hunt

◈ Stretching and sighing and yawning are art forms for you. Regard each occasion as a potential performance opportunity.

◈ Give yourself permission to do just about anything that has integrity and is fueled by compassion. —Azariah Smithie

VIRGO: Below are hunches and guesses about the topic "How to Be a Virgo." My readers provided some ideas, which are noted.

◈ "Love your mistakes and foibles," Virgo astrologer William Sebrans advises his fellow Virgos. "They aren't going away. And it's your calling in life—some would say a superpower—to home in on them and finesse them.

"Why? Because you may be able to fix them or improve them with panache—for your benefit and the welfare of those you love."

◈ Take care of yourself as well as you care for others. —Geoffrey Huckabay

◈ You can't and won't tolerate unprofessional behavior or a lack of manners and etiquette. Why should you? In the whole world, there are enough skillful people with integrity for you to exclusively stick with them.

◈ Write as many lists as you damn well feel like writing. List-making is the Truth and the Way for Virgos. —Cara Inmungilun

◈ Of all the signs in the zodiac, you know best that the most useful truths can't be entirely told with abstractions. Key ingredients are concrete facts and specific details.

◈ Hooray! A fresh, new project! Analyze the daylights out of its potential, craft an exquisite plan to accomplish it, and then spend more time and work than strictly necessary to bring it to fruition. —Amari Wenendero

◈ When your humor and patient focus are amply engaged, you have extraordinary power to create elegant and interesting versions of harmony. —Janicia Waymer Hasko

LIBRA: Below are hunches and guesses about the topic "How to Be a Libra." My readers provided some ideas, which are noted.

◈ You are a translator. Among your life purposes are:
  • To serve as an intermediary between disparate elements
  • To lubricate and facilitate conversations between people who might not otherwise understand each other

- To find mutuality between apparent contradictions
- To weave paradoxes into amalgamations
- To never give up on finding the most elegant way to understand a problem

◈ Find beauty in literally everyone and everything. Seriously. There is no good reason you can't or shouldn't do this.

◈ Know what it takes to please everyone, even if you don't always choose to please everyone. Know how to be what everyone wants you to be when they need you to be it, even if you fulfill that wish only now and then.

◈ Learn to argue with skill and élan. To nurture your vitality, engage in regular debate that amuses and educates you.

◈ More than any other sign, you can tolerate and even thrive amidst ambiguities and gray areas.

◈ Creating aesthetically pleasing environments is crucial to being a Libra.

◈ *Do not* give others all that you have and, in the process, forget to keep something for yourself.

◈ Be reverent and respectful about the language you write and speak and think. Understand that the way you use words will make or break your power to fulfill your goals.

◈ So much about being a Libra is the search for interesting stimulation. You are driven to find people, places, ideas, and things that invigorate you with ever-fresh thoughts and feelings.

SCORPIO: Below are hunches and guesses about the topic "How to Be a Scorpio."

◈ There are blessings in every abyss. You, of all the signs in the zodiac, have the greatest capacity to find those blessings and make them yours.

Likewise, there is an abyss in each blessing. You, of all the signs, have the most power to make sure your experiences in the abyss don't detract from but enhance the blessing.

Take maximum advantage of these superpowers! Be an expert in zeroing in on the opportunities seeded in the dilemmas. Show everyone how to home in on and enjoy the delights in the darkness. Be an inspirational role model as you extract redemption from the messes.

◈ Use tasteful disguises. Establish secret identities in several different venues. Own a deluxe squirt gun and a knife made of foam rubber.

Do something ingeniously Machiavellian to a person in authority.

Be merciful to the young souls you know who are living their first lifetime.

Study the Death card in the Mother Peace tarot deck and use it to predict your upcoming renaissance and revitalization.

Make friends with a snake and coax it to go for a walk with you, or buy a rubber snake and pretend it's real as the two of you take a stroll.

Use your ex's picture on a dartboard so you won't act out more literal revenge fantasies.

◈ You know more about how karma works than all the other signs. Scorpio-style intelligence typically has a fine intuitive grasp of how today's realities evolved out of the deep patterns and rhythms of the past.

But that doesn't mean you perfectly understand how

karma works. And I urge you to be eager to learn more. Become even savvier about how the law of cause and effect impacts the destinies of you and your allies.

Meditate on how the situations you are in now were influenced by actions you took once upon a time. Ruminate on what you could do in the near future to foster good karma and diminish weird karma.

◈ Who can simultaneously love and hate, support and undermine, celebrate and demean with more panache than you? No one!

◈ Be like the guardian of a cave of wonders that goes so deep that even you can't find its end.

◈ Now and then, you slip into phases when you're poised on the brink of either self-damage or self-discovery. You wobble and lurch on the borderline where self-undoing vies with self-creation.

Whenever this situation arises, here are key questions to ask yourself: Is there a strategy you can implement to ensure that you glide into self-discovery and self-creation? Is there a homing thought that will lure you away from the perverse temptations of self-damage and self-undoing?

The answers to these queries are always yes—*if* you regard love as your top priority and *if* you serve the cause of love over every other consideration.

◈ Remember that not everyone can handle your honesty, sometimes not even you.

◈ Cherish wisdom more than knowledge. Serve soul more than ego.

SAGITTARIUS: Below are hunches and guesses about the topic "How to Be a Sagittarius." My readers provided some ideas, which are noted.

◈ Love vastly, powerfully, and with great depth. Get to the point. Keep it moving. Exult in having the big picture in mind. —Darrell Sanchez

◈ Trust your gut instincts. While the world is telling you to take the safe, well-planned route, your inner itinerary provides alternative counsel. Listen to it. —Janell TheSelkie Oelrich Schreiber

◈ At random occasions, erupt with sudden epiphanies about the mystery and meaning of whatever-the-hell-this-crazy-game-is-we're-all-playing. Scream it out to everyone. Run away laughing with senseless joy. —Mandy Macklin

◈ Be fiercely allergic to fraud and injustice. With relish, rip the mask off the pathetic imposters. With glee, undo the corrupt work of the entitled greedheads. —Anna E. Woolverton

◈ Never fake your way through anything. If you are scared, say so. If you don't know how to do something, ask for help. If you feel insecure, tell other people and request feedback. —Kathleen Youmans

◈ Of all the signs in the zodiac, you Sagittarians know best how to have fun even when life sucks. Your daily rhythm may have unraveled into a tangle of boring or annoying tasks, and yet you can still summon a knack for enjoying yourself.

And how are your instincts for drumming up amusement when life doesn't suck? Are you as talented at whipping up joy and inspiration when the daily rhythm is smooth and groovy?

When you're at your best, the good times spur you to new heights of creating even more good times.

◈ If thou hast pain, transmute it into pleasure. If thou hast guilt, wallow in it until it brings ecstasy. If thou hast hatred, burn in it until thou art ablaze with the infernal truths that will set thy soul free. —Babalon Frieze

CAPRICORN: Below are hunches and guesses about the topic "How to Be a Capricorn." My readers provided some ideas, which are noted.

◈ How to Be a Capricorn: Achieve everything you want while being true to your rigorous principles and expressing high levels of integrity.

◈ I hereby authorize you to worry, worry, and worry some more. Stew and simmer as you weigh all the options and mull the correct actions.

But when the time is right, end your fretting with crisp decisiveness. Shake off any residual doubt that still clings to you. And then undertake robust action to transform the situation that provoked your righteous brooding.

◈ I feel you Capricorns are wise to commune with rocks, dirt, mud, sand, and clay. I think you should regularly touch the actual earth with your hands and bare feet.

If I'm out hiking with a Capricorn friend, I might urge them to sniff blooming mushrooms and lean down to kiss the exposed roots of trees. Direct encounters with natural wonders are magic potions and miracle medicine for you.

Moreover, you flourish when you nurture close personal relationships with anything that might be described as foundational. Your words of power are *kernel, core, gist, marrow,* and *keystone.*

◈ All our Capricornian climbing can feel exhausting until we realize we're getting younger and less burdened as we go. —Asha Sanaker

◈ Becoming our own fathers can feel arduous for us Capricorns until we're old and sage enough to be good at it. —Asha Sanaker

◈ You are not "royalty" in the abusive, oppressive way. People look to you to guide them because you have patience, care, and strength. You serve as anchor and support. You take on lots of responsibility because you can, you're asked to, and you like to.

◈ Develop disciplined, well-planned strategies to achieve more freedom. —Alicia Dominic Keenon

◈ Embrace your fully realized empowerment without having to negate the power of others. —Lisa Fairman

AQUARIUS: Below are hunches and guesses about the topic "How to Be an Aquarius." My readers provided some ideas, which are noted.

◈ Aquarian actor Tallulah Bankhead testified, "Nobody can be exactly like me. Even I have trouble doing it."

◈ Dream up creative solutions to problems that haven't materialized yet. Then apply your discoveries as you address problems that already exist.

In other words, Aquarius, your uncanny facility for glimpsing the future can be useful as you enhance your life in the present. Your almost psychic capacity to foretell coming trends can be instrumental as you fix glitches in the here and now.

◈ Be a humble know-it-all who is smart enough to realize none of us can ever do more than scratch the surface of the Great Mystery. —Laura Monnig

◈ Let your swirling, whirling intuition alight on the stony, muddy earth for longer and longer intervals. Allow your third eye to wear sunglasses every now and then. —Sara Elize

◈ Keep getting rid of things that are not yours. —Amber Xanthos

◈ Aquarius haters describe this as being an Aquarius monologue: "Help! I think I'm having a feeling. There are five, right? Which one is it? I can't remember. Who cares?" —Kathleen Hansen

◈ But Aquarius lover Chandira Hensey offers a counterargument to Aquarius haters: "We may be called aloof and dispassionate, but the truth is we feel everything and need to work diligently to screen out the constant chatter we absorb. We benefit by escaping to wild places where the airwaves are quieter and where we can think our own thoughts and feel our own feelings."

◈ There is a subset of the Aquarius (Aquari-us) tribe that calls itself Aquarithem (Aquari-them). They think in seven dimensions instead of six. They celebrate the end of the world twice a year, not just once, as the Aquarius tribe does. Instead of claiming an unlimited Artistic License and Poet License, Aquarithems insist on wielding Artiztik Lizenses and Poetik Lizenses.

PISCES: Below are hunches and guesses about the topic "How to Be a Pisces." My readers provided some ideas, which are noted.

◈ You're one big harmonious contradiction! You travel through and live in heaven and hell, plus all the sprawling real estate in between.

Other signs might be simply torn between the wild and tame, between the yes and no, between the black and white.

You are spread-eagled across the entire spectrum, forever tugged and heaved in the labyrinthine crosscurrent interweave of motley commingled with patchwork, mosaic coalesced with mottle, paisley amalgamated with plaid.

◈ Surround yourself with people who don't condemn you for being spaced out or dreamy, but rather know how to have fun with you in the spacey dreaminess. —Elizabeth Kirkpatrick

◈ Sometimes, you may feel you're under the influence of a debilitating spell or hindered by a murky curse. Pisceans are prone to such worries.

But here's a secret. More than any other zodiac sign, you have the power to escape from spells. Even if you have never studied the occult or read a witch's grimoire, you possess a natural facility for the natural magic that disperses curses. From the depths of your psyche, you can summon the spiritual force necessary to cleanse the gunk and free yourself.

Do you believe me? Now would be a perfect time to prove to yourself that what I've said here is true.

◈ Cry. Write poetry. Cry about your poetry. Sing. Cry about your singing. Cry about your crying. —Cheryl Means

◈ See way too much. Know way too much. Yearn for way

too much. Give way too much. Take way too much. — Mebbie Jackson

◈ My Piscean friend Luna wrote me an email that sums up how I sometimes feel about you. I'll repeat it here in hopes it will inspire you to be perfectly yourself.

Luna said, "Every time I meet someone who was born within two weeks of my birthday, I end up with the impression that they are the loopiest and wisest person I've met in a long time. They are totally ridiculous and worthy of profound respect. They are unhinged and brilliantly focused. They are fuzzy-headed dreamers who couldn't possibly ever get anything practical accomplished, and they are lyrical thinkers who charm me with their attunement to the world's beauty and impress me with their understanding of how the world works. Hahahahaha. Luckily for me, I know the fool is sacred."

◈ Is it better to seek spiritual enlightenment than to wander around lost in your fantasy world? Maybe. Maybe not. Who's to say your fantasy world isn't where you can find spiritual enlightenment?

◈ Float in the salt watery sea foam, always gravitating toward the waves of melancholy ecstasy. —Renee Schildkraut

Loving The Catalytic Abyss

Guidelines for Loving the Catalytic Abyss at the Heart of the Luminous Nothingness:

- ∞ Empty ourselves out gladly. Release the clutter exuberantly. Create a clear, free space full of sweet absence.
- ∞ With blithe daring, lower our expectations all the way down to the Zero Point of Unexpected Healing.
- ∞ Cheerfully surrender every remnant of delusional hope that might blunt our brazen courage.
- ∞ See if we can imagine a dark, fertile unknown seeded in the blankness.
- ∞ Open a howling welcome in our wild hearts for the messy, unpredictable enigmas that well up from the disappearance.
- ∞ Say, "I revere and commune with the confounding and regenerative beauty of ambiguity and paradox."
- ∞ Emancipate ourselves to glimpse fresh, raw truths that resemble no truths we ever knew before.

Oracular Homework #103 ≡▼

For all signs: The German word *Nachkussen* refers to the kinds of kisses that compensate for all the kissing that has not been happening, all the kissing that has been missed or omitted or lost.

If it has been too long since you've kissed anyone, you need *Nachkussen*.

If a lover hasn't kissed you lately with the focused verve you long for, you need *Nachkussen*.

If you yourself have been neglecting to employ your full artistry and intensity as you bestow your kisses, you need *Nachkussen*.

Element 1

If we never team up with allies who quest for wonders and marvels, our own quest for wonders and marvels may atrophy.

If we choose allies who quest for wonders and marvels, our own quest for wonders and marvels may thrive.

Chapter 4

Your Sly Miracle Quest
+
My Sly Miracle Quest
=
Our Sly Miracle Quest

The Spiritual Power of Pleasure

Proposed experiment: Assume your drive to experience pleasure isn't a hindrance to your spiritual growth, but is essential to it.

Proceed on the hypothesis that cultivating joy can make you a more ethical and compassionate person.

Research the possibility that when you feel good, you're more generous spirited toward others.

Imagine that delight has an interesting teaching for you every day.

To Honor the Dazzling Muses

Here's an interview that author Vimala Blavatsky did with me.

Vimala Blavatsky: You have been known for many years as the heavyweight champion of horoscope columnists. Why, then, was your first book a burst of experimental poetry, your second book a "docu-fiction memoir," and your third and fourth books blends of philosophy and storytelling and psychology?

You did publish an astrology book in 2010, but it was in Italian, not your native tongue! Millions of your fans can't read it! Why haven't you tried to create best-selling astrology books?

Me: From a marketing perspective, it may seem like a bad business move not to have expeditiously followed up on the success of my horoscope column with an astrology book or three. But I long ago pledged to honor the promptings of my inner guides above all other motivations.

As much as I love writing "Free Will Astrology," the dazzling muses who pilot my creative urges have been unambiguous in their desire for me to first write the books you cited.

As best as I can tell, their dream has been to help me ripen a host of skills and gather a wealth of knowledge in many different fields. For me to be a horoscope writer was a part of a complicated blueprint that included many additional facets.

Ironically, this may turn out to be an excellent marketing strategy. I suspect I am one of those oddballs whose income increases in direct proportion to my devotion to pleasing the muses.

And, oh, by the way, those inscrutable shepherds now have me working on 12 astrology books, one for each of the signs, as well as this book about the lessons I've gleaned while working as an oracle.

Vimala Blavatsky: Because you pack your horoscopes with doses of wry humor and adventurous imagery, some people think you don't take astrology seriously.

Me: On the contrary, I think my humor and imagery, along with my passion for crafting language free of clichés, demonstrate how much respect I have for astrology. With the intellectual vigor I apply to writing my oracles, I feel I've shown that astrology may have more credibility than its lowbrow practitioners have afforded it.

Vimala Blavatsky: Don't you risk playing the same role the low-brow astrologers do: enticing people to take on a superstitious approach to life and seducing them into believing their fate is determined by supernatural forces beyond the influence of their willpower?

Me: My primary gift is predicting the present rather than fore-casting the future. I seek to awaken my readers to the hidden agendas and unconscious forces at work in their lives. With that information, they can respond intelligently to the totality of what's happening instead of merely to superficial appearances.

When I'm doing my job well, I also inspire people to realize how much power they have to solve their problems. I want to be a friendly shocker who helps unleash their imaginations, giving them the power to create their destinies with the same liberated fertility that great artists summon to generate their masterpieces.

Vimala Blavatsky: Do you consider yourself a guru figure? How can you nurture your readers' ability to seize control of their own lives if they're busy attributing to you supernatural levels of charisma?

Me: I could be deluded about this, but I sincerely believe I infuse my horoscopes with abundant suggestions to be skeptical of me and to seek, above all, the guidance of one's own inner teacher.

Vimala Blavatsky: How do you write your column? Do you use actual astrological data or just go into a trance and let your imagination run free?

Me: I draw up a weekly chart for the sun, moon, and major aspects impacting each sign. It's the framework within which I ruminate and improvise. As I conduct each new divination, of course, I have years of study and research to draw on. I have also acquired extensive empirical evidence about what is useful for my readers and what isn't.

The artistic aspect of the work is harder to pin down. One of my guiding principles, though, is to treat each sign's horoscope as a communiqué to a friend—to speak as intimately about the mysteries of the moment as if I were addressing a close ally.

Where do my inspirations come from? My dreams, transmissions from readers, overheard conversations, meditation, lots of reading in a variety of texts both sacred and profane, and the intensive cultivation of my own receptivity. I am also constantly absorbing the books and websites of astrologers I respect.

In addition, I rely on periodic fact-finding missions I call whirlygigs. During these forays, I steep myself with the intention of attracting lessons I don't know I need. I meander through the world at random, going places I've never been and striking up conversations with strangers, both human and animal, with whom I may ostensibly have little in common.

Vimala Blavatsky: You confuse me in the way that you praise rational thought and the scientific method, yet reserve the unconventional right to believe in astrology, angels, miracles, and other woo-woo.

Me: Thousands of astounding, inexplicable, and even supernatural events occur every day. And yet most are unreported by the media. The few that are cited are ridiculed. Why?

Here's one possible reason: The people most likely to believe in wonders and marvels are superstitious, less educated, and prone to having a blind, literalist faith in their religions' myths.

Those who are least likely to believe in wonders and marvels are skilled at analytical thought, well educated, and yet prone to having a blind, literalist faith in the materialist perspective. That spurious ideology dogmatically asserts that the universe consists entirely and only of things that can be perceived by the human senses or detected by instruments that scientists have thus far invented.

The media is largely composed of people from the second group. It's virtually impossible for them to admit to the reality of events that elude the rational mind's explanations, let alone experience them. If anyone from this group manages to escape peer pressure and cultivate receptivity to the miraculous, it's because they have resisted the unsophisticated way that wonders and marvels are framed by the first group.

I aspire to be immune to the double-barreled ignorance. When I behold astonishing synchronicities and numinous breakthroughs that may seem to violate natural law, I'm willing to consider the possibility that my understanding of natural law is too narrow. And yet I also refrain from lapsing into irrational gullibility. I'm willing to entertain mundane explanations for apparent miracles.

Vimala Blavatsky: Can you sum up your approach to seeing the world?

Me: My outlook combines the rigorous objectivity of a scientist, the "beginner's mind" of Zen Buddhism, the "beginner's heart" taught by Jeff Brown, and the compassionate friendliness of the Dalai Lama. I blend a scrupulously dispassionate curiosity with a skepticism driven by expansiveness, not spleen.

To pull this off, I must be willing to regularly suspend my theories about the way the world works. I accept with good humor the possibility that what I've learned in the past may not be a perfectly reliable guide to understanding the fresh phenomena right in front of me.

I'm suspicious of my biases, even the rational and benevolent ones. I open my wild heart as I strip away the interpretations that my emotions might be inclined to impose.

"Before we can receive the unbiased truth about anything," wrote my teacher Ann Davies, "we have to be ready to ignore what we would like to be true."

At the same time, I don't want to turn into a hard-ass, poker-faced robot. My feelings remain fluidic and receptive. My natural affection for all of creation hovers at the front of my awareness. I enjoy the power of tender sympathy as it drives me to probe for the unimaginable revelations of every new moment.

"Before we can receive the entire truth about anything," said Ann Davies, "we have to love it."

Vimala Blavatsky: I promised three of my friends with PhDs that I would ask this question, though it doesn't reflect my personal views: How can an intelligent person believe astrology has any merit?

Me: There's no need to "believe" in astrology. As my astrological colleague Antero Alli says, "I don't believe in astrology; I use it because it works. And it seems to work best as a language, not a belief system or a religion or a science."

At its best, astrology opens up and fecundates our imaginations and inspires us to play with practical visions of what's beautiful and useful.

Where Does Help Come From?

I get many requests from people who are slogging through challenging dilemmas and would like my personal advice.

I wish I could help! The inquiries are often well thought-out and infused with emotional intelligence. I feel poignant pangs of empathy.

Unfortunately, I can't respond. My various projects are delightfully consuming; I can't add further tasks, no matter how interesting they might be. But I've developed a response to people who seek my direct input. I offer it below.

Dear Beloved Champion:

I'm honored that you regard me as a potential helper who might provide answers or solace. But it wouldn't be responsible for me to offer advice without knowing more about the complexities of your problems. And I can't give the time necessary to explore those complexities.

As you seek to clarify your situation, I suggest you go on a retreat. During this time of withdrawal from the world's madness, you would try to avoid all media and to be as silent and relaxed as possible.

You don't necessarily have to travel to a distant sanctuary. You can do it in your own home. And there's no need to strive to do the retreat perfectly. Do the best you can.

During the first part of your retreat, spend a few hours visualizing in your mind's eye the entire story of your life, from your earliest memory to the present moment.

During the second phase of your retreat, establish contact with the highest source of wisdom and love within you. You can call this source God or Goddess or your Guardian Angel or Higher Self. Spend luxurious time in dialogue with this source, making sure to ruminate on these questions:

◈ "What is it I want more than anything else?"

◈ "What is true about me? Who am I, really?

◈ "What is the best way to serve the mission I came to Earth to carry out? What are the best gifts I have to offer people, animals, and the earth?"

◈ "What path will allow me to ultimately learn the most about wise love?"

◈ "How do I need to change so as to get what I want, carry out my life's mission, and learn about wise love? What influences and attitudes do I need to eliminate?"

During the third phase of the process, write a mission statement: what you want to accomplish by the time you die many years hence. Then create an overall plan of the actions you will take to fulfill that mission statement. Include three actions you will take in the next month to get more serious about accomplishing your mission.

During the fourth phase, visualize the following scenarios in lush detail:

◈ That God, Goddess, Life, and Something Very Big and Mysterious and Intelligent loves you

◈ That the entire universe is conspiring to give you the lessons and blessings and kicks in the ass and liberations you need exactly when you need them

◈ That you are primed and eager to welcome love and guidance

You Are a Prophet

One of my beloved tasks as an astrologer of the soul is to help readers learn to distinguish between the wasteful, demoralizing use of the imagination and the uplifting, regenerative use of the imagination.

A good way for me to earn the right to discourse on this subject is to keep learning more about how to distinguish between my own wasteful, demoralizing use of the imagination and my uplifting, regenerative use of the imagination. I was not adept at this early in my adult life. My skill has improved, but is still far less than expert.

Here's the foundation of my meditations: Our imagination is the most important asset we possess. It's our power to create mental pictures of things that don't exist yet and that we want to bring into being. It's like the magic wand we use to shape our future.

We are all prophets. Our imaginations tirelessly churn out images of what we will be doing later. The featured prophecy of the moment may be as simple as a psychic impression of ourselves eating a fudge brownie at lunch or as monumental as a daydream of building our dream home.

Our imagination is a treasure when it generates scenarios aligned with our deep desires. In fact, it's an indispensable tool in creating the life we want. We call on it to formulate images of the conditions we'd like to inhabit and the objects we hope to wield.

But for most of us, the imagination is as much a curse as a blessing. We may use it conjure up fearful or distasteful premonitions that are at odds with our conscious values.

That's in part the result of having absorbed toxic programming from the media and influential people.

Chaotic, disturbing, and even sickening fantasies regularly pop up into our awareness, many disguising themselves as rational thoughts and genuine intuitions. Those disheartening fantasies may hijack our psychic energy, directing it to exhaust itself in dead-end ruminations.

Every time we entertain at length a vision of being rejected or hurt or frustrated, every time we dwell on a memory of a painful experience, we blast ourselves with a hex.

Meanwhile, ill-suited longings are also lurking in our psyche, impelling us to want things that aren't healthy for us and that we don't need.

Whenever we surrender to the allure of false and trivial and counterproductive desires, our imaginations are practicing putrid magic.

This is the unsavory aspect of the imagination that Buddhists dub the "monkey mind." It's the part of our mental apparatus that endlessly exudes pictures in the manner of an agitated critter. The teacher Jeff Brown adds a crucial nuance. He says our "monkey hearts" are forever churning up forlorn, fractious, frightful feelings that are at the roots of the monkey mind's disquiet.

Is there an antidote? Maybe. If we move away from locating our sense of self in the relentless surge of the monkey mind's and monkey heart's slapdash chatter, we may become gracefully attuned to the life that's right in front of us.

Whether our imagination is in service to our righteous desires or in thrall to our compulsive commotion, there is one constant: Its prophecies play a prominent role in shaping what happens to us. Many of our visions of the future do come to pass. The situations we expect to occur and the experiences we rehearse and dwell on are often reflected back to us as actual events that confirm our expectations.

The well-documented placebo effect in drug research, for which there is plentiful evidence, has broader implications. So much (not all!) of what unfolds in our lives, for good and for ill, is shaped by what we believe will happen.

Does that mean our mental and emotional projections help create the future? Let's consider that possibility. What if it's at least partially true that what we presume will happen does tend to materialize?

Here's the logical conclusion: It's downright self-destructive to keep infecting our imaginations with pictures of loss and failure, doom and gloom, fear and loathing. The far more sensible and practical approach is to expect blessings.

That's one reason why I'm reverent in composing my divinations for you, my readers. If I'm to be one of the influences you invite into the intimate sanctuary where you hatch your self-fulfilling prophecies, I want to conspire with you to disperse fear and invoke relaxation and joy.

Divinatory Homework #104 ≡

For all signs, here's an invitation:

Glide inward and downward even as you spiral home-ward and upward.

Keep going until you gently collide and merge with the shrewdest and craftiest and kindest source you know—call it your higher self, your holy guardian angel, the Divine Wow or Blooming HaHa, the genius of nature, or your wild luminous soul bloom gusto.

As you are gloriously entangled there in blissful sagacity, pose this inquiry: "What do I need to become aware of that I wouldn't even know to ask about?"

Syndication

The first newspaper that published my horoscope column was the *Good Times* in Santa Cruz, California. Publisher Jay Shore hired me. May blessings shower him all his life and every one of his future lives, too! He only paid me $15 per week, but since I would have done the job for free, it was a treasure.

Two years later, another paper signed on: the *Santa Barbara News & Review*. My friend Jeff Greenwald was the cultural and features editor there. Not exactly nepotism, since he and I aren't blood related. Suddenly, I was raking in a total of $30 per week.

For the first time, I fantasized about the possibility of being syndicated. While I didn't aspire to create generic, boring horoscopes like famous astrology writers Sydney Omarr and Jeane Dixon, I noticed their columns were published in hundreds of daily newspapers.

Would those bastions of mainstream media shove Omarr and Dixon aside to publish my weird poetic oracles? Not likely. Readers of the *Chicago Sun-Times*, the *Times Picayune of New Orleans*, and the *Kalamazoo Telegraph-Press* wouldn't appreciate my advice about doing dreamwork as a dyadic technique to enhance their sex lives.

But the fantasy began to grow that maybe I could carve out a new market for my column in the alternative newsweeklies of the US and Canada. These were the progressive-leaning media located in mid-size to large urban areas. Some had originated as "underground newspapers" during the hippie era but evolved into more sophisticated cultural interpreters. Might they be willing to experiment with my witty little astrology column?

I couldn't afford to hire a marketing company to assist me, or even a friend who would work for cheap. The plan to get more widely syndicated had to be my job.

In those ancient days before the internet and text messaging existed, I conducted my crusade by snail mail and telephone. With the help of scissors, glue, and Kinko's copy shops, I whipped up homemade promotional materials and sent regular waves of inquiries to all the alternative newsweeklies I could find out about in North America. The research had to be done at the local library, since there were no such things as "online" and "Google."

Hallelujah! It worked! At least slightly. New papers accepted my column for publication! *The Chico News and Review* in Chico, California ($10 a week), and the *Blade Citizen* in San Diego County ($10). Plus, the *Santa Cruz Express* offered me a hefty raise if I would move my column from the *Good Times* to its pages. Wow. Suddenly, I was raking in $110 per week!

Fortunately, my avant-funk rock music career and my mega-bestselling poetry book were subsidizing food and rent. (No, they weren't. Just kidding.)

But after my slight upgrade, I added a second hotplate. Now I could have two pots cooking at once—hot rice and veggies in the same meal! I got a used mattress to replace the one-inch foam pad I'd been tossing and turning on since leaving college.

I honed my game. Intensified my marketing. Tried the tips and clues about self-marketing suggested by Jay Conrad Levinson's book *Guerrilla Marketing*.

I sent alternative newsweekly editors red nine-by-12-inch envelopes decked with wacky commemorative stamps and excerpts of the funniest bits from my column.

I made friends with the receptionists and classified ads people at prospective publications. Always called back right on time when someone told me, "Maybe we'll try you in nine months when our ad revenues go up."

Oh—and very important!—I worked to improve my writing skills. That might have helped a little. I also steadily added to my astrological knowledge, reading every half-interesting book I could find on astrological theory in the library and used bookstores. Among the authors who taught me the most were Alan Oken, Liz Greene, Isabel Hickey, Linda Goodman, and Marc Edmund Jones. My first and best mentor, Dane Rudhyar, continued to inspire me.

By then, three quirky, artful creations were making headway as syndicated features in the alternative newsweeklies. They were Lynda Barry's comic strip *Ernie Pook's Comeek*, Matt Groening's *Life in Hell* comic strip, and *Straight Dope*, a question-and-answer column written by pseudonymous author Cecil Adams. I took their success as a sign that there was hope for me.

A year after Chico and San Diego came aboard, a Kansas City weekly signed on for $4/week. My first non-California account! Maybe I was no longer preaching to the woo-woo crowd.

A few other new publications came calling, too, including a Massachusetts newspaper that placed my column on the same page as "Shoe Corner," a column for senior citizens interested in buying comfortable shoes.

A few years later, with 15 papers in tow, I signed on with Alter-Net, the progressive syndicate. The advantage that organization had over a self-marketer like myself was that it had regular, friendly contact with the main editors and publishers at many of the papers I wanted to be part of.

At first, AlterNet took 50% of the money the papers paid for my column. Later I negotiated my share up to 75%.

Explosive growth didn't follow, but there was a new buzz about my work. My big breakthrough erupted during the first Gulf War. Enraged by the tragic explosion of American militarism and imperialism, I filled my horoscopes with witty politically progressive rants interwoven with personal forecasts.

A raft of new alternative newsweeklies signed on to publish my column, including the *New York Press*, *The Stranger* in Seattle, the *Baltimore City Paper*, the *Metro Times* in Detroit, and the *Philadelphia City Paper*.

Thanks, Gulf War! Within a month after American troops had finished decimating Iraq, my syndication had grown to 42 newspapers.

I discuss this bizarrely fortuitous development further in "Not Sticking to Astrology," a piece later in this book.

Up All Night

For many years, my writing schedule was 9 p.m. to 5 a.m. When I worked on my horoscope column, I customarily started after nightfall and soldiered on till dawn. My bedtime was 5:30. I would wake up eight and a half hours later at 2 p.m.

Why? If I stayed up all night, I reasoned, I could tap into the psychic airwaves with optimal clarity. What better way to feel out my readers' moods than if I was awake while they were asleep and dreaming?

When I was growing up, I gathered abundant evidence that telepathy was real. But since so many adults told me it wasn't, I doubted my own experience. The reservations dissolved once I found my calling. Information that flowed into me via telepathy became crucial in my efforts to craft 12 weekly love letters. Today, I am adept at what I do—addressing my readers' depths—because I learned to apprehend and interpret the fantasies and feelings, they spin out all night long.

★

In more recent years, I have kept a schedule akin to the majority of the world's adults: sleeping at night and working during the day. But the capacities and faculties I developed during my long training as a night laborer have remained steadfast.

When I first made the transition, I derived encouragement from poet Linh Dinh. At the beginning of his career, he often stayed up late and wrote, blissfully wrestling with epiphanies till the sun came up. The power of the darkness unleashed his bottomless fertility. He was able to conjure inspirations that were harder for him to access during the shiny time when wide-awake people poured out tsunamis of chatter.

Dinh's routine changed as he aged, though, in part because he got married and chose to keep more conventional hours.

But his early imprint remained vigorous inside him. "Now I can write at any time of the day," he says, "because I always carry the night inside of me."

It's not as if I never woke up early during the first half of my career as a horoscope columnist. I made a few exceptions.

One dramatic transgression of my sacred sleep ritual happened at a key moment in my career's evolution.

Over 70 newsweeklies were publishing my column when Doug Simmons, editor of New York's *Village Voice*, called me with an offer: Leave the *New York Press*, a paper of modest circulation that had paid me $75 a week for the previous three years, and jump to the Pulitzer Prize-winning *Voice*, circulation 200,000. My new paycheck would be $500 per issue.

Simmons asked me to fly cross-country from my home north of San Francisco for a 9 a.m. confab in New York two days hence. I agreed, even though the meeting would take place at 6 a.m. California time, the hour when I would customarily have just fallen asleep.

I'm a tea drinker, never coffee—except that morning in Lower Manhattan, when I needed an extra boost. Simmons and I hashed out the deal in a café a few blocks from the *Village Voice* offices in Cooper Square in the East Village. There was no hashing, though, really. I accepted exactly what Simmons offered.

Soon, my horoscope column was splashed weekly near the

front of one of my favorite publications. The *Voice* was not only New York's biggest weekly newspaper, but was also distributed nationally.

I could barely grasp my astounding fortune. Years before, when I had been coming of age as a writer, I had studied the prose in the *Voice* to improve my craft. Among my inspirations were virtuoso writers like Robert Christgau, Molly Haskell, Greil Marcus, James Wolcott, Jon Pareles, and Vivian Gornick.

The *Voice* had won two Pulitzer Prizes before I arrived and captured a third during my time there.

For 13-plus years, "Free Will Astrology" appeared without fail in every issue of the *Voice*. It wasn't a coincidence that during this time, my syndication empire expanded from 70-some to 130-some.

Enchantments for You #3

ARIES: Secret Superpower: Generous Risks

TAURUS: Secret Superpower: Ecstatic Duty

GEMINI: Secret Superpower: Rowdy Bliss

CANCERIAN: Secret Superpower: Fertile Chaos

LEO: Secret Superpower: Joyous Upheaval

VIRGO: Secret Superpower: Unauthorized Healing

LIBRA: Secret Superpower: Friendly Shock

SCORPIO: Secret Superpower: Subversive Enlightenment

SAGITTARIUS: Secret Superpower: Guerrilla Splendor

CAPRICORN: Secret Superpower: Sacred Transgression

AQUARIUS: Secret Superpower: Dissident Love

PISCES: Secret Superpower: Rebellious Apotheosis

Element 2

If we don't ceaselessly conjure and nurture and refine and experiment with the love mojo within us, it will confuse us. It may damage and desecrate our intelligence.

If we ceaselessly conjure and nurture and refine and experiment with the love mojo within us, it will hone our perceptions and amplify our intelligence.

Chapter 5

Your Love Mojo Artistry
+
My Love Mojo Artistry
=
Our Love Mojo Artistry

Be Alert for the Subtle Miracles

How can we outwit and escape the numbing trance that every-day routine seems to foster? What can we do to stay alert to the subtle miracles and intriguing mysteries and numinous beauty that surround us on all sides?

Some possibilities:

∞ Make it a daily practice to refresh the ways we perceive the world. Can we imagine what it would be like to change how we use our eyes?

∞ Scan for opportunities to play and for creatures that like to play. Regularly test the hypothesis that playing is a prime strategy for liberation.

∞ Assume that the entire world is a constantly chang-ing source of oracular revelation that has meaning for us—perhaps a meaning we have never before realized or understood.

∞ Experiment with what happens when we use empathy and intuition to imagine how animals and other people experience life.

∞ Don't take things too seriously or too personally or

too literally.

∞ Expose ourselves to provocative myths and intriguing symbols. Seek out stories that bend and twist our beliefs. Be open to exploring events and phenomena that elude rational explanation.

∞ Give our unconscious minds the message that we want to learn more and more about how to feel deeply.

∞ Cultivate a willingness, eagerness, and receptivity to being surprised.

Feed Your Imagination
with Beauty ⟳

Think of all the stories, images, and sounds you invite into your
beautiful head.

Do you absorb a relentless barrage of distressing news reports
and movies brimming with brutality and gossipy tales of decline
and degeneration? Does your diet consist primarily of repulsive
memes that agitate your revulsion?

If so, that's the equivalent, for your psyche, of eating rotting
vulture intestines and crud scraped off from the inner wall of a
dumpster behind a McDonald's and pitchers of trans fats recov-
ered from the deep fryer in the kitchen at a Dunkin' Donuts.

On the other hand, maybe you seek out, at least part of the
time, stories that loosen your fixations and riffs that stretch your
understanding of the human condition and news about situations that are working well.

If so, you're taking decent care of your precious insides. You're
practicing good imaginal hygiene.

Nigerian writer Ben Okri: "Beware of the stories you read or
tell; subtly, at night, beneath the waters of consciousness, they
are altering your world."

Diane di Prima: "The only war that matters is the war against
the imagination. All other wars are subsumed by it."

Me: The delusional drive for perfection that fuels fundamentalism is a weapon in the war that di Prima references. In its natural state, the imagination yearns to be free to explore ever-fresh
variety and mystery and paradox, which perfectionism eschews.

Elizabeth Gilbert: "You need to learn how to select your

thoughts just the same way you select your clothes every day. That's a power you can cultivate. If you want to control things in your life so bad, work on the mind. That's the only thing you should be trying to control."

I invite you to read this fine article on imaginal hygiene by educator Morgan Brent: https://tinyurl.com/ImaginalHygiene.

Taking a Break from the Collective's Monkey Mind

One possible goal of meditation is to empty our minds of their obsessively generated thoughts, habitual rationalizations, and addictive images.

Alas, much of the media functions as a reverse meditation machine: a manic chaoticizer. Not only does it stir up our own mental clatter, but it also floods us with seething surges of other people's personal pandemoniums.

Furthermore, it delivers this rattling racket with entertaining words and brilliant colors and crystalline sounds, driving it as deeply into our psyches as our own vivid flotsam.

What might ameliorate the effects of the media's relentless reverse meditations? Can you regularly clear a space for the counsel of the still, small voice within?

I suggest a once-a-month day-long fast from all media: a luxurious immersion in the Wild Silence.

Using our fears and superstitions and delusions as a power source, our monkey minds and monkey hearts are churning out fake news about ourselves all the time.

One possible remedy: Treat our inner fake news with the same healthy, exuberant skepticism we do toward politicians' and media's fake news.

Auguries for You #4

ARIES: Bless your appetite. May it be voracious and unapologetic.

I send you much respect for your buried needs and half-conscious yearnings. May they flow into clear view for you to embrace and celebrate.

Congratulations for your willingness to name the unspeakable truths and acknowledge the embarrassing fears.

May you be willing to rebel against your self-image for the sake of gaining access to deeper reserves of mojo and inspiration.

TAURUS: Philosopher Alan Watts said the whole world is wiggling all the time. Clouds, trees, sky, water, humans: Everything's constantly shimmying and jiggling and waggling.

One of our problems, Watts said, is that we're "always trying to straighten things out." We feel nagging urges to deny or cover up or eliminate the wiggling. "Be orderly," we command reality. "Be neat and composed and predictable."

But reality never obeys. It's forever engaging in what it does best: flickering and fluctuating and flowing.

In accordance with your astrological potentials, Taurus, I encourage you to rebel against any tendencies you might have to resist the eternal wiggle. Instead, relish it. Rejoice in it. Align yourself with it. It's your birthright to do so.

GEMINI: In the version of astrology I find most interesting, reincarnation is a foundational hypothesis. In each lifetime, a soul chooses a particular astrological sign because the qualities of that sign are what the soul wants to learn about.

In other words, being born a Gemini doesn't mean you're automatically a consummate wizard at being a Gemini. On the contrary, in this lifetime you're a Gemini in order to learn the art of being one.

You're here to get the hang of what it's like to be smart and versatile and adaptable and changeable. Your assignment is to keep yourself endlessly entertained and build a strong center of gravity as you weave your life together with a variety of lively activities and ideas and friends.

CANCERIAN: The ancient Greek mythic hero Orpheus possessed an abundance of what we call emotional intelligence. His feelings were profound, well wrought, and lyrical. He had a virtuoso talent for rousing sublime passions in others.

The music he played on his lyre inspired warring soldiers to stop fighting. Wild animals listened raptly. Workaholics ceased their compulsive toil. When he gave concerts in the underworld, even the cold-hearted rulers of that infernal realm were charmed.

Was Orpheus a Cancerian? I think so.

LEO: Why do people love you? What attracts them to you? Can we identify the qualities in you that provoke adoration?

It's hard to generalize or summarize, of course. But one factor that generates excitement in others is your role as a radiant benefactor of uplift and inspiration.

Below are epithets I have dreamed up to refer to Leo people

who have provided me with that blessing.

- ∞ Succulent Dazzle
- ∞ Molten Luminosity
- ∞ Splashy Fire Bliss
- ∞ Reverent Reveler
- ∞ Shimmering Joy Beam
- ∞ Opulent Delirium
- ∞ Passion Donor
- ∞ Incandescent Rapture
- ∞ Wild Soul Throbber
- ∞ Fluidic Gleam Blessing
- ∞ Sacred Heart Salvation

VIRGO: Eighteenth-century painter Joshua Reynolds said that a "disposition to abstractions, to generalizing and classification, is the great glory of the human mind."

To that lofty sentiment, his fellow artist William Blake responded, "To generalize is to be an idiot; to particularize is the alone distinction of merit."

So I may be an idiot when I make the following generalization, but I think I'm right. Now and then—not frequently—it may be in your best interests to rely on crafty generalizations to guide your decisions. Getting bogged down in details at the expense of the big picture—missing the forest for the trees—is a potential pitfall that you can and should avoid.

On the other hand, you are the zodiac's champion particularizer. It's your birthright to express that predilection in all its glory. Have at it!

LIBRA: I stumbled upon an engineering textbook for under-graduates. There was a section on how to do technical writing, as opposed to the literary kind. It quoted "To Helen," a poem by Edgar Allan Poe:

> Helen, thy beauty is to me / Like those Nicean barks
> of yore / That gently, o'er a perfumed sea, / The weary
> way-worn wanderer bore / To his own native shore.

The book then gave advice to the student: "To express these ideas in technical writing, we would simply say, 'He thinks Helen is beautiful.'"

But it's best for you Libras not to take shortcuts like the engineering textbook. For the sake of your emotional health and spiritual integrity, don't indulge in treating the world as if it were stunted, abbreviated, or sterilized.

SCORPIO: I will name three tasks that are among the hardest any human can attempt. They are more difficult for you Scorpios than they are for other astrological signs. Paradoxically, you also have the greatest potential to excel at them and perform them with maximum verve.

Here they are:

∞ Interrupt and overthrow negative trains of thought in the midst of their flow through your mind.

∞ Negotiate partial solutions to complex problems. Do the half-right thing when it's hard to do the fully right thing.

∞ Understand that to graduate from weird karma that has persisted, you must accept the situation as it is, acknowledge any role you played in precipitating and prolonging it, and be gratitude for all it has taught you.

SAGITTARIUS: Over the years, you've explored expansive ideas about what characterizes a good time. You have a fertile imagination as you dream up interesting ways to amuse and please yourself. I like that about you.

Sometimes it gets extreme, true, but it's a valuable capacity.

In the coming years, I'm guessing you will add to this colorful tradition with further novel variations of the definition of "pleasure" and "happiness."

My advice: Enjoy your experiments without apology. Explore the inexhaustible possibilities. Be willing to play and improvise as you add to your repertoire of bliss and joy and excitement.

To paraphrase the Wiccan credo: As long as it harms no one— including yourself—anything goes.

CAPRICORN: No one knows the scientific reasons why long-distance runners sometimes get a "second wind."

Nonetheless, such a thing exists. It enables athletes to resume their peak efforts after seemingly having reached a point of exhaustion.

Metaphorical versions of this happy event occur for you Capricorns more often than they do for all other zodiac signs. You are the champion of second winds.

AQUARIUS: Aquarian chemist Spencer Silver was a co-inventor of Post-it notes, those small pieces of paper you can temporarily attach to things and then remove to attach again and again.

Speaking about the process he went through to develop this crafty convenience, he said, "If I had thought about it, I wouldn't have done the experiment. The literature was full of examples that said you can't do this."

I'd like to make him one of your patron saints. Like him, you have vast potential to make practical breakthroughs that may seem unlikely.

With Silver as your inspiration, I hope you periodically ignore conventional wisdom as necessary—even your own. One of your main assignments in life is to respect your intuition when it suggests you consider improbable accomplishments.

PISCES: In the autumn, the sweet gum tree in my yard is a paradoxical sight. As its green leaves turn red and fall to the ground, it seems to announce that it's slipping into a state of dormancy.

But at the same time, it sprouts hundreds of spiky, bright green balls full of seeds, as if to declare it's bursting with irrepressible vitality.

This phase of the sweet gum's life is an apt metaphor for the way you Pisceans periodically mix endings and beginnings. You have the potential to develop a knack for growing in vitality as a part of you fades away.

Fear Versus Intuition

I love to help readers learn to distinguish between their fearful fantasies and authentic, accurate intuitions.

A reliable way for me to earn the right to discourse on this subject is to keep learning more about how to distinguish between my fearful fantasies and my authentic, accurate intuitions. I doubt I will ever gain full proficiency at this skill. But I'm making progress. I'm better at it than I used to be.

In the history of civilization, has there ever been a time when this skill was less than critical? I don't think so. But it's even more essential nowadays. Humans are in the midst of a thrilling and unnerving pivot point. Decrepit habits of thought are unraveling. Structures that have kept us enthralled to fake values are crumbling. The coming decades will be ripe with opportunities to forge a world that empowers the soul to flourish.

As the monumental mutations proliferate, many so-called leaders cram our imaginations with scary visions and angry emotions. They sell us the delusion that their visions of gloom and doom are rooted in logical analysis.

In the face of their toxic propaganda, it's wise to remember that we have the power to shun their fearmongering. As a partial antidote, we can tune in to the guidance of the demure but potent voice within us—the muse-like intuition that will, if we allow, lead us capably through the zigzags of our destiny, even when we experience the personal ramifications of civilization's colossal transformations.

★

Knowing the difference between our fearful fantasies and our authentic, accurate intuitions is a spiritual superpower.

Let's explore what it means to grasp the distinctions between the frightening, alienating pictures that pop into our imaginations and the warm, clear directions available from the deepest source within us.

Many people confuse these two. I've done it myself on countless occasions. When an alarming future possibility wells up in our imagination, we worry it's a sign that our intuition is foreshadowing a real event that will literally assail us.

For instance, we may fantasize about getting in a car accident or falling down a flight of stairs. Maybe we dream of a loved one becoming sick or a beloved pet getting lost.

On a few occasions, demoralizing fantasies like these are authentic warnings from our deeper knowing. Maybe we should indeed drive more carefully or urge our loved one to get a medical check-up. But mostly, these dire scenes invading our mind are not accurate premonitions. True intuition is rarely fueled by fear. It's not prone to motivate us with dread.

Our true intuition emerges from the part of us that knows love is the ultimate law. It blooms in the spirit of affinity and intimacy. Like a slow-motion fountain of lucid compassion, it reveals the objective truth about the riddles before us. It shows us the big picture.

Forbidding fantasies, on the other hand, burn and itch and demoralize us. They drain our energy and cloud our judgment. They fill us with obsessive urges to run and hide or act desperate and melodramatic.

I don't believe our true intuition is always calm and emotionally neutral. It isn't, necessarily. But I will say this: The feelings that accompany true intuition aren't alienating. They don't arouse hate or revenge, and they don't encourage us to act superior to others. When true intuition flows, we are usually empowered, not rendered hopeless or helpless.

True intuition may provoke our anger. But if so, it's an invigorating rage that leads to clarity and constructive action.

True intuition may show us difficult truths, but it offers directions about how to deal courageously with those truths. True intuition may suggest changes and adjustments, but it does so in ways that groom our poise and grace.

I will emphasize this point: True intuition may not reveal that everything will turn out fine or that we can keep living exactly as we have been. True intuition isn't falsely optimistic. But if it does alert us to how we need to transform, it does so with love and aplomb, not with loathing and panic.

Here's another key theme. Just as our true intuition never works by spooking us, neither does it flatter us with grandiose suggestions about how faultless and superb we are.

It may even inform us to correct our attitude or abandon a delusion or fix a wrong conclusion. It may tactfully but firmly show us that we have been suffering from some ignorance and need to wise up.

True intuition reveals the story of our lives from our soul's point of view, not our ego's. It's the voice of our inner teacher.

The certainty that true intuition provides is never strident or overconfident, but reliably humble and impeccable.

Now is a perfect moment to ruminate on these ideas and add insights of your own. I invite you to have fun flushing away any disquiets and perturbations and trepidations that may have distorted your relationship with your true intuition.

I'm giving myself the same invitation, too. I always need to do more work!

PS: One way to facilitate the process is to cut back on the amount of horrifying and disorienting images we allow to flow into our imagination from the TV, internet, newspapers, movies, and other mass media.

Relationship with Intuition

"Intuition" refers to the capacity to get insight without calling on logic and rational thinking. It seems to enable us to skip steps as we quickly and directly home in on a clear insight. We may have the sensation that the crisp, lucid realization has been fully formed for some time, and has been waiting for us to pounce on it.

Surprisingly, many scientists don't regard intuition as being the province of pseudoscience. Researchers have studied it in lab experiments.

But as I meditate on intuition here, I speak as a poet and creative artist, not a scientist.

In seeking intuitive help, one reliable spur comes from formulating specific, timely questions, like:

◈ "What is it I most need to learn right now?"

◈ "Who is it I most need to learn from?"

◈ "What practical measure can I initiate to live my life with more vigor and rigor?"

◈ "How could I attract new experiences that will enhance my intelligence and decision-making?"

Intuition often reveals the action we need to take *next*. It doesn't necessarily show us the entire plan of the big picture and all the particular steps required to assemble the big picture.

So we shouldn't try to pressure intuition to give us a mountaintop perspective. Instead, we might ask, "What one or two things should I do in the immediate future?"

Four more things I'll mention about intuition: One is to work with dreams. That takes study and expertise. Our nightly adventures speak a different language from that of our waking life.

But if we develop even a modicum of skills at translation, we can draw a steady stream of useful clues from our other brain in that other world.

Dreams have been crucial in helping me do shadow work—dealing with aspects of me that are unripe and dumb. And that has helped me transcend my imprints and conditioning, thereby fostering my true intuition.

Another good practice for intuition is to ask the question, "What does my death say?" On one's deathbed, what does one want to look back at and say, "That was important. That was important. That was important. No, that wasn't so important." This exercise can be a tonic informant that helps intuition focus and work with maximum efficiency.

Another aid to intuition, at least for me, is walking and moving. Nature hikes and strolls around town often rouse realizations that turn out to be useful and enduring. I take a notebook or recorder with me to capture them.

Here's one more aspect of my relationship with intuition. I'm most successful in accessing sudden outbreaks of fresh truth when I have gone as far as I can in doing research, thinking hard, employing logic, and being objective and reasonable. This usually involves invoking the help of the scientific method.

Then I hand over my ruminations and questions to intuition and say, "What more can you tell me, given that I've come this far with all my analysis? What treasure can you add?"

Disappear Fear

Here's your mantra: "I disappear my fear. I resurrect my audacity."

Say it or sing it. Let it flow out of you upon waking each morning as you lie in bed. Make it the last sound on your lips as you drop off to sleep.

Have fun with it. Dip into your imagination to come up with different ways to let it fly. Say it as your favorite cartoon character might say it, or like a person with a Russian accent, like your inner teenager, like a cockatoo, like the person you'll be when you're 87 years old.

"I disappear my fear. I resurrect my audacity. I disappear my fear. I resurrect my audacity."

★

If that spell isn't right for you, here's another idea.

Be scarier than your fears. If an anxious thought leaps into your mind, bare your teeth and growl, "Get out of here or I will demolish you!"

If a demon visits you in a nightly dream, chase after it with a torch and sword, screaming, "Begone, foul spirit, or I will burn your mangy dreck!"

Don't tolerate bullying in any form, whether it comes from a critical voice in your head or from supposedly nice people trying to guilt-trip you.

"I am a brave conqueror who cannot be intimidated!" is what you could say, or "I am a gorgeous monster of love and goodness who will defeat all threats to my integrity!"

Arguments with Goddess ✶

In addition to the Slam Book, I have used other methods to encourage interactions with my audience. They have helped me cultivate my $I^2 <-> $ THOU practice.

One is below, my Arguments with Goddess service.

ARGUMENTS WITH GODDESS

Our Prayer Hagglers are standing by, ready to study the protests and complaints you want Goddess to ponder and respond to.

Send us your outraged, rebellious, poignant appeals. Tell us exactly what makes you mad and sad and bad. Don't be inhibited about casting your pleas in the form of arguments.

Within 72 hours, we will translate and relay your petitions to Goddess from the depths of our meditations. We will be sure she understands your precise discomforts.

Be consoled and hopeful! We have extensive training in conversing with Goddess in her native tongues. She listens attentively to our elegant and eloquent flourishes. She responds creatively.

We know just how to offer up your quarrels and disputes as rapturous supplications she will regard with compassion.

Telepathics Anonymous

Early in my horoscope-writing career, I began urging my readers to contact me telepathically, either while awake or during dreams or in any state in between those two.

Would that actually work? I didn't know at first. But it was a fun prospect. Then, as now, I aspired to solicit influence and teaching from everywhere. Why not invite my readers to interweave with me via the realm that mystery religions and esoteric philosophies have referred to as the astral plane or astral world?

I was joyfully surprised when the psychic contacts flowed in. How amazing and uncanny! The evidence was unimpeachable: I was receiving a steady stream of information, images, questions, and feelings from strangers responding to my writing.

To harness the phenomenon, I developed techniques as a medium. Sometimes I engaged in automatic writing, transcribing the messages. On occasion, I did stream-of-consciousness narrations into my tape recorder.

As gleeful as I was at the discovery, I was also overwhelmed. In the early phase of my career as a semi-famous beacon, I was untrained and unpracticed in weeding out what was disorienting and draining from what was interesting and useful.

But gradually I learned. When I did, I had another reliable modality that empowered me to be tutored and transformed.

For years, I didn't talk much about this phenomenon. But at one point I founded an organization that served as an iconic tutelary for my psychic work. Below is the text I have distributed now and then in various venues, including my column.

Welcome to Telepathics Anonymous, a 12-step program for those who are not yet fully cognizant of how the thoughts and feelings of others spill over into their own.

Are you one of the millions of stubborn rationalists suffering from the delusion that your psyche is an utterly separate and sealed-off territory?

Telepathics Anonymous offers proof that you are in continual extrasensory contact with more souls than you can imagine.

As a get-acquainted gift, Telepathics Anonymous will present you with an omen concerning the future of your relationship with love exactly 95 hours and 19 minutes from right now.

How to Not Be a Know-It-All

Here's an interview I did with journalist Mark C. Anderson at the *Monterey County Weekly*. He is @MontereyMCA on Instagram and Twitter.

Mark C. Anderson: Whenever I read your column, I muse about how almost every horoscope has information that's personally meaningful to me and that I can use. I'm an Aries, but I love meditating on Taurus, Gemini, Libra and all the rest. At the same time, you really do know my Aries idiosyncrasies. You help me be a better Aries. How can both things be true?

Me: There's an amusing riddle about the job I do that I've never figured out. It's part of the fun, and it's always evolving. In the early days, I kept asking myself, "How can this thing I do possibly work? How can people draw so much help and inspiration from a sun sign column?"

Eventually, I realized there are powers in play I don't know about or comprehend. Some Dazzle Beyond My Conscious Awareness creates the horoscopes. One source of this Dazzle comprises my readers, who are in touch with me via email, social media, personal contact out in public, and telepathy.

A psychic once told me there are two types of psychics: narrow-band and broad-band. She said she was a narrow-band psychic, who teaches and works with individuals, whereas I am a broad-band, reading and communing with the energy of large groups.

In my dreams, I regularly attend various schools where I study what it is to be a Pisces or Virgo or Aquarius and all the rest. On occasion, my teachers there are readers I have met in waking life.

Mark C. Anderson: In my experience, you don't dispense pronouncements from on high, and you don't act like a know-it-all. You respect your readers' free will. You often invite them to respond—to be collaborators with you as they consider your suggestions.

Me: When I first offered oracles to the public, I thought of my imagination as a holy shrine that fed from my soul's depths. Later my emphasis shifted. Now I regard my imagination as a holy shrine that feeds both from my soul's depths and from my soul's interactions with other souls.

Everything I create is in part a collaboration with the people and spirits and animals who have touched me, moved me, taught me, changed me. Through my empathetic exchanges with them, I have grown smarter and kinder and wilder.

My aesthetic ethic is that I'm a star and you're a star. I am devoted to developing and expressing my unique individuality, and that happens best as I nurture and am nurtured by your unique individuality.

Years ago, I got an illustrative email from a woman in Northampton, Massachusetts. She wrote, "Thank you. You have helped me become the person I want to be. You have inspired me to become me." I was ecstatic to hear that. She didn't say, "You helped and inspired me to become more like you."

One of my favorite aspirations is to be of service to people as they strive to access parts of themselves that weren't previously accessible, that were oppressed, that were occluded by their conditioning.

Mark C. Anderson: A recent column references the fourth-century woman mathematician Hypatia, philosopher Martin Buber's idea that stories can heal, musician Brian Wilson's encounter with the Ronettes' song "Be My Baby," a suspension bridge in India made from the living roots of fig trees, a chess master's match with a computer named Deep Blue, and the US Congress's failure to give Harriet Tubman a pension in her old age. Then you invoke poet Adrienne Rich, comedian Sarah Silverman, a plea to make Pluto a planet again, and observations about the wind from a nature walk. As far as I know, you have never missed a deadline. What's your secret for staying fresh and freaky and persistent?

Me: After the first 30 months of writing my column, I realized that if I were going to do it until I was an elder—which I wanted—I would have to generate a hefty quotient of delight, both for my readers and myself. To accomplish that, I've worked industriously to become a good listener pumped up on curiosity and beginner's mind. I've made it my vocation to discover the sacred in the profane and the profane in the sacred. One of my most intense pleasures, pursued daily, is to be swept away with insights and experiences I've never had before.

Mark C. Anderson: That theme comes up often in your writing. "Evil is boring" is one of your iconic mottoes. I also love your 11th Commandment, "Thou shall not bore God."

Me: Nor shall thou bore Goddess!

Mark C. Anderson: Amen and awomen, as you might say.

Me: The best way to avoid dreary ruts is to cultivate the capacity to be taught, amazed, charmed, and entertained. I am ambitious to keep this strategy at the heart of my everyday actions. When I wake up each morning, I say a prayer to life: "Surprise me today, s'il vous plaît! Show me what I don't know! Route me in the direction of interesting riddles!"

I assume the Divine Wow Formerly Known as God is like me. She, too, wants to be intrigued and beguiled. She rejoices at having her mind changed. She longs to fulfill her quest for marvelous stories. That's why she launched this mysterious art-game ritual project in the first place.

My bedrock operating principle: To the degree that we bore ourselves and bore each other, we fail to give the Divine Wow the gifts and blessings and stories she created us to provide.

With my libido in fully aroused sublimation mode, I bring her such gifts and blessings and stories. I play fondly and fiercely in her theater and laboratory.

Element 2

If we don't recruit regular delight and enchantment, our intimate relationship with the Great Mystery will decay.

If we recruit regular delight and enchantment, our intimate relationship with the Great Mystery will flourish.

Chapter 6

Your Crafty Delight and Enchantment
+
My Crafty Delight and Enchantment
=
Our Crafty Delight and Enchantment

Sacred Trails

It may turn out that the "blemish" is essential to the beauty.

The "deviation" could be at the core of the strength.

The "wrong turn" might be crucial to getting you back on the path with heart.

★

In light of the hypotheses above, here's a good question to ask: "How will the sacrifice I'm enduring make me available for an interesting assignment and unexpected fulfillment in the future?"

A robust affirmation: "Surrender will make me potent in ways I can't imagine yet."

A wise warning: Getting premature relief from the suffering might stop you from harvesting the suffering's deepest lessons.

★

My wishes for you:

◈ That your apparent breakdowns mutate into breakthroughs

◈ That each spiritual emergency spawns a soulful emergence

◈ That your scary trials lead to sacred trails

The Surprising Truth

I subscribe to Robert Anton Wilson's theory that information, by definition, must contain elements of surprise. If it doesn't deliver ideas, feelings, facts, or perspectives we haven't contemplated before, then it's at least partially rhetoric or propaganda.

In my creative work, I assume that if I steadily come upon insights I have thought about in the past, I'm not working hard enough. I aspire to break down existing cultural forms, not embody and reinforce them. It's my job to be surprised, confounded, scrubbed of certainty.

That's why the use of language is so crucial. It's the primary way we spawn new realities and evolve older ones. In the Biblical myth of Genesis, naming was the power of the first man, Adam. He created the world by naming everything.

But these days, the act of naming is largely corrupt. Who names? Mostly corporate sources, including entertainment and news conglomerates. And those who claim to be in rebellion against corporate sources are often naming in reflexive reaction to them—and are thus conditioned by them.

Can we take back the power of naming? The odds are against us. In the $26 billion pop music industry, for example, we seldom hear novel information that hasn't been articulated countless times before. To be successful, a song must invoke well-worn ideas and emotions.

If it's unfamiliar, if it expresses qualities of love or relationship that haven't been previously named by authorities or celebrities, it's unlikely to get heard.

★

In Ursula K. Le Guin's story "She Unnames Them," Eve decides to reverse her mate's work. She yearns to return to a primordial state when the misunderstandings caused by words no longer stand between her and the rest of creation.

So Eve unnames all the animals, from the sea otters to the bees. When she's done, she marvels at how they feel "far closer than when their names had stood between myself and them like a clear barrier."

What Are Your Liberating Thoughts? (((ⵔ)))

Question: What are the most liberating thoughts you've ever had?
Possible answers:

∞ "If new evidence presents itself, it's okay to change my beliefs."

∞ "I get to choose who's in my life and who isn't."

∞ "I am not my history."

∞ "I can't change something that has already happened, so I will stop worrying about it."

∞ "I am not, nor will I ever be, conventionally beautiful."

∞ "I don't have to respond to people when they say stupid shit to me."

∞ "I am not responsible for the happiness of others."

∞ "I can choose the most uplifting interpretation of disturbing events."

∞ "Life is an ever-changing experiment and infinite game. There is no single right way to live."

∞ "What other people think about me is none of my business."

∞ "To be alive in this moment is the only thing I really have to do."

∞ "I can change the way I want to engage with the world whenever I want to."

∞ "I will not continue working for an unethical or hostile boss. I will only work for people who are generous and kind."

∞ "The world is not mostly about me."

∞ "I am allowed to change my mind."

∞ "We cannot live in a world that is interpreted for us by others. An interpreted world is not a home. Part of the terror is to take back our own listening. To use our own voice. To see our own light." (Elaine Bellezza said this.)

∞ "I am not obligated to play the character someone else has cast me as in their personal screenplay."

∞ "What I feed will grow."

∞ "I could be mistaken."

∞ "Nothing ever happens the same way twice."

∞ "People will show me who they are if I am paying attention."

∞ "If I'm facing a seemingly impossible dilemma, it may mean both options are wrong."

∞ "Boredom is a lack of imagination."

∞ "I don't understand."

∞ "It is OK to be a legend in my own mind."

∞ "Thoughts are not facts."

∞ "I can't get what I want if I don't ask for it."

∞ "I'm not responsible for how people respond when I'm standing up for myself and my health."

∞ "I won't compare my insides to other people's outsides."

∞ "If I don't like who I am, I can change whenever I want."

∞ "I am not responsible for the version of me that you created in your mind."

∞ "I did the best I could do with what I knew at the time."

∞ "Gratitude nullifies fear."

Thanks to My Adversaries!

My puny but illustrious career as a syndicated astrology columnist might never have happened if it weren't for a Taurus astrologer named Robert Cole.

Before I dreamed of writing horoscopes myself, he was creating
a weekly horoscope column for the *Good Times* in Santa Cruz.

I read it on occasion. He wasn't a skillful writer, but I appreciated how he playfully departed from the same old boring format
of conventional horoscope writers. "A Sagittarius with a big nose
and big feet will approach you with an invitation to drink coffee
next to a redwood tree," he once wrote for Aquarians.

As Robert Cole grew more confident of his value to the Santa
Cruz community, he decided to assert his Taurus prerogative
and ask *Good Times* publisher Jay Shore for a raise in pay. Shore
refused, and Cole quit in a huff.

Shore immediately placed an ad in the classifieds section of his
paper, advertising for a replacement. Luckily for me, as I mentioned before, my bicycle had been stolen. As I perused the "For
Sale" section of the *Good Times* classifieds, I spied his solicita-
tion for a new astrologer.

I dashed off my audition column, leading with my perfect
spelling and grammar. Were there other applicants? I didn't know
and still don't. Two days later, Shore hired me. The following
Thursday, he published my first offering in the *Good Times* without a single edit. My long career had begun.

But wait! There were complications. Robert Cole was incensed
that I had dared to become his substitute. He wrote letters to the
editors of three Santa Cruz newspapers, each of which published

his complaint.

Cole ranted against Jay Shore and me. Shore was a "capitalist pig," and I was a scab who had colluded with the greedy boss. Although Cole knew nothing of my astrological training, he called me a fraud with no skill in the ancient art.

That wasn't sufficient revenge for him, though. Somehow, he found out where I lived and mailed me a series of five angry letters. Early on, he demanded that I resign from my new job and stand with him in solidarity against the capitalist pig. "No compromise!" he told me.

But I didn't quit. He got so agitated that he condemned me to everlasting obscurity and insignificance. "You're a flash-in-the-pan, Brezney," he wrote in one of his personal letters to me, spelling my name wrong. "You're a brief toxic blip on the scene. You'll never last. You'll fade into oblivion. You'll lose your powers. I will still be here inspiring readers with my astrological advice long after you're gone."

This message felt like an old-fashioned curse. But it didn't debilitate me. It didn't fill me with fear and trembling. Rather, it energized me. I was motivated to make sure his maledictions would never come true. I resolved to prove him wrong.

Over the years, his curse turned out to be a wonderful influence in my life. It was by no means my sole or even primary stimulus to make myself into a great horoscope writer. But it helped. It played a role in galvanizing me to continually go deeper in my understanding of astrology and improve at the art of writing.

My self-appointed competitor got a job writing horoscopes for another weekly newspaper in Santa Cruz. He also published a book, *The Book of Houses: An Astrological Guide to the Harvest Cycle in Human Life.*

In 1992, at age 44, he died, failing to see his hex come to pass. I felt no joy in his demise. On the contrary, I was and have always been grateful to him for assisting me in fulfilling my soul's code.

Amazingly, Robert Cole was an important catalyst in my life.

The early days of my gig as a horoscope writer benefited from another use of the *via negativa*.

Other than Robert Cole, there were no role models in the astrological community who cultivated a frisky, amusing approach. Many of them felt defensive about being dismissed as kooks, which is why they overcompensated by being ponderous and tediously serious.

I had heard of one astrologer who had a more lighthearted style. The Cosmic Muffin, also known as Darrell Martinie, did a spirited radio show on Boston's WBCN. I never actually tuned in—that was before the internet made all stations available globally—but a few friends on the East Coast had told me it was charming.

Were there any horoscope columnists who avoided being generic and bland? I didn't know any.

"You want to have a good time, so go along with the ideas of buddies you like and be happy," advised syndicated astrologer Carroll Righter in one of his daily horoscope columns.

"Be direct, take initiative, and strive to get to the heart of matters," admonished famous horoscope writer Sydney Omarr.

"Routine jobs can be cleared away at last," counseled syndicated astrologer Joyce Jillson, adding, "Go through your residence and start cleaning closets and drawers."

One widely published horoscope columnist offended me more

than the others: Jeane Dixon.

Her use of astrology was everything I didn't want mine to be: obsessed with celebrities, expressed with cliché-ridden language, and rife with pandering to her readers' narcissism.

Her political beliefs were anathema to me, as well. Among the right-wing politicians she counseled were racist Senator Strom Thurmond and Republican Thug Presidents Richard Nixon and Ronald Reagan.

I didn't hate Jeane Dixon. On the contrary, I loved her for providing such a lucid symbol to define myself in opposition to. In studying her approach, I got good ideas about how not to shape my own career in astrology. She was a perfect choice to serve as my anti-role model.

Reader Mail

Receiving diametrically opposed opinions of my work's value has medicinal value. It helps keep me from believing too strongly in either the insults or the praise.

I'll provide extremes exemplifying the range of reader communications that have arrived over the years.

Here's one:

> Where is the real Rob? We have been following you for years. Whoever has taken your place should dress up as a clown. Bring back the original guy please and dump the ridiculous impersonator. Can't bear to read his bullshit.

Here's another one, which came after I encouraged my readers not to vote for Donald Trump:

> You used to be smart, at least for the last 20 years I've been reading you. But now I see you're an idiotic, misinformed, ignorant, delusional, misguided dirtbag.
>
> PS: You don't have any fucking right to write about anything besides astrology.

Below is another, in which a Sagittarius reader hated how I invoked the metaphor of a windmill.

> I advise you to quit your job. You do not write horo-

scopes at all. You write hard to follow musings full of ridiculous analogies. I am not a windmill. I am nothing like wind blowing through a windmill. I work my ass off and I can't work any harder. Stop insulting me with your motivational douchebaggery.

You are a con artist who is diluted and full of himself.

Here's the horoscope he didn't like:

When the wind blows at 10 miles per hour, a windmill generates eight times more power than when the breeze is five miles per hour. Judging from the astrological omens, I suspect there will be a similar principle at work in your life during the coming weeks. A modest increase in effort and intensity will make a huge difference in the results you produce. Are you willing to push yourself a bit beyond your comfort level in order to harvest a wave of abundance?

I will provide one further example of messages that arrive from the "Quit Your Job, Brezsny" crowd. They are incited by the fact that while I am a cisgender heterosexual man, I'm also a champion of gender fluidity. I recognize a billion and one different flavors of gender identity and sexual identity. I want everyone to feel perfectly free and empowered and unafraid to embody and express any variation they please.

Because I periodically make public declarations to this effect, I attract nasty communiqués from people who are addicted to the fixation that there can't and shouldn't be anything else besides pure male and pure female. The hate mail I get can't compare with the toxic messages that LGBTQIA+ people experience far too often, of course.

Here's an email I got from a zealot after I published a horoscope that praised gender fluidity.

> I am not EVER going to be a woman, not EVER going to dress like one, not EVER going to smell like one, not EVER going to cut off my dick to resemble one.
>
> Your "horoscopes" are the most retarded, nonsense filled pieces of drek I've ever read. Perhaps if you pulled that head of yours out of your ass, you might be able to write a REAL horoscope.
>
> Just go to Thailand and have your dick cut off. Then YOU act like a fucking woman, BITCH.

Here's the horoscope I wrote that the Angry Guy objected to:

> Upcoming adventures might make you more manly if you're a woman. If you're a man, the coming escapades could make you more womanly. How about if you're trans? Odds are that you'll become even more gender fluid.
>
> I may be exaggerating a bit. The transformations I'm referring to may not be visible to casual observers. They will mostly unfold in the depths of your psyche.
>
> But they won't be merely symbolic, either. There'll be mutations in your biochemistry that will expand your sense of your own gender.
>
> If you respond enthusiastically to these shifts, you will begin a process that could turn you into an even

more complete and attractive human being than you already are.

I'm pleased that I get more messages of thanks and praise than dismissal and scorn. Below is an email from a reader who likes what she sees:

> You interpret the tales the wind people have always been trying to shoulder-tap whisper at us. You tantalize our souls' taste buds with addicting teachings of how to grow one's glow. You are the arrow piercing news delivery from the left right above within & below. You open our hearts' windows to let in tornados hurling mind-blowing ocean-deep wowwwwws.
>
> So just wanna say thanks a priceless bazillion, to you, the co-teacher of the great mystery and sneaky angels hiding in the snow. For every time I read, I learn a little bit more than a lot, and now am engorged with the desire of knowing how much breathtakingly beautiful know there is to know.

Below are five more love notes to me.

◈ You write unassailable legal briefs in rainbow-colored chalk on sidewalks.

◈ As I ponder all you have written, I am bewildered by the love I feel for you. You are a fierce angel sweeping past in a cool storm of wings, tenderly slapping me in the face while passing by, roaring a divine song all around me and in my bones. I give you my gratitude.

◈ Your love notes from the Universe have done more to keep me happy and balanced than just about anything else. Although I have never met you, you seem to have an unobstructed view of the interior of my psyche and an unerring sense of precisely what I need to hear at any given time to help me to either stay or to get to where I need to be to be my happy, whole, and creative best self.

◈ You are a prolific coyote whose mind is part labyrinth, part cathedral, part jungle, part macrochip. (What's a "macrochip"? You inspire me to invent new words and worlds.)

◈ You write with such radical beauty, skilled sweetness, and seemingly infinite imagination. You are a literary trickster and a feisty optimist, and I'm grateful for your work.

But... but... but...

My horoscopes don't work for everybody! Here's what the editor of the *Metro Times*, a Detroit newspaper, wrote when he fired me in May 2014 after I had appeared there for 19 years.

> In the wake of announcements of the "superweekly" created by the merger of the two newspapers *Metro Times* and *Real Detroit*, some readers have one burning question that outshines all others: Will the new paper keep the "Horoscopes" column by Cal Garrison or the "Free Will Astrology" column by Rob Brezsny?
>
> Over the years, some of our readers have voiced frustration over Brezsny's literate style, such as, "I want to find out what's going to happen next week, and suddenly I'm hearing about an article about Japanese

poetry that appeared in *The New Yorker*? Or hearing about a piece of art that was left on the moon by astronauts? What does this have to do with me?"

These readers find solace in the straightforward horoscopes of Cal Garrison, who's much more likely to tell you to break that thing off, or that you should ask for a raise or something. Far from dancing around the future and quoting magazine articles, Garrison talks to readers as if she were that old friend who knows you need some sense shaken into you.

For readers who prefer Garrison, we have great news: You will see her "Horoscopes" column in place of Rob Brezsny's starting next week, in our paper and up on our website.

PS: Six years after the *Metro Times* switched to Cal Garrison, the newspaper restored "Free Will Astrology" to its pages.

Let's climax this discussion for now with some praise. First from a reader named Libby Heppler. She writes: "Dear Rob: I read you each week in Detroit's *Metro Times*. I love it. It's so spiritual, it's not. It's so earthy, it's cosmic. It's the anti-hero's hero's horoscope! Thanks."

Now from reader Valerie Luzadis: "Thank you, Rob, for your continued care of us all with your pithy, witty, and always on-the-mark advice, questions, and suggestions. They help ease the effort to make real change to this trauma-based, violent world with love, joy, and gratitude."

Oracular Homework #105

Below are three homework assignments for all signs.

Homework Assignment 1. Who laid a curse on you in the past? Who said you would never accomplish your dreams? Who discouraged you, foiled your plans, or hoped to prevent you from fulfilling your soul's code?

Whoever those subverters and detractors were, whether they were relatives or enemies, teachers or bosses, I encourage you to diminish the grip they have had on you.

Push hard. Be a rowdy warrior as you shrink, shred, and dismantle their influence. Be a fierce defender of your integrity and self-respect as you banish their power over you.

What actions can you take to ensure you won't be inhibited or limited by their negative expectations in the future? How can you triumph over their ignorant cruelty?

★

Homework Assignment 2. How can you use your enemies and adversaries as teachers? What healing transformations might you unleash by responding to the influences of people who don't like you, want to prevent you from succeeding, or have beliefs that are opposed to yours?

One useful lesson to learn is how to detach from your hatred and fear of them—not let them poison your mood. Another teaching is how to keep from buying into their opinions about you.

If you work toward your dreams even when you know there's someone who expects you to fail, you hone your willpower. You build up your courage and stamina in ways that aren't possible when everyone loves you and approves of you.

I will go so far as to advise you to identify your own *reverse mentor*. This might be a person who is working in the same field as you or who has skills similar to yours, but who is making different choices than you.

While reflecting on this person's life and work, formulate a clear and vigorous picture of what you don't want to become.

Homework Assignment 3. Say the following aloud: "No. No. No. Nonononononono."

Again. Say, "No. No. No. Nonononononono."

Take it further. Speak the following aloud: "No. No. No. Nonononononono. I can't go along with you on that. No. No. No. I won't take on more responsibilities. No. No. No. No. I don't agree with your views, and I won't let you invade my space or violate my boundaries. No. No. No. Nonononononono."

Now compose 10 more negative affirmations sculpted for your specific needs. Practice them until you can chant them in your sleep. That way, you can say "no" in your dreams, too.

For extra credit: While practicing your refusals, maintain a cheery, blithe, or ebullient tone of voice, stripped of defensiveness and malice.

Redemption Story

My weekly astrology column is called "Free Will Astrology," but for many years it was "Real Astrology."

Here's the story of where "Real Astrology" came from.

Around the time I started writing horoscopes decades ago, I co-founded the rock band Tao Chemical in Santa Cruz. Our local popularity grew inexorably as we gigged regularly, offering a blend of performance art, poetry, and songs with melodic tunes and impeccable grooves.

Tao's drummer and manager Rick Walker was a virtuoso musician who employed rhythmic riffs gathered from many cultures. Our fan base loved the way we embodied the punk values of sarcasm and satire and anarchy, but also expressed joy, optimism, and uplift.

Some punks loathed us for being New Wave, though, and some New Wavers detested us for being punk. Both punks and New Wavers disdained us for being neo-hippies. As is often the case, the purists disapproved of experimenters who blended and blurred genres. How ironic that they were imitating the corporate marketing mavens they allegedly despised.

Here's another factor that roused scorn. We, the members of Tao Chemical, were feminists and advocates for LGBTQIA+ people. Since many of that era's Santa Cruz punks were macho homophobes, they denounced this aspect of our message.

There wasn't an official Cancel Culture back then, but we experienced an early, perverse form of it. One of Tao Chemical's members even got beat up by punks who reviled our activism.

There was one guy—I'll call him Rennie Nova—who took a

special dislike for me and us. He brought his posse to Tao Chemical shows to harass and heckle us.

After the first such foray, he upped the ante. He announced to me that he would cast black magic spells against us. During our next two shows, he and his crew stood in the audience drawing upside-down pentagrams in the air, burning black candles and putrid incense, and scowling at us with their curse faces.

I countered by doing spells of psychic self-defense and the psychospiritual equivalent of Tai Chi: expressing no anger or distress, but affirming that their cartoony behavior would bounce off us and fly back to them.

Next, we called on ritual assistance from four women who called themselves the Dyke Punk Witch Brigade. One night, they joined us onstage at the nightclub Shelley's Too. As the band played our song "Scare Me," our colleagues cast a counter spell designed to sic bats on Rennie Nova and his team.

Amazingly, three bats with long ears soon materialized inside the club and dive-bombed our nemeses until they fled.

That was the last time they dared to show up at a Tao Chemical concert.

In addition to being an early leader of Perverse Cancel Culture, Rennie Nova was a punk musician who called his band "Real Music." I loved the idea of adding the descriptor "Real" to the generic term "music."

As my ultimate revenge against him, I stole his trick: taking "Real" and tacking it on to "Astrology." My column's title, which had previously just been "Rob Brezsny's Astrology," became "Rob Brezsny's Real Astrology." Once again, an adversary served as a beloved resource.

The Greatest Gift You Can Give Yourself

The greatest gift you can give might be the gift you yourself were never given.

Give that gift.

The most valuable service you have to offer your fellow humans may be the service you have always wished were performed for you.

Offer that service.

An experience that wounded you could inspire you to help people who have been similarly wounded.

Heal yourself by healing others.

★

Author V (formerly Eve Ensler) tells us, "You have to give to the world the thing that you want the most, in order to fix the broken parts inside you."

Love Cues and Clues: Write a
Love Letter to Yourself ◎

For all signs: I invite you to write a love letter to yourself.

Say unscripted and surprising words of adoration that fly into your soul brain. Be extravagant and uninhibited as you tally the qualities in yourself that are impressive and amusing.

Your recklessly affectionate appreciation could begin with an invocation like the testimony below.

"I love me with astonished blissful fury. I love me with sense-less luminous alacrity. I love me with tender howling joy. Why? Because I am a ticklish, gorgeous, aching, enchanting Unknown— the raciest and spiciest and zestiest Unknown I could ever create."

Element 2

If we don't cultivate excellent, noble, righteous desires, we will be held hostage by mediocre, stingy, degrading desires.

If we cultivate excellent, noble, righteous desires, they will liberate us from at least some of our suffering.

Chapter 7

Your Righteous Yearnings
+
My Righteous Yearnings
=
Our Righteous Yearnings

Be Tastefully Gonzo

Be tastefully gonzo and gracefully racy.

Walk sleek and lithe like a supernatural mischief champion.

Think chunky and sing funky.

Dream upside-down and breathe inside-out.

Laugh incorrectly and change everything you look at.

Be a wonder-plucker and a thunder-sucker.

Expunge guilt with ruthless compassion and erase shame like
a legendary joker.

Do no harm and take no shit.

When I Do Personal Horoscope Readings

I haven't done personal horoscope readings for years. There's too much other fun work to do! Writing my column! Creating audio horoscopes! Authoring books! Recording music!

But during the phases of my life when I sit face-to-face with curious seekers who want help in untangling their riddles, I prepare with diligent reverence. My first move is to send a set of guidelines to meditate on during the days before our session.

I provide these guidelines below. Maybe they will be of use if you are ever shopping for an astrologer to help illuminate your mysteries.

When I do a personal chart reading, it's crucial that I talk WITH you, not AT you. I summon my best service when we are in dialog.

It's also essential not to set myself up as a flawless fount of divine wisdom. For me to act like an all-knowing expert tends to shut down your access to your inner sources of knowing.

I've been wary of certain styles of fortune-telling ever since a fortune-teller told me when I was young that I would leave the earth at age 29. I spent that year of my life looking for omens of death in my dreams. During the week before my 29th birthday, I cowered in fear and left the house only to brandish my fists at the night sky.

But I survived. And I vowed that in my own role as a fortune-telling astrologer, I would never plant seeds in people's psyches that made them feel helpless to control their destiny.

My motto: Good astrology doesn't impair your willpower, but galvanizes it.

If I do a chart reading for you, my goal is to help you know more about yourself in the here and now. Is it useful to speculate about what might come your way in the months and years to come? Maybe. I'll do that if I think it will enhance your joie de vivre and lust for life.

My playful but accurate intention is to conspire with you to read your own mind. Together, we discover unconscious inclinations lurking in your depths. We figure out where you are located in your long-term cycles and how to identify your highest potentials.

Here's my unruly rule: Astrology isn't a fixed set of strict formulas. It's a web of evocative symbols that liberates your imagination and inspires you to reframe the stories you use to understand your life.

If you and I are investigating your natal chart, I want us to collaborate as we conjure up dynamic new perspectives about your soul's code. Some of our improvisations may ring true for you, while others may feel less applicable. You get to decide. I'm your assistant, not your director. I'm your teammate, not your manager.

The reading I do with you consists of two sessions: the exploratory session and the main reading. During the exploratory session, I get to know you better and find out what you want to glean from our conversation. Because a chart can be read on many different levels, this first step is crucial.

During the exploratory session, I ask you to provide three questions or issues you want addressed during the main reading. This is an important part of the process and is emblematic of my approach. I expect you to participate with your curiosity and intelligence fully unfurled.

During the exploratory session, I love it if you tell me an important dream or series of related dreams. The adventures you live as you're sleeping can help focus our research into your mysteries. But if you don't have any dreams to offer, don't worry about it.

The main session lasts about 90 minutes. If we had had an informative exploratory session, I will arrive for our dialog with focused intuitions about how to proceed. Even so, I encourage you to interrupt me, question me, or add your own input at any time during the process.

PS: I can't imagine conducting a reading without your participation. There's no way I want to be alone dictating my thoughts into a recording device and then sending you an mp3. You need to be with me, co-creating our experience, either in-person or on the phone or via Zoom.

Divinatory Homework #106 ≡

For all signs:

You may find it uncomfortable to figure out how your problems are necessary, how you are attached to them, and how you might be reluctant to give them up. But that's what I'm asking you to do.

  ∞ What part does your suffering play in holding your world together?

  ∞ How do your most intractable dilemmas help you avoid reaching goals you are unconsciously afraid or too timid to strive for?

  ∞ In what sense do your thorny frustrations entertain you or keep you from being bored?

  ∞ Do you ever find yourself bragging to others about the stress and hardships you endure?

  ∞ Are your exasperating predicaments essential to the construction of your self-image?

Write out your answers and mail or email them to yourself.

Losing What's No Good for You

A psychic once told me that my first name "Rob" is an apt description of my spiritual function.

"You're here on earth to rob people of their godawful belief that life is a miserable ordeal," she advised me.

"Your job is to steal away the habits that sap their life energy; to rip off the sorry dogmas that divert them from the wondrous feats their imaginations are capable of."

I don't know if I have fully earned that glowing promise, but I aspire to do so.

Training Our Imaginations to Do Magic

In the dictionary, the first definition of "magic" is "the art of producing illusions as entertainment by the use of sleight of hand and deceptive devices."

A more appealing definition doesn't appear in most dictionaries. It's my adjustment of an idea by occultist Aleister Crowley: "Magick is the science and art of causing practical changes to occur in accordance with our true will—under the rigorous guidance of love."

(I prefer using Crowley's spelling, "magick," which distinguishes it from the less interesting kind.)

What is our true will? It's the psychospiritual fuel we access to implement our life's mission. It's the driving force that empowers us to know and express our soul's code.

Here's the catch: Our true will is fully available only if we anchor it in love. And we must ceaselessly reinvigorate and reinvent our devotion to that practice. We can't just do it on happy days when we're in a good mood. It must be a daily task.

Another catch: We must train our imagination to serve our true will. That's hard work! It requires us to do what doesn't come naturally: to stop it from conjuring fear and illusions that leak our psychic energy.

★

When we cultivate a vivid perception of being intimately interwoven with the greater rhythms that create and sustain life on our planet, they naturally assist and guide us as we carry out our true will.

When we have identified, defined, and tapped into our true will, we are united with the inexhaustible energy of those greater rhythms.

When we affirm our desire to perform magick that serves love, beauty, justice, and truth, the greater rhythms provide us with the most useful expressions of their specific personal support and inspiration.

In response to the above definition of magick, a reader asked me, "Is this done by retraining negative thoughts to be positive thoughts?"

Here's how I replied: That's complicated! I suggest that when negative thoughts come up, we trace them back to their source. Are they based on objective truth? Or are they partially or entirely generated by fears and delusions? If the former, we should take measures to respond constructively to the legitimate worries. If the latter, let's pivot hard as we substitute positive thoughts for the irrelevant negativity.

The reader responded: "That's much easier said than done. I am flooded with negative thoughts that have a hint of truth to them, but at the same time I am too stern with myself. The negative thoughts are exaggerated. And I can see where the truth lies in them, but I can't seem to reclaim my power over them. It's like knowing the truth isn't enough. I am at odds with myself."

I replied: The retraining takes practice and diligence and commitment. Can't happen overnight. I suggest you compose a vow that you will work on steadily for a year and a day.

Here's a useful practice. I invite you and me, dear reader, to write down brief descriptions of five pleasurable moments we have experienced. Then we will authorize our imaginations to dwell lushly on these memories for 20 minutes.

If we catch ourselves slipping into a negative train of thought, we will interrupt it immediately and compel ourselves to return to our fantasies about the Big Five Ecstatic Moments.

Let's try this once a day for 30 days.

I am in favor of critiquing what some observers call "toxic positivity." When we refuse to look at difficulties and insist on being compulsively optimistic, we spawn monsters.

At the same time, I think toxic negativity is at least as big a problem. The sheer immensity of cynicism and nihilism is so pervasive that most of us take it for granted. It's the air we breathe.

My hypothesis is that our moment in history is more thoroughly under the wicked curse of pessimism than most other ages.

But it's also true that humans have always been under that spell. Modern science has gathered vivid evidence that we literally take pleasure in feeling negative emotions. We may even willingly dive back into misery again and again for the same reason we eagerly climb aboard a roller coaster or go bungee jumping: We get a rush from it.

That is, the pleasure/reward centers of our brains light up and release dopamine. And we can get addicted to whatever causes our brain to release dopamine, whether it's chocolate or screaming arguments.

What can we do about the fact that our brains are predisposed to generate and dwell on disturbing, demoralizing, and draining thoughts?

Andrew Newberg, MD, and Mark Waldman write: "To overcome our neural bias for negativity, we must repetitiously and consciously generate as many positive thoughts as we can."

"When you generate a minimum of five positive thoughts to each negative one, you'll experience an optimal range of human functioning."

Newberg and Waldman don't advise us to never say no. They don't believe it's unhealthy to express skepticism and discernment and resistance when appropriate. They simply argue that we have a neural bias, a built-in biological predilection for fear-based reactions, which may have served our distant ancestors but is now a debilitating handicap.

More: https://tinyurl.com/d3jhcxh.

"I've found a nice balance," writes EarthMover, one of my readers, "between living like someone who has overdosed on delusional optimism and someone who thinks everything and everyone sucks. I can see things as they really are instead of through either rose-colored glasses or trash-colored glasses.

"That means I can cultivate true objectivity, not the fake cynical kind. I free myself from negative emotional biases that used to cloud my ability to see the partially hidden beauty all around me.

"At the same time, I'm not addicted to the idea that I should be eternally happy and blithe and sweet. When the dark moods descend on me, I trust them. I know they are openings into equally sacred perceptions and insights."

Tips to Promote Self-Management ((⧉))

Tips to promote rigorous self-management:

◈ Steal away from deals that erode your confidence.

◈ Be bigger and wilder than your forgivable ignorance.

◈ Trade certainty for freedom.

◈ Craft yourself into an ever-renewing promise.

◈ Love the tricks that rouse your holy mirth.

◈ Live in the flood of your playful assent.

◈ Invent a new truth in an unknown world at least once every awakening.

◈ Change everything you touch into the most soulful version of itself.

Divinations for You #5

ARIES: Let's talk about growth. While the points I'll discuss are useful for all the signs, they are especially crucial for you Aries to consider.

- ∞ Not all growth is good for you. It may stretch you too far too fast—beyond your capacity to integrate and use it.
- ∞ Some growth that will ultimately be good for you doesn't feel good to you at first. It might force you to transcend comforts that are making you stagnant. Discomfort and pain may arise.
- ∞ Some growth that's good for you may meet resistance from people close to you. They might prefer you to remain as you are. They may even experience your growth as a problem.
- ∞ Some growth that isn't particularly good for you may feel good. For instance, you could enjoy working to improve a capacity or skill that is irrelevant to your long-term goals.
- ∞ Some growth is good for you in certain ways, but not good in other ways. You must decide if the trade-off is worth it.
- ∞ Some growth is utterly healthy for you, feels pleasurable, and inspires other people.

TAURUS: For thousands of generations, our early ancestors were able to get some of the food they needed through a practice known as persistence hunting. They usually couldn't run as fast as the animals they chased.

But they had a distinct advantage: They could keep moving

relentlessly until their prey grew exhausted. In part that's because they had far less hair than the animals, and thus could cool off better.

I propose we adopt this theme as a metaphor for you. The way I interpret the Taurean modus operandi, you don't need to be extra fast or super ferocious or cunningly devious to get what you want. A lot of your success can come from discovering your equivalent of persistence hunting.

GEMINI: More than most, you are attuned to the world's hums, murmurs, and whispers. Some important clues you need arrive via ripples and rustles and whirrs.

There may be people around you, however, who are more attracted to and conversant with clangs and bangs and jangles. They may imagine that the only information worth paying attention to is the stuff that's loud and noisy.

I trust you have a knack for knowing when to resist the appeals of the showy clamor. One of your potential talents lies in being a subtlety specialist who thrives on nuance and undertones. You can often attract the most meaningful fun by cultivating your natural capacity to listen mysteriously.

CANCERIAN: Practitioners of the Ayurvedic healing tradition tout the curative power of regular self-massage.

Taoist author Mantak Chia goes further. He suggests you visualize sending smiles and fond wishes to your kidneys, lungs, liver, heart, and other organs. These acts of kindness bolster your vigor, he believes.

I invite you to try these two practices. Here's another: Give yourself compliments and praise. Speak the words aloud. Address yourself as you would a beloved person or animal.

One more recommendation: Regularly get or make yourself symbolic gifts. They will be talismans stimulating your intention to cultivate gleeful self-care.

It's your birthright as a Cancerian to be adept at all the practices I have named here.

LEO: I'd love for you to give your best gifts without worrying about whether they will be received in the spirit with which you offer them. But that's not realistic. It's unlikely your best gifts will ever be perfectly received in the spirit with which you offer them. I advise you to give them anyway.

I would also be ecstatic if you never had to tone down your big, beautiful self out of fear that others would be jealous or intimidated. That's not a viable possibility, either.

But I will note that you Leos, more than any other zodiac sign, can be charmingly fearless in expressing your big beautiful self as your offer your best gifts to people who receive them with grace and appreciation.

VIRGO: Now and then we may be able to whip up a catalytic breakthrough in a magic moment.

But it's rare to undergo rapid, dramatic transformations in short periods of time. "True life is lived when tiny changes occur," wrote Leo Tolstoy.

That's why it's usually delusional to be forever pining for a big miraculous intervention that will fix everything.

The most likely way to alter our course is slowly and gradually, by conscientiously revamping our responses to the small daily details.

Beauty and truth and love and justice usually emerge in their glory only over the course of a painstaking, step-by-step, trial-and-error process.

"All that I made before the age of 65 is not worth counting," wrote Japanese painter Hokusai. "At 73, I began to understand the true construction of animals, plants, trees, birds, fishes, and insects. At 90, I will enter into the secret of things. At 110, everything—every dot, every dash—will live."

You Virgos often have a special talent for these perspectives. I regard you as an excellent choice to serve as teachers and role models for the rest of us.

LIBRA: We change everything we look at by gazing at it and forming ideas about it. Nothing remains exactly the same when we enter into a relationship with it.

So why not regard ourselves as makers of meaning at least as much as understanders of meaning? Why not proceed on the hypothesis that our highest expression, our way of collaborating with the Divine Intelligence, is to create?

We could regard spiritual practice to be as much about playing as about defining—transforming what we are given even more than figuring out the nature of what we are given.

Since we can never completely know what is ultimately true, why don't we generate approximations of the truth that are imbued with love and beauty?

Inspired by my Libran teacher Norman O. Brown, we might aspire to find "words used not to interpret the world but to change it; not to advertise this world but to find another. To pass from this world to the next; from ordinary to extraordinary language."

The approach I am describing here doesn't come naturally to some Libras. And yet one of my favorite Libras, Norman O. Brown, was a wizard in wielding it.

So were all the following Libran philosophers: Friedrich Nietzsche, Michel Foucault, Edith Stein, John Dewey, Hannah Arendt, Philippa Foot, Mary Daly, Judith Jarvis Thomson, Rosi Braidotti, Sunny Bergman, Isabelle de Charrière, Jasna Koteska, Denis Diderot, Henri Bergson, Samuel Taylor Coleridge, Samuel Adams, Ishwar Chandra Vidyasagar, and Miguel de Unamuno.

Based on this evidence, I conclude that even though it may be a strenuous challenge, Libras can become skilled at being makers of meaning as much as understanders of meaning.

SCORPIO: The world isn't full of iconoclastic visionaries who specialize in imagining the future of intimate matters. Most modern innovators seem devoted to seemingly more glamorous and critical matters like artificial intelligence, 3-D printers, and smart chips implanted in our brains.

But my truth is this: Revolutionizing how we do our inner work and craft our cherished bonds is key to transforming the world. There is therefore a pressing need for geniuses who place their imaginations in service to creating a more emotionally intelligent culture.

If you're interested, it's your birthright to make this talent one of your specialties.

SAGITTARIUS: Self-described skeptics sometimes say to me, "How can any intelligent person believe in astrology? You must be suffering from a brain dysfunction if you suppose that planetary movements reveal any useful clues about our lives."

If the "skeptics" are truly open-minded, as authentic skeptics should be, I offer a mini-lecture to correct their misunderstandings.

I say that I don't need to "believe" in astrology. I use astrology because it works pretty well. It doesn't work perfectly—what does?—but it provides helpful information with enough frequency and profundity as to be useful.

For instance, I have a working hypothesis that Sagittarians enjoy better-than-average insight and luck with themes involving home, roots, foundations, stability, self-knowledge, and security every year from late February through the month of March.

It's irrelevant whether there's a logical theory to explain why this might be. I simply advise my Sagittarian friends to seek enhancements in situations related to the subjects I named. If they are successful at least 65 percent of the time, which they often are, I regard that as a big win.

For the sake of comparison, I will mention a purely scientific approach to making the world a better place. An executive at the UK's biggest pharmaceutical company admitted that most prescription medicines are far less than totally effective. "The vast majority of drugs only work in 30 or 50 percent of the people," said geneticist Allen Roses of GlaxoSmithKline.

For example, hepatitis drugs work for 47 percent of patients. Migraine medicines used to treat acute attacks are effective for 52 percent. Thirty percent of Alzheimer's patients benefit from the standard drugs and 62 percent of clinically depressed people respond to SSRI antidepressants. Only half of those who suffer from rheumatoid arthritis get relief from the usual treatments.

I suspect there's a similar principle at work in every useful modality, whether it's based in science or psychology. Is astrology potentially valuable to a greater percentage of the population than GlaxoSmithKline's drugs? That's my theory.

CAPRICORN: A typical Capricorn cultivates fervent passions, even to the point of obsession. Few other people may know the magnitude of your zeal, though, because you often pursue fulfillment with methodical, business-like focus.

But I wonder if maybe it's a good idea to reveal more of the raw force of your driving energy. It might humanize you in the eyes of potential helpers who see you as too strong to need help. And it could motivate your allies to provide more of the support and understanding you'd benefit from getting.

PS: I will be pleased if you expand your capacity to welcome the care and inspiration offered by others.

Write out this quote from author Hélène Cixous and keep it in a place where you will see it every so often: "It is easy to love and sing one's love. That is something I am extremely good at doing. But to be loved, that is true greatness. Being loved, letting oneself be loved, entering the magic and dreadful circle of generosity, receiving gifts, finding the right thank-you's, that is love's real work."

AQUARIUS: A reader calling herself Rebellioness collaborated with me to imagine five revolutionized approaches to the art of rebellion. I present them here for your use. Of all the signs, you Aquarians are most likely to take them to heart.

∞ Experiment with uppity, mischievous optimism.

∞ Invoke insurrectionary levels of wildly interesting generosity.

∞ Indulge in a cheerfully insolent refusal to be chronically fearful.

∞ Pursue a cheeky ambition to be as wide awake as a cheeky messiah in service to blithe dissidence.

∞ Bring reckless levels of creative intelligence to all expressions of love.

PISCES: Poet Emily Dickinson revealed to a friend that there was only one commandment she ever obeyed: "Consider the Lilies."

Japanese novelist Natsume Sōseki told his English-speaking students that the proper Japanese translation for "I love you" is *Tsuki ga tottemo aoi naa*, which literally means, "The moon is so blue tonight."

I invite you to be regularly inspired by these approaches. More than any other sign of the zodiac, your duty is to be lyrical, sensual, aesthetic, imaginative, and festively non-literal.

Element 3

If we don't cherish the inspiring struggles available to us, they will teach us useless lessons.

If we cherish the inspiring struggles available to us, they will illuminate and disperse our dangerous ignorance.

Chapter 8

Your Nimble and Nuanced
Emotional Expertise

+

My Nimble and Nuanced
Emotional Expertise

=

Our Nimble and Nuanced
Emotional Expertise

Interpret All Omens Favorably

There is no such thing as an inherently bad or ominous astrological configuration.

No such thing as a planetary transit that signifies destruction or doom.

No such thing as aspects in our chart that justify our fear.

All omens deserve to be interpreted in ways that provide guidance and teaching.

All omens are revelations about how to successfully wrangle with our problems, perpetrate liberation, ameliorate suffering, find redemption, and perform the tricky maneuvers and ingenious tweaks that enable us to slip free of our mind-forged manacles and discover the deeper meanings beneath our experiences.

The Blessings of Saturn

In my view, Saturn is the planet that traditional astrologers understand least. Some spread irresponsible distortions about it.

I won't dwell on discussing faulty conceptions about Saturn. Even though they are at best incomplete and at worst misleading, they tend to provoke fear even in people who know better.

I will sum up by saying that too many old-school practitioners regard Saturn as the cosmic equivalent of a crabby old tyrant whose intention is to limit our freedom. They suggest that when transiting Saturn conjuncts or forms squares and oppositions to planets in our natal charts, we will endure cramped, depressed periods. Our dreams will be stymied. We must accept less satisfaction and meaningfulness than we want.

But I believe this is a lazy misrepresentation of Saturn. I have mentioned it only to stimulate your skepticism.

Let's speak about Saturn in ways that are closer to the truth: Saturn the teacher, Saturn the organizer, Saturn the archetype that potentially heralds an influx of creative discipline and clarifying structure.

Here's a shocker, at least to some orthodox astrologers: In Western Hermetic Qabalah, Saturn embodies the Great Mother, Binah on the Tree of Life. She is an outer signifier of the Goddess who gives birth to every creature—who imparts to each of us our special form and function.

In one sense, we humans are all one: I am you and you are me and they are we and we are all together. But in another sense, each of us is exquisitely special and unique, a miraculous one-of-a-kind character unlike any other ever created in all of eternity.

And from an archetypal perspective, it is the Great Mother, symbolized by Saturn, who gives us our inimitable life. You are you in all your specific, unrepeatable glory, because the Great Mother has made you exactly so.

If there is ever a time when Saturn appears to be a harbinger of frustration and limitation, it is because she is figuratively nudging us to stop trying to be what we are not—and devote ourselves more fully to being who we really are.

Saturn the Great Mother loves us with a sweeping scope that is unimaginable to us when we try to understand from the ego's viewpoint. Saturn will do everything possible to influence us to live the exact, specific, singular life we were created to embody.

Let's say you were born with the potential to be a kindergarten teacher who specializes in awakening children to the world's beauty. If you instead decide—because of bad conditioning you received growing up and your overexposure to the distorted values of mainstream culture—you want to be a rock star or dental hygienist or bookie, Saturn may obstruct your path. She will push you away from being a rock star or dental hygienist or bookie—and in the direction of being a kindergarten teacher.

Here's the fact of cosmic matter: The archetypal energy Saturn symbolizes is your expert servant and kind mentor. She loves you and wants you to be what you were born to be. If she seems to hurt your feelings or prevent you from advancing, it is only and always and absolutely because she wants you to find meaning and be fulfilled by doing what your soul's code intends.

If you cooperate with Saturn, she will help you own your rightful power. She will strip you of flaky, aimless tendencies and liberate you to be your competent self without squandering your energy on low-priority goals. With Saturn as your healing guide, you will evolve toward being the gorgeous genius you were born to be, unhampered by trivial yearnings and false ideas about yourself.

If you welcome Saturn to work her magick, she will help you add organization to your life, enhancing your efficiency. She will encourage and support you to be more focused. She will direct you to rely less on authorities and take your fate into your own sovereign control. She will marshal you to vigorously translate your potential into practical expression.

If Saturn comes to call and you authorize her to intensify her gifts, frivolous and irrelevant ambitions lose their clench on your imagination. You feel a mandate to stop messing around with time-wasting activities. Abracadabra and poof: You are unburdened of any desires you might have to wander all over the place in quest of nothing in particular. Hallelujah and hosanna: You are delivered from the temptation to frolic along dead-end paths just for the entertainment value of such recklessness.

When Saturn leans into your destiny, you get opportunities to boost your knack for finishing what you start. You find it easier to calm your restless heart and commit yourself to a single choice out of the many options that float into your sphere.

When Saturn becomes available to boost your potency, you may be inspired to renounce mediocre pleasures and misaligned priorities. You will attract assistance, some of it unexpected, as you cease fiddling around on the peripheries and gravitate to the core of the key issues.

Best of all, you will figure out where you truly belong—as opposed to being half-sure of where you *sort of* belong.

In conclusion, my advice is to respond with grateful enthusiasm to the pressure exerted by this expert servant and kind mentor.

The sooner you hone your self-discipline and refine your focus, the less likely it is that you will spend any time writing "I will not squander my riches" a billion times on Saturn's blackboard.

I suggest that during full moons, you say a reverently rowdy prayer to the Great Mother Saturn, asking her to reveal a vision of how to order your life with just the right mix of freedom and responsibility as you become more of the unique miracle you have the potential to be.

PS: For the ancient Romans, Saturn's influence was anything but baleful. As the vine-growing deity who ruled over a golden age, Saturn was synonymous with abundance.

The holiday in Saturn's honor, Saturnalia, was a seven-day feast of freedom and pleasure. Businesses and schools were closed, enslavers served the people they had enslaved, grudges were forgotten, and parties raged nonstop.

Impossible Dreams

A few weeks into writing my horoscope column, way back at the beginning, I realized how much I wanted to give my readers a psychologically and soulfully savvy experience.

Not trivial advice about making money and accumulating power and getting laid. Not banalities about how to be sentimentally happy. Not barren language crammed with platitudes.

I recognized that if I wanted to write a regular column week after week, year after year, I would have to continually reinvent my reasons to be excited about the work. If I failed to do that, I would be boring, and my counsel would grow feeble.

To accomplish my exalted ambition, I would have to unearth ever-new ways to rebel against my own formulas. I'd have to refrain from relying on shticks. My holy-as-fuck duty: to keep overthrowing my mental habits again and again.

There was good news and bad news. I was brimming with curiosity, but I was young and immature. I was clever but callow. An intuition wormed its way into my awareness and wouldn't go away: that I wasn't nearly as wise as I might someday be.

And so I set an intention to use my column as a teaching device for myself. I asked the muses who had conjured up this breakthrough opportunity to deepen my emotional intelligence and develop robust compassion and sharpen my perceptions.

Above all, I wanted help in crafting a spiritual vision that offered benevolent disruption and practical healing. "Make me into a friendly shocker," I begged the muses. "Show me how to console and liberate my readers, how to build their confidence and guide them to bravely face the darkness, tell them they are

perfect just the way they are and yet to always be ready to transform into a higher-octave version of themselves."

Even back then in my rookie phase, I was immune to the
appeal of religious authorities who taught that life on the material
plane was to be demeaned, disowned, and transcended. Whatever spiritual influences might flow from me, I vowed they would
exalt the beauty of our daily lives, our actual bodies, and yes, even
our complicated egos.

I had majored in religious studies at Duke University and had
done extensive readings of the world's sacred texts. But as my
column ripened, I grew clear that I wanted to offer an iconoclastic brand of spirituality that wasn't in thrall to the New Age
or Buddhism or Christianity or Sufism or any other tradition,
even my favorites.

I aspired to dive down deep and dig up strange and wonderful
and paradoxical truths from the shadow realms. And I wanted to
be loose and flexible and mercurial and experimental as I plied
that serpentine quest.

To be profound and playful was my aim. Rigorous and vigorous, but blithe and rowdy. Penetrating and lilting. Intense and
lyrical. Uncompromisingly in search of what was authentic and
useful, but buoyantly entertaining.

Eventually, I realized I would have to borrow extensively from
both great minds and great souls—and not just the great minds
and great souls that bloomed from a particular ideology or tradition or gender or race or nation.

I also guessed I would need to be influenced by flamboyant tricks and confusing tweaks and mysterious twists of fate. I
couldn't rely merely on the greats for my illuminations. I needed
the outriders, the outliers, the outlandish and outrageous outcri-

ers and outlanders and outravers.

Epiphany after epiphany struck me in those early days as I grasped the fact that I aspired to achieve seemingly impossible dreams for my readers and me: to be both intellectually dexterous and emotionally intelligent. To be spiritually adept and soulfully frisky. To be psychologically innovative and wildly practical.

Have I succeeded in fulfilling my intentions? At least to some degree, I think.

But I am still a work in progress. Still pushing to revolt against who I am so as to become even more of who I am.

Pluto Demoted?

Some readers ask me, "Why do astrologers still give so much importance to Pluto? It's not a planet anymore." Below is my response.

Since 2006, when Pluto was "demoted" from a planet to a dwarf planet by a few astronomers, nothing has changed for astrologers about Pluto in its role as a signifier of mythopoetic meanings.

All that has changed are the ideas about Pluto that reside in the minds of the 424 mostly male astronomers who were at the conference in Prague in 2006. By the way, over 9,500 other astronomers weren't consulted about the change in definition.

"I'm embarrassed for astronomy. Less than 5 percent of the world's astronomers voted." So said planetary scientist Alan Stern about the action taken at the IAU conference. He's chief of NASA's New Horizons mission to Pluto.

Speaking of the guidelines by which the astronomers disbarred Pluto, Stern said, "The definition stinks, for technical reasons." He said that by the terms of the definition, Earth, Mars, Jupiter, and Neptune shouldn't be considered planets, either.

Not quite 5 percent of the world's astronomers can juggle interpretations about the nature of the heavenly bodies, but their province is different from astrologers'. To those who speculate about mythopoetic meanings, Pluto is still the symbol of the underworld—the heavenly body that speaks to us about our connection to the underside of life, to the soul's perspective, to the secrets and hidden depths in any situation, to the realm of dreams and death and altered states.

This doesn't imply that the meanings of Pluto for astrologers will remain forever static. As explorers of consciousness, we will continue to refine and enrich our understanding of its metaphorical importance.

One astro-mythologist, Roxanna Sergeievna, has suggested there's poetic justice in visualizing Pluto as a "dwarf planet." In mythic stories and fairy tales, dwarves are often magicians who have transformative powers and possess hidden storehouses of fantastic riches. They live beneath the earth or underneath bridges, which are symbols of transition and reify the dwarves' role as guardians of thresholds.

As heroes proceed on their epic quests, dwarves may demand difficult tasks from them. If the heroes are to be successful, they must in some sense die, psychologically if not literally. Success in carrying out the dwarf's assignment brings the heroes wealth and magical interventions.

Every detail of the above description is an apt poetic meditation of the astrological meaning of Pluto.

In the best-known version of the Greek myth, Persephone is dragged down into the underworld by Hades, whose title is "Pluto."

But in earlier, pre-patriarchal tales, Persephone descends there under her own power, actively seeking to graduate from her virginal naïveté by exploring the intriguing land of shadows.

"Pluto" is derived from the Greek word *ploutos*, meaning "wealth." Psychologist James Hillman says this refers to the psyche-building riches available in Pluto's domain. Hades, he says, is "the giver of nourishment to the soul."

The goddess Hecate also lives in the underworld. Her meanings largely overlap Pluto's. According to poet Robert Graves, she is the wizard of sorcery, "the goddess of ghosts and night-terrors, of phantoms and fearful monsters."

On the other hand, Graves notes, Hecate "presides at seed time and childbirth; she grants prosperity, victory, plentiful harvests to the farmer and rich catches to the fisherman."

How can a single deity embody such contradictory archetypes? Graves: She symbolizes "the unconscious in which beasts and monsters swarm. This is not the living hell of the psychotic, but a reservoir of energy to be brought under control, just as Chaos was brought to cosmic order under the influence of the spirit."

Sounds like Pluto, too!

Psychologist Carl Jung: "Whoever loves the earth and its glory, and forgets the 'dark realm,' or confuses the two (which is mostly what happens), has spirit for his enemy; and whoever flees from the earth and falls into the 'eternal arms' has life for an enemy."

Revelatory Homework #107 ≡

For all signs: If you are soggily embroiled in the trance of numbing routine, astrology can pry open your habit mind and illuminate patterns that have been opaque to you.

Astrology can unveil the sweeping swooping vista of your life story, decluttering pinched ideas and shriveled expectations you have about yourself.

Astrology can purge your imagination of repetitive self-talk, rebirthing you into previously uncharted perspectives.

But reliance on horoscopes may also have downsides. If you're superstitious, it might make you even more so. If you are prone to be passive and tempted to believe that life is a story that's out of your control, astrology might further crush your willpower. If your inclination to trust magical thinking far outstrips your skill at critical thinking, you could become ungrounded and cut off from your lodestar and wellspring.

That's why, as much as I love astrology, I'm also wary of its potential to bamboozle and victimize.

Where do you stand in your capacity to draw on astrology's gifts? Are you at risk of succumbing to its liabilities? Are you primed to hunt for its treasures?

Mercury Retrograde ◈

I'm a rebel maverick dissident heretic. Contrary to orthodox doctrine, I reject the dogma that periods when Mercury is retrograde warrant outbreaks of fear and worry.

They do not portend massive snafus in communication and connection.

We are not far more liable to commit costly gaffes and veer off on wrong turns.

My rebel maverick dissident heretical instincts tell me that there are propitious possibilities to take advantage of during phases when Mercury is retrograde. Here are three:

∞ We can refine and deepen the ways we exchange information.

∞ We can heighten our commitment to saying precisely what we mean and meaning exactly what we say.

∞ We can be extra thoughtful and imaginative and ingenious about how we interweave ourselves with valuable people and resources.

Here's my anecdotal testimony, gleaned through extensive research into my personal experience these last few decades: The mistakes I make are as numerous and flagrant when Mercury isn't retrograde as when it is.

The evidence is unambiguous: There are zero correlations between eruptions of my foolishness and the extremely regular and lengthy phases when Mercury appears to be moving in reverse to its more common orbit.

But what about all the other billions of people in the world? Have they painstakingly gathered data that contradicts mine?

Have they conducted exacting experiments to test the hypothesis of Mercury's ill omens?

No, they have not. All the information we have to go on concerning the phenomena associated with Mercury retrograde is as subjective and anecdotal as mine. There are no objective, rigorous studies.

Now let's consider a further accusation against the planet closest to the sun. Could the truth be that when it's retrograde, we shouldn't begin anything new? That we risk spawning malignant fortune if we launch fresh projects and seek novel connections and make new agreements? I have personally known 23 astrologers who have assured me that's true.

Here's some evidence I have gathered: During a Mercury retrograde a few years ago, my acquaintance Marnie delayed accepting a dream job offer as editor of a magazine she loved. By the time Mercury safely returned to "normal," the magazine had hired another applicant. She still regrets her action.

Ready for some actual factual data? Some of America's biggest, most enduring Fortune 500 companies began when Mercury was retrograde. They include Disney, Goodyear, and Boeing.

Whatever we may think about the corruption of massive corporations, we can't pretend that Mercury retrograde interfered with their ability to become what they wanted to be.

Over the years, I have gathered many stories like that of my acquaintance Marnie. I've watched people amp up their anxieties as they proceed on the assumption that the current Mercury retrograde is a time of bad luck. And then they suffer what seems to be bad luck.

Here's the other side of my research: I have observed many friends and acquaintances and relatives who don't keep track of times when Mercury is retrograde. They therefore expect no misfortune and massive inconvenience to happen, and—what do you know?—misfortune and massive inconvenience don't occur.

According to traditional astrologers, each complete Mercury retrograde cycle lasts an average of 55 days. Since there is an average of three Mercury retrogrades per year, we are in some part of the Mercury retrograde phenomenon for at least 165 days per year—about 45 percent of the time!

That is a *longgggg* time to imagine ourselves as being under a bad spell!

But wait! There's more! Also streaming our way—always, always—are other astrological configurations that traditional astrologers interpret as malefic, miserable, and menacing.

One major example is the moon void-of-course aspect. A comically absurd profusion of astrologers regard it with the same fear and loathing they do Mercury retrograde. And the moon void-of-course is also a regular, predictable, and frequent occurrence: about 160 times annually, or 44 percent of each year's 365 days!

Many astrologers also view certain planetary configurations with trepidation. When Mars is square to Jupiter (at a 90-degree angle) or Saturn is opposed to the sun (a 180-degree angle) or Venus is square to Saturn, they might advise their clients to be extra cautious and express at least a modicum of fear and loathing. Squares and oppositions are scary, troublesome, stress-provoking!

There are not a million of all these problematic omens per year. But there are hundreds. I haven't tallied the data (it would be a waste of my time), but if Mercury is retrograde 45 percent of each year and moon is void-of-course 44 percent annually, we might be in one or the other at least 60 percent of the time.

To that terrifying figure, we would be duty bound to add all the squares and oppositions, as well as other prickly aspects like the semi-squares (45 degrees), sesqui-quadrates (135 degrees), and inconjuncts (150 degrees). I'm ballpark estimating we would have to wake up quivering with apprehension at least 256 mornings every year.

I refuse that assignment. I reject that mandate. I will not default into chronic nervous vigilance in the face of all the supposedly foreboding signals.

PS: Traditional astrologers regard each Mercury retrograde phenomenon to consist of eight phases:

- ◈ Pre-Shadow Phase
- ◈ Pre-Shadow Phase Intensified
- ◈ Mercury Retrograde Station
- ◈ Mercury Retrograde Phase Intensified
- ◈ Mercury Retrograde Phase
- ◈ Mercury Direct Station
- ◈ Post-Shadow Phase Intensified
- ◈ Post-Shadow Phase

So, for example, one of Mercury's Pre-Shadow Phases started on April 25, 2022. Its Post-Shadow Phase finished on June 18, 2022. We were allegedly under a grim curse for 56 days.

Here's one of my favorite astrologers, Antero Alli (https://tinyurl.com/AnteroAlliMap), on Mercury retrograde:

When Mercury goes retrograde, I tend to notice new twists and turns in the way people think, talk, and otherwise attempt to communicate.

I have also noticed how many astrologers, both amateur and pro, overreact and warn others of the Dire Straits of Mercury Retrograde! Beware of Things Going Badly!

Rubbish, I say. Personally, I look forward to Mercury retro periods.

Though I don't confess to understand why or how daily events can become askew during these brief periods, I don't see Merc retro as necessarily bad or ill-fated.

In fact, I see it as a creative state where we can expect the unexpected and try new things—that is, if we're open to novelty.

If we have become overly entrenched in our comfort zones and owned by the deep force of habit, then perhaps Merc retro can coincide with a time of frustration.

However, it doesn't have to be that way if we're open to doing things differently from "business as usual."

During Merc retro, maybe there's no such thing as "business as usual."

Another of my favorite astrologers, William Sebrans (https://otherwiseworld.com), gives 10 ways to appreciate times when Mercury is retrograde.

1. Misunderstandings are now attributable to impersonal forces or gods on vacation. That is, we are

for the time being in the clear and temporarily off the hook.

2. We expect things to not work, so when they do, we are happier than before, when we expected them to work.

3. We can spend hours tossing out crap, purging email sludge, and organizing our micro-universes. We are entitled to call it productive work. No need to rush forward when it is salutary to shuffle backward for a spell.

4. We are forgiven in advance for impatience and frustration, but we are also given extra permission to blow off the pressure and be calmly accepting of what we are usually supposed to get upset with. Think: customer service.

5. For a few weeks, we get to hear less New Age murmurings about the Divine Flow, the power of creative visualization, and the power of surrender to Shakti. We are allowed to focus on getting the job done any damned way we can figure it out.

6. If we are believers, we can find proof of the retrograde effect. If we are non-believers, we can find proof of the non-retrograde effect. Either way, we are vindicated.

7. We can watch more Merchant Ivory period films and feel good about ourselves.

8. We can handwrite letters and craft arty postcards, while justifying the less efficient retrofit communication as mandated by Divine Decree.

9. We can slow down.

10. We can slow down and repeat ourselves.

Love Cues and Clues: How to Be with Each Sign ⊚

Here are tips on how to get the most out of your connections with other signs of the zodiac.

◈ With Sagittarius: Think bigger and go further than you normally do. Encourage them to show you the fun they love best. Be willing to make messes in the name of getting educated and entertained.

◈ With Libra: Seek out beautiful things together. Collaborate to create beautiful experiences together. Relish talking about beauty. Be the most beautiful version of yourself.

◈ With Cancer: Give them extra care when they feel needy and extra space when they feel self-protective. Allow them to infuse you with their creative energy and be interested in how that might change you in interesting ways.

◈ With Taurus: Be earthy and imaginative with them. Be practical and effervescent together. Be gradual and thorough together. Be creative and steady together. Be affectionate and ethical together.

◈ With Aquarius: Collaborate in making the flow of intriguing ideas crackle and splash. Be willing to get weirder than you might typically be. Expand your notion of what "fun" might consist of.

◈ With Capricorn: Laugh at hypocrisy together. Make ambitious plans together. Take a brave stand together. Have fun riffing on ways you could boost your prestige and reputation by expressing maximum integrity.

◈ With Virgo: Encourage them to express their finesse, elegance, and smart problem-solving abilities. Collaborate with them to do good deeds that heal and uplift. Let them influence you to be more precise and discerning than you might normally be.

◈ With Pisces: Join together in feeling deeply about whatever life brings. Enjoy the imaginative fluidity they express—and let them influence you to be fluid, too. Sing and cry together.

◈ With Gemini: Be interested in meeting and playing with all their sub-personalities. Encourage them to entertain you with the way they talk. Admire their knack for making quick changes.

◈ With Aries: Proceed on the assumption that spontaneity leads to truth. Give them openings to lead the two of you on surprising adventures. Encourage them to show you how to play with fire.

◈ With Leo: Playfully brag to each other. Even playfully try to out-brag each other. But also show them how clearly you see and appreciate their luminous gifts. Dare them to show off.

◈ With Scorpio: Dive down together, going deeper than you could have by yourself. Figure out how to enjoy working on interesting problems together. Exult in the sensual pleasure of basking in mystery.

Mars within Us

According to the Western Hermetic tradition, which is my spiritual path, we harbor the archetypal qualities of each planet within us.

So, for example, Mars, the heavenly body in the sky, is one visible manifestation of an archetype that permeates the Great Everywhereness, including the interiors of human beings.

What is the Mars archetype? Richard Tarnas, one of the world's best astrologers, describes it like this:

> Mars represents the principle of energetic force. It symbolizes that part of the psyche which impels us to act, to assert ourselves, to struggle, to press forward and against, to be courageous and vigorous, to be competitive or combative.

So the rocky planet Mars doesn't beam out vibes that manipulate our behavior. It doesn't twist and tweak us with gravitational pull.

But we can analyze its movements to provide signs and omens as we speculate on how the Mars archetype may be at work at any particular time and in any particular culture or person.

What's your relationship with anger and aggression and forceful energy? Are you skilled at harnessing those qualities to serve constructive goals?

Do you make them work for you in your efforts to change

situations that need changing? Have you developed proficiency in your ability to fight fairly and wisely for the world you
want to live in?

I hope so! The questions I just posed provide a reliable frame
for evaluating your use of what astrology regards as the power
symbolized by the planet Mars: the fierce urge to defend and protect what you love; the strong-willed intention to create excellence
and truth and justice and beauty; the determination to work tirelessly in behalf of your noble and inspiring desires.

I honor your efforts to craft your share of the Mars force with
grace and intelligence. I pray you are guided by your higher intelligence to find elegant and effective ways to express this potent
aspect of your life force.

Oracles for You #6

ARIES: Afrikaner author Laurens van der Post told a story about a conversation between psychologist Carl Jung and Ochwiay Biano, a Pueblo chief.

Jung asked Biano to offer his views about White people. "White people must be crazy because they think with their heads," said the chief, "and it is well known that only crazy people do that."

Jung asked him what the alternative was. Biano said that his people think with their hearts.

That's your assignment, Aries: to think with your heart. Not all the time, necessarily. Try doing 20 percent of the time and see how that works for you.

For extra credit, you could also try feeling with your head.

In my opinion, you Aries people have a special potential to develop these capacities.

★

TAURUS: I invite you to dream and muse about your true sanctuary; your sweet, energizing, love-strong root-source, the haven where you can freely be high and deep, vigorous and tender, flexible and rigorous; the oasis where you are the person you have promised yourself you can be.

To stimulate and enhance your insightful feelings about these matters, experiment with the following activities.

∞ Visualize memories that empower you. Regularly dose your imagination with images and scenes that evoke calm and joy.

∞ Seek out adventures and situations that imbue you with

confidence and poise and self-possession.
- ∞ Keep reinventing and reinvigorating your vital traditions. Shed traditions that have lost their meaning for you.
- ∞ Cherish and foster your reliable sources of inspiration.
- ∞ Continually renew and redefine and refine experiences that enrich you emotionally.
- ∞ Identify influences that nurture you. Treasure your relationship with them.
- ∞ Tend tenderly to your web of close allies. Take care of whom and what takes care of you.
- ∞ Practice the arts of adoration and reverence and awe.

GEMINI: "When I grow up, I'm not sure what I want to be." Have you ever heard that thought bouncing around your mind, Gemini?

How about this one: "Since I can't decide what I want to be, I'll just be everything."

If you have been tempted to swear allegiance to either of those perspectives, I invite you to update your relationship with them.

It's not unhealthy for you to have some ambivalence about commitment, nor is it pathological to be receptive to myriad possibilities. But if you hope to claim your birthright as a Gemini, if you long to ripen into your authentic self, you will have to become ever-more definitive and specific about what you want to be and do—even if that changes and evolves over time.

CANCERIAN: In your mind's eye, drift back to a turning point in your past that didn't go the way you'd hoped.

But don't dwell on the disappointment. Instead, change the

memory. Visualize yourself then and there, but imagine you're in possession of the wisdom you have gathered ever since.

Next, picture an alternative ending to the old story—a finale in which you pull off a better result. Then bask in this transformed state for five minutes.

Will this change the past? Not in a literal way. But it may rearrange your feelings about the past, and that could transform how you're affected by it in the future.

Here's a related exercise: Drift back to that historical turning point. Use your imagination and ingenuity to recast the plotlines that have unfolded in your story since then. Come up with alternate meanings for the old event, including at least one redemptive interpretation.

Is it possible that adventure cracked open opportunities that would not otherwise have come your way? Did it alter your understanding of how life works in ways that made you more effective and soulful?

The exercises I'm describing here are especially felicitous for you Cancerians. Of all the signs in the zodiac, you have the most power to reshape your memories.

LEO: You can listen a person's soul into existence. Your receptive interest in the inner life of those you love can awaken their dormant potentials.

The teacher Richard Moss says, "The greatest gift you can give another is the purity of your attention."

Early in life, some Leos regard this activity as at best irrelevant to their life's work. They are more focused on being listened to than listening.

But as Leos mature, many see the wisdom of developing an active investment in listening. They realize that the influences of potent individuals can serve as magic spells that help activate their own treasures.

Here's Leo philosopher Paul Tillich's counsel: "The first duty of love is to listen." I'll add that a prime duty of loving yourself is to listen.

VIRGO: Capricorns may be the hardest workers of the zodiac, and Tauruses the most dogged. But you Virgos have the potential to be among the smartest workers.

When you're at your best, you efficiently surmise the precise nature of the tasks at hand, and you do what's necessary to accomplish them.

There are no false starts or reliance on iffy data or slapdash trial-and-error experiments. You have an elegant touch as you find innovative shortcuts that produce better results than would be possible via the grind-it-out approach.

LIBRA: Experiment: Present the following dare to a person or persons with whom you would like to go deeper: "You think you know me, but it's possible you know just a tantalizing fraction. Would you like to experience the rest of the story?"

If anyone expresses interest, take them on a tour. Reveal the sides of you that are too mysteriously interesting to show the general public, or too intimate to reveal to anyone you don't trust, or so potent they might intimidate those who aren't poised or self-possessed.

SCORPIO: Is it really love? That's always a good meditation for you Scorpio passion connoisseurs. Here are some rigorous, vigorous, Scorpio-style guidelines.

- ∞ Love asks you beautiful, unanswerable questions. —poet Carl Sandburg
- ∞ Love brings to life whatever is dead around us. —theologian Franz Rosenzweig
- ∞ Love works best when two solitudes welcome and respect and nurture each other. —Rainer Maria Rilke
- ∞ Love is the only game where two can play and both win. —author Erma Freesman
- ∞ Falling in love is a lot like dying. You never get to do it enough to become good at it. —my Scorpio friend Elise
- ∞ Love is like a shrine in the wilderness where eternity adores the lightning as it roves. —mash-up of me and Pablo Neruda

SAGITTARIUS: How do I love thee, Sagittarius? Let me count the ways.

First, I adore it when you give your companions a personalized dose of the primordial force of nature described by French philosopher Teilhard de Chardin.

"Some day after we have mastered the winds, the waves and gravity," said de Chardin, "we will harness for God the energies of love; and then for a second time in the history of the world, humans will have discovered fire."

Here's another way you please me, Sagittarius. More than any other zodiac sign, you put into action the ideal expressed by author Antoine de Saint-Exupéry: "Love does not consist in gazing at each other, but looking outward together in the same direction."

CAPRICORN: When the young Capricorn director Richard Lester got his big break, he took full advantage. It happened in 1964, when the early Beatles asked him to do their first movie, *A Hard Day's Night*, Lester's innovative approach to the project propelled his career to a higher level that brought him many further opportunities.

Writing of Lester's readiness, critic Alexander Walker said, "No filmmaker appeared more punctually when his hour struck."

That capacity to be in the right place at the right time is one of your great potentials, Capricorn.

AQUARIUS: Of all the signs in the zodiac, you have the greatest potential to be a psychonaut: a feisty explorer of consciousness.

With this in mind, I invite you to cherish this counsel from Aquarian anthropologist and author Walter Evans-Wentz:

> Accept the possibility that there is a limitless range of awareness for which we now have no words; that awareness can expand beyond range of your ego, your self, your familiar identity, beyond everything you have learned, beyond your notions of space and time, beyond the differences which usually separate people from each other and from the world around them.

PISCES: Sixteenth-century Italian poet Torquato Tasso described one of love's best blessings. He said your lover can reunite you with "a piece of your soul that you never knew was missing."

You Pisceans have great potential for finding and creating such relationships. It could be your specialty.

Have you met such wonders? Can you go deeper with allies who could become such wonders?

Element 3

If we don't treat our personal destiny as a holy art-game-story, we forfeit the ecstasy of crafting our souls into creative masterpieces.

If we treat our personal destiny as a holy art-game-story, we earn the ecstasy of crafting our souls into creative masterpieces.

Chapter 9

Your Holy Art-Game-Story Masterpiece
+
My Holy Art-Game-Story Masterpiece
=
Our Holy Art-Game-Story Masterpiece

Wishes for You

I wish you torrents of ecstatic empathy and gleeful sympathy. May the planet Neptune conspire with you to rouse these bounties.

I wish you fluidic, kaleidoscopic insights and "ah-ha!" epiphanies that lead to cathartic integrations. May the planet Mercury conspire with you to attract these exaltations.

I wish you the ripening of lucky trends you've worked hard to earn, resulting in miracle cures that incite your generosity and spur adoration to flow your way. May the planet Venus conspire with you to galvanize these favors.

I wish you rowdy rambling adventures that inspire you to weave together diverse threads of your destiny, empowering you to claim more of your fully synergized potency. May the planet Mars conspire with you to propel these blessings.

The Horoscope-Writing Process

How do I write my column?

I am always writing it. Even in my sleep. Even now. In my soul's rumpus room, I'm collating and integrating impressions from all that happened earlier today, like the Ukrainian reporter's trembling voice and sobs on the car radio. Like a YouTube video in which a gray wolf unleashes a howl, and many nearby creatures of the forest answer back with cries and shrieks and songs of their own.

I'm hearing in my mind a song my daughter Zoe sent me, a Cambodian folk ballad by a woman telling the story of her parents' deaths during the genocide of the 1970s.

I'm considering the kind-hearted criticism that a reader offered regarding my horoscopes: "Some of us can't change as fast as you think we can."

I'm recalling the taste of a Nightcap Whisky Dark Chocolate Bar mailed to me by a reader who said, "Thanks for literally saving my life with your poetic horoscopes."

I'm wondering about my dream last night, which brought me to a jubilee tea party and happy reunion with my first poetry teacher, now gone from this earth for the last 25 years. She and I wore red silk and pharaoh crowns.

I'm fondly recalling an orange feral cat and black feral rabbit gingerly checking each other out in the overcast wetland outside my window. I wondered if they would mate or fight or just be friends.

Will some of these traces and signs turn into future horoscopes? Maybe. Maybe not. I know that the poignant, precious feelings they roused will influence my mood as I write. They pulled me closer to the wild heart of the Great Mystery. Touched and toned me into a more resonant receptacle for the secret story that's unfolding just below and above the reach of our conscious awareness.

The aesthetic moral of the story: The "Free Will Astrology" column creates itself in and through me. It gathers raw materials from everywhere and uses them to compose its educated guesses and playful theories.

Since the beginning, I have vowed to be an amplifier for the voice of the collective. I aspire to tune into the undercurrents of the zeitgeist and express them with lyrical lucidity.

Caveat: As an amplifier, I have numerous filters—cool special effects like dream reverb and prophetic echoes and playful pitch-shifting glitches.

Or maybe the better metaphor is that I've taken a pledge to be a funhouse mirror that tricks the collective into laughing at and thereby breaking down its fixations and delusions.

Or how about this: I'm offering metaphorical four-dimensional Mobius strips that brave experimenters can steal for their own and incorporate into their quest to follow the path with heart.

Help! Don't let me get trapped inside these metaphors. Metaphors should liberate, not confine.

The horoscope muses run my life with a clear intention: to flood me with raw clues that I'm supposed to weave into oracles.

The experiences and information they deliver might come

from any direction, from any level, from any source—even influences I don't like or respect—and I had better be alert for them!

I strive to be aware of the difference between my personal stuff and the collective stuff, though often that's an artificial distinction. Personal stuff and collective stuff overlap a lot.

Another element of my column-writing process is more formal and scientific, if it's possible to apply that last word to such a poetic art.

I use a house system, wherein each sign is paired with one of the 12 houses according to the location of the sun. For instance, the last week of July and first three weeks of August are the solar month of Leo, and they constitute the fourth-house period for Taurus.

During the fourth house phase of anyone's cycle, childhood patterns may come up for review. It's a propitious period to meditate on how our original family relationships may still be coloring our current relationships. We might generate good fortune for ourselves if we purge our current domestic situation of bad old habits and recreate it in accordance with our highest values.

Do our roots need attention? Could our foundation benefit from fixing or bolstering? What's our dynamic with the fuels we rely on for maximum functioning? These are useful fourth house questions.

In the charts I draw up, I also note what houses the moon and major aspects are affecting. When Luna is in the sign of Cancerian the Crab and passing through Taurus's third house during the astrological month of Leo, I might tell Bulls to deepen and refine their emotional intelligence as they focus on communicating clearly—especially in the areas of home and family and foundations and roots.

That's the framework, but I'm not chained to it. I never want to get too attached to a system, since that would numb my antennae and shut out information. My main discipline while working on the column is to cultivate receptivity.

Here's another element, the obvious secret I mentioned before: If I seem prolific, it's because I don't have to rely solely on my own powers. The whole world offers me its generative energies, and I accept its generous gift.

Effects of the Moon on Earth

Fundamentalist materialists and practitioners of scientism have assured us that the moon doesn't impact living creatures in any way. Nope. Never. Impossible. Case closed.

I must once again intervene, invoking science to educate the science abusers. Shall we examine the actual evidence?

But first, this: As you know, dear readers, I don't believe the planets beam down invisible rays that mold historical trends or shape the destinies of individual humans. I harbor no farfetched theories that the gravity of Mars and Jupiter somehow manipulates the behavior of Earth's organisms.

On the other hand, I think the evidence is clear that the moon does in fact tangibly affect life forms. Its influence is not merely symbolic.

Below is a portion of the substantial data that demonstrate the fundamentalist materialists and practitioners of scientism are poorly informed about the subject.

- ∞ Biological activity on Earth really is affected by the gravity of the moon: https://tinyurl.com/mtdevrky.
- ∞ Longitudinal observations call into question the scientific consensus that humans are unaffected by lunar cycles: https://tinyurl.com/mpn4k4h9.
- ∞ The moon alters moods: https://tinyurl.com/4nfarf26.
- ∞ There's an association between lunar phase and sleep patterns: https://tinyurl.com/2p8w64ts.
- ∞ Here's a study of the physical fitness index, heart rate, and blood pressure of men during different lunar phases:

https://tinyurl.com/2p95evm8.

∞ There's evidence that lunar phases affect human sleep: https://tinyurl.com/2p92aa7f

∞ The moon has subtle effects on our sleep and mental health: https://tinyurl.com/bsuhvxna.

∞ Here's an analysis of the synchronization of human sleep with moon cycles: https://tinyurl.com/2bzrcwsa.

∞ Moon cycles exert an influence on menstruation and sleep patterns: https://tinyurl.com/5a7h47y4.

∞ Here's an analysis of the effects of full-moon definition on psychiatric emergency department presentations: https://tinyurl.com/2p9cnwvy.

∞ Shark encounters with humans are more likely during a full moon: https://tinyurl.com/ycxcdffy.

∞ The gravitational tugs of the sun and moon send significant tremors through California's San Andreas Fault. They could potentially trigger full-blown earthquakes: https://tinyurl.com/39ut5vt9.

Lunar Eclipse 💎

Lunar eclipses occur three times every year. Of these, 29 percent are total eclipses.

The phenomenon is striking. Compulsive rationalists assert there's no meaning to it—just as they may say there's no meaning to a heron flying into view, carrying a flounder in its beak, as you gaze at the sunset on your birthday; and no meaning to seven swans swimming along a creek on the winter solstice, a creek where no swans have appeared in the 13 years you've been observing it; and no meaning to a narrow shaft of rain falling only on your father's grave and nowhere else, as you visit the grave on the anniversary of his death.

But who wants to live life without speculating on the symbolic power of unusual events? Not me. Below are possible meanings of a lunar eclipse.

During the day of the eclipse, as well as two days before and two days after, assume you have extra power to gently or roughly wake yourself up out of any trance you're in. You have an enhanced ability to liberate aspects of your psyche that might have been acting like an automaton.

A lunar eclipse is a favorable time to break free of a bad habit. You'll attract help from both expected and unexpected sources if you focus on deprogramming a negative behavior pattern, substituting it with a positive one.

As nourishing and consoling as memories can be, they sometimes trap you in stale grooves that are better escaped. A lunar eclipse may signify you now have the power to love the past as you leave it behind—and rumble forward to a new chapter

Uranus

Let's have fun riffing on the meaning of the planet Uranus in our personal charts. I believe it signifies the talents and superpowers we harbor that would be most beneficial to others. If we fully develop these potentials, they will express our unique genius and be useful to our fellow humans.

I invite you to brainstorm about the nature of your Uranian talents.

Spiritual teacher A. H. Almaas believes that a genuinely creative act is always motivated by generosity.

If that's true (and I agree it is), here's the question: How do we explain the ego-obsessed "geniuses" who treat people carelessly even as they churn out their supposedly brilliant art?

Here's my answer: Those are not authentic geniuses. Genius is by nature benevolent.

★

You've heard the term "Higher Self"? We might define it as a genius aspect of your intelligence that is usually beyond the reach of your conscious awareness but is always looking out for you and offering you guidance—if you take the trouble to tune in to it.

Fun fact: Your Higher Self is itself evolving. One of its goals is to activate the genius that comes fully awake through a synergetic melding of Higher Selfishness and Higher Selflessness: "where your deep gladness and the world's deep hunger meet," in the words of Frederick Buechner.

Resolved: There's no contradiction between:

> being a highly individuated, creative person devoted
> to developing our own maximum potential and enjoy-
> ing life to the fullest
> and
> being a spiritual freedom fighter dedicated to the lib-
> eration of other humans and to the transformation
> of civilization into a paradise that serves and exalts
> all creatures.

The two tasks can blend quite well.

Divinatory Homework #108 ≡

For all signs, regarding their response to Uranian imperatives:

◈ Which aspects of your soulful beauty are potentially of greatest service to the world?

◈ How can you express your uniqueness in ways that activate your most profound generosity?

◈ What could you personally do to make the world a better place for our descendants?

◈ What gifts and blessings constitute your finest legacy?

Do It Now ⟳

Do it now.

It's always a favorable time to diminish the past's power to obstruct you; always a propitious moment to work on dissolving and healing painful memories.

It's always a fabulous phase to recommit yourself to your righteous ideals with such vivacity that you render your stale conditioning irrelevant.

It's always a pivotal period to dismantle enervating habits that aren't in alignment with your soul's code.

What planetary archetypes might be of service?

∞ Invoke Mars to energize the force of creative destruction.

∞ Ask Mercury to supply fresh ideas about the most dynamic strategies to implement.

∞ Call on Uranus to rouse visions of the future you can use to supplant the decayed visions.

∞ Welcome the help of Venus to infuse your actions with love and lyricism.

As Above, So Below ⟳

"As above, so below" is a maxim at the heart of the Western Hermetic tradition. It implies that the nature of the cosmos is intimately reflected here on earth—and vice versa.

Everything we imagine to be far away and out there has a parallel in the here and now, right up close. A miniature heaven resides within each of us, even if we have only partially activated its full potential.

The astrologers I respect say that we all contain the archetypal essences of the planets. A little bit of Mars lives in your reproductive system and the corresponding parts of your psyche; Jupiter inhabits your solar plexus and feeds your will.

I act as if the hypothesis "As above, so below" is a useful perceptual filter. I urge my teammates to experiment with it in their daily practice.

Now and then, though, I recommend exercising caution about promoting unity.

Writer Hanna Blank sets the right tone. "My cat attempted to adorn a prayer rug with a hairball, and I had to stop her," she says. "There are some instances in which we do not wish all things to be interconnected."

What things don't you want interconnected?

Element 4

If we don't try to ease the suffering of others when we have the chance, our own suffering will fester. If we only think about injustice when we're directly affected by it, our personal injustices will ossify.

If we try to ease the suffering of others when we have the chance, our own suffering will be more curable. If we express concern for injustices endured by people with whom we have no connection or similarity, we will be smarter about escaping injustices we personally experience.

Chapter 10

Your Generosity Medicine
+
My Generosity Medicine
=
Our Generosity Medicine

Utter Pragmatism

Hypothesis: The most pragmatic strategy we can practice consists of making continuous efforts to align our thoughts and feelings with the highest ideals we have thus far been able to comprehend.

★

Hypothesis: A second pragmatic strategy we could practice is to act like a person in love.

Even if we are not technically in the throes of passion, we can pretend we are. We can simulate and approximate the state.

Everywhere we go, we might exude the charismatic blend of shell-shocked contentment and blissful turmoil that washes over us when we're infatuated.

We invite our allies to soak up the tender, libidinous wisdom we exude.

We dispense free blessings and pure slack like rich saints who are sure our souls live for all eternity.

What Nourishes You Emotionally and Spiritually?

The world is filled with things that provide you with mediocre nourishment. Resources that enrich you with teachings and blessings are smaller in number.

To say it from another slant: You derive scant sustenance from the vast majority of people, songs, images, words, stories, environments, and sights. From a rare few, you glean illumination and inspiration.

★

So what nourishes you emotionally and spiritually?

I'm not talking about what provides measly entertainment and meager diversion. Not referring to stimuli that flatter or anesthetize you. Don't mean lackluster time-wasters that wanly distract you.

What wonders make you smarter and stronger? Who sees and appreciates your essence? What adventures teach you riveting and pivotal lessons?

I want to hear you exult about the beauty that replenishes your soul flesh and the symbols that titillate your wisdom and the divine interventions that prove to you your destiny is fueled by sacred mystery.

I invite you to take inventory of these untamed and untamable treasures. Make decisive moves to be in ongoing communion with them. Strategize about how best to nurture them back.

Love Everything about Life?

I dream I love everything about life. I dream that each event I have ever experienced or will ever experience is cherished and sublime—even the painful and puzzling interludes.

I dream I have personal possession of the universe's most splendid creation: consciousness.

I dream torrents of praise and gratitude for the mercurial flashes and shimmers that whirl inside my head. I dream I'm amused and amazed that I can think thoughts whenever I want to—soaring, luminescent, flamboyant thoughts or shriveled, rusty, burrowing thoughts, thoughts that can invent or destroy, corrupt or redeem, bless or curse.

I dream I wallow and revel in rolling flows of feelings. Are they poignant or intoxicating? Salty or like nectar? Condensed or capacious? Akin to thunderstrokes or labyrinths? I adore them all. I welcome every one. I relish the privilege of harboring such blessed intensity. I exult in commanding such extravagant life force.

I dream of being blessed with an additional lustrous, luxurious stroke of luck. I dream of owning and operating an imagination—a prodigious tool I use to shape the astonishments life gives me. It's a resplendent and sumptuous instrument that sanctions me to find eternity in every blade of green weed, every whispered blue word, every touch of electric flesh.

I would love for you to dream similar dreams.

Love Cues and Clues:
Golden Repair ⊚

Kintsukuroi and *kintsugi* are Japanese words that mean "golden repair." They refer to the practice of fixing cracked pottery with lacquer that's blended with actual gold or silver.

Metaphorically, the words suggest that something may become more beautiful and valuable after being broken.

The wounds and the healing of the wounds are integral parts of the story, not shameful distortions to be disguised or hidden.

"Break a vase," wrote author Derek Walcott, "and the love that reassembles the fragments is stronger than that love which took its symmetry for granted when it was whole."

Oracular Homework #109

ARIES: Describe the differences between what your ego needs and what your soul needs.

TAURUS: "Make your work your play and your play your work," advises Hall of Fame basketball coach Phil Jackson. I believe that cultivating this enlightened state is a Taurus birthright. How are you doing with that? Are you making progress toward fulfilling your potential?

GEMINI: What's your favorite rule to break? Why? What pleasure does it provide?

CANCERIAN: What would the people who love you best say is the most important thing for you to learn?

LEO: Is it possible there's something you really need but you don't know what it is? What might it be?

VIRGO: What feeling do you love to feel more than any other?

★

LIBRA: If you had to choose one wild animal to follow, observe, and learn from for a month, which would it be?

SCORPIO: Tell or write a story called "How I Created Something Out of Nothing."

SAGITTARIUS: What two gifts could you give yourself to enhance your sense that your life is intensely meaningful?

CAPRICORN: Whether or not we believe in gods, we all worship something. What idea, person, thing, or emotion do you feel reverence for?

AQUARIUS: Of all the ridiculous situations you've ever been in, which is your favorite?

PISCES: What is the most soulful thing you've ever done? The most soulful thing you've never done? The most soulful thing you will do in the future?

Love Cues and Clues:
So Much to Love

It's always the right time to unleash a flamboyance of Love Bombs. That's what's going to happen now.

There was so much to love, I could not love it all; I could not love it enough.
    —poet Louise Bogan

Say to those you love: I have sipped the gusts of your dusky gaze, and so I am eternally mobilized.
    —my rendering of a poem by poet Sohrab Sepehri

I profess the religion of love; it's the belief, the faith I keep.
    —author Ibn 'Arabi

Holding your hand, I can hear your bones singing into mine and feel the moon as it rolls through you.
    —author Sara Eliza Johnson

I ask you please to speak to me forever.
    —poet Alejandra Pizarnik

Raw light spills from your eyes, utterly naked, awakening an intoxicating shimmer of adventure.

  —poet Al-Saddiq Al-Raddi mashed up with author Hermann Hesse

You are my inspiration and my folly. You are my light across the sea, my million nameless joys, and my day's wage.

  You are my divinity, my madness, my selfishness, my transfiguration, and purification. You are my rapscallionly fellow vagabond, my tempter and star. I want you.

  —playwright George Bernard Shaw

Love is everything it's cracked up to be. It really is worth fighting for, being brave for, risking everything for. And the trouble is, if you don't risk everything, you risk even more.

  —novelist Erica Jong

I love you more than it's possible to love anyone. I love you more than love itself. I love you more than you love yourself. I love you more than God loves you.

  I love you more than anyone has ever loved anyone in the history of the universe. In fact, I love you more than I love you.

  —a voice in your dream

Your body needs to be held and to hold, to be touched and to touch. None of these needs is to be despised, denied, or repressed.

But you have to keep searching for your body's deeper need, the need for genuine love.

Every time you are able to go beyond the body's superficial desires for love, you are bringing your body home and moving toward integration and unity.

—author and theologian Henri Nouwen

I love you with what in me is still changing.
I love you with what in me is unfinished.

—author Robert Bly

He who is in love is wise and becoming wiser, sees newly every time he looks at the object beloved, drawing from it with his eyes and his mind those virtues which it possesses.

—author and philosopher Ralph Waldo Emerson

Love, love, love, that is the soul of genius.

—composer Wolfgang Amadeus Mozart

Fall in love over and over again every day. Love your family, your neighbors, your enemies, and yourself. And don't stop with humans. Love animals, plants, stones, even galaxies.

—authors Mary Ann and Frederic Brussat

No work is more worthwhile than to be a sign of divine joy and

a fountain of divine love.
—author Andrew Harvey

The giving of love is an education in itself.
—activist and diplomat Eleanor Roosevelt

Love is a great beautifier.
—author Louisa May Alcott

The most vital right is the right to love and be loved.
—author and activist Emma Goldman

I want enough time to be in love with everything.
—author Marina Keegan

Unfuck the World

I renounce any denunciations I may have carelessly hurled toward our beautiful Earth and its inhabitants when I was under the spell of bad ideas, delusional attitudes, or unloving influences.

I invite you to do the same.

★

UNFUCK this. UNFUCK that. UNFUCK these and those.

UNFUCK all the stuff out there and in here.

UNFUCK the people, places, and situations that don't know they need to be UNFUCKED.

UNFUCK every little nuance and every big deal that would make life more fun and interesting for all of us if they were UNFUCKED.

UNFUCK the whole world.

★

The definition of UNFUCKWITHABLE: When you're so at peace with yourself and so at home wherever you go that no one can rile you up and knock you out of your groove.

Caveat: There is an important distinction between not giving a fuck about what people think of you and not giving a fuck about other people's feelings.

★

I consulted my 117 spirit guides to ask if I should give a fuck.

Their unanimous response: "Fuck yes, you should give a fuck."

So I do.

Love Cues and Clues: Clues to Your Loved Ones' Mysteries ◎

"Everyone carries with them at least one piece to someone else's puzzle." So wrote Rabbi Lawrence Kushner in his book, *Honey from the Rock*.

I agree. You have in your possession clues to your loved ones' destinies—secrets they may not have discovered themselves.

Wouldn't you love to hand over those clues? To make a gift of the puzzle pieces needed by those you care for?

Search your depths for insights you've never communicated. Tell truths you haven't found a way to express before now. Assume you have the power to mobilize your companions' dreams.

Fortunes for You #7 ෴

ARIES: Below are hunches and guesses about the topic "How to Be an Aries." My readers provided some ideas, which are noted.

∞ Aries says, "Just because I'm an Aries doesn't mean I will fall into an astrologer's assumptions about who an Aries is 'supposed to' be or how we're 'supposed to' act. And I'm being a thoroughly intense Aries by telling you so." —Elisa Jean

∞ If you don't vividly ask for and eagerly welcome the exciting gifts the Universe has in store for you, you may have to settle for trinkets and baubles. Never settle. —Monica Ballard

∞ When people don't get it done fast enough for you, be ready and able to DO IT YOURSELF. And don't waste any time or energy being mad at the slowpokes.

∞ Even when your courage has a touch of foolhardiness, even when your brazen quest for adventure makes you a bit reckless, you can be resourceful enough to avoid dicey consequences. Maybe more than any other sign of the zodiac, you periodically outfox karma.

∞ You like challenges—especially those that you consciously choose and especially those that aren't imposed by others.

∞ If someone tells you that you are too aggressive, invade their personal space and demand to know what the hell do they mean by that!!!

∞ Smile when you have absolutely no reason to. Smile when your reasons for smiling are still in the future. Smile as you concoct outlandish, farfetched reasons to smile.

∞ When you Aries are at your best, you are attracted to people who tell you exactly what they think, who aren't shy about being purely themselves, and who dare to be as vigorous as you.

TAURUS: Below are hunches and guesses about the topic "How to Be a Taurus." My readers provided some ideas, which are noted.

∞ How to be a Taurus: Eat, drink, and be merry, for tomorrow, you get to do it again! —Francesca Maria

∞ What's truly meant for you will wait for you until you are ready for it. —Yeshe Matthews

∞ Who you will be has always loved who you are.

∞ Taurus says, "As a Taurus, I have found that many places can be home. The forest can be home. The river can be home. The birch trees can be home. I bring pieces from those other homes and make them part of my home at home."

∞ Make it your gift to be in communion with every level of reality. Conspire to heal fragmentation and schisms. Unite heaven and earth. Keep paradises and hells in touch with each other. Never let the past forget about the future, and vice versa. Turn dreams into waking-life experiences, and vice versa.

∞ You can be led and inspired and guided—but never driven. —Lacey Wren

∞ Tell your favorite people the god-awful truth when they need to hear it and no one else will do it. But do it kindly.

GEMINI: Below are hunches and guesses about the topic "How to Be a Gemini." One of my readers provided some ideas, which are noted.

∞ When you Geminis are at your best, you don't merely tolerate dualities. You enjoy and embrace them. You work with them eagerly and may even endow them with sparkly magic.

While many non-Geminis regard oppositions and paradoxes as at best inconvenient and at worst obstructive, you often find how the apparent polarities are woven together and complementary.

That's why so many of you are connoisseurs of love that's both tough and tender. You can be effective in seemingly contradictory situations that confuse and immobilize others.

∞ My family is used to me exclaiming while driving "I need to keep my eyes on the road but LOOK AT THAT LOOK AT THAT!" as I gaze at whatever random hawk or cow or horse or waterfall or cloud I happen to spot. —Jenny Nalley Boyd

∞ Network until you almost but not quite explode with excitement as you pinball among all the fun connections.

∞ People may be inclined to come to you with their secrets because you are so good at seeing and sympathizing with more than one side of the story. But you should perhaps let them know you're not a rigorous secret-keeper.

∞ Don't be everyone's messenger. But be the messenger for as many people as is amusing for you.

∞ Your mind is sometimes a lush and beautiful maze that you get lost in. Is that a problem? Now and then it is, yes.

But just as often, it's a blessing.

As you wander around amidst the finery, not sure of where you are or where you're going, you often make discoveries that awaken your dormant potentials. You luck into unforeseen insights you didn't realize you needed to know.

My advice: Next time you're in an amazing maze, don't be in a mad rush to escape. Allow the dizzying but dazzling expedition to offer you all its rich teachings.

CANCERIAN: Below are hunches and guesses about the topic "How to Be a Cancerian." My readers provided some ideas, which are noted.

∞ Cancerian says, "In some ways, we are the most stubborn of signs. We are prone to telling others, 'You can't make me do it!' This may be counter-productive and overly and unnecessarily self-protective, yes. But it also assures that we have a reliable, unassailable core." —Kool Nancy

∞ If you don't feel close to or trusting of the family members that life gave you, go find some others you like better. You Cancerians have the right to get the family that serves you best.

∞ When you are the attentive, nurturing parent of your own inner child, you have made it all the way home to the ultimate home. Now go and play. —Suzane Langlois

∞ Just by being you, alter and shape the entire mood of any environment you're in. Be the lodestar or mother lode or mother lode star.

∞ Cancerian says, "I feel all my feels and I know all my

feels are real but not necessarily based on truth. Tricky to do! I honor every deep flow within me without necessarily regarding it as objective evidence about the rest of the world."

∞ Never leave the house except to go to the store to buy stuff for the house. Get a job where you can work at home. Have lots of children. Do their laundry for them until they are 36 years old. —Amanda Yallos

∞ You rarely take the straightforward route anywhere. Like the crab, you're inclined to move sideways or even backward to get where you need to go.

There's nothing wrong with that! It might be an antidote for people you know who are superficial and simplistic in their directness.

LEO: Below are hunches and guesses about the topic "How to Be a Leo." My readers provided some ideas, which are noted.

∞ Leo says, "My Leonine magnanimity invites everyone to do as I do: Glow like the sun, unleashing the full radiance of their hearts both outward and inward, flooding their surroundings with nourishing beauty as they flood themselves. My sovereignty inspires and welcomes the sovereignty of all." —Sharon McCarthy

∞ Carpe the hell out of every fucking diem! —Dee Ashford

∞ On a regular basis, show how high you can leap and yet always land on your feet.

∞ Question your own power? That's OK, I guess. But only if your power isn't working in service to love.

∞ Assume there is no limit to how much generous vivacity

you can summon and express.

∞ Fondle and nuzzle as much as possible. Tell your lovers EXACTLY where it feels good.

∞ Assume there is no limit to how much generous zest, brio, zip, spice, and zeal you can summon and express.

∞ One of the experiments I hope you will enjoy in the coming years is to work on loving another person as wildly and deeply and smartly as you love yourself.

In urging you to do so, I don't mean to imply I have a problem with you loving yourself wildly and deeply and smartly. I endorse your efforts to always keep increasing the intensity and ingenuity with which you adore and care for yourself.

But here's a secret some Leos don't know: Learning to summon a monumental passion for other souls may enhance your love for yourself.

VIRGO: Below are hunches and guesses about the topic "How to Be a Virgo." One of my readers provided an idea, which is noted.

∞ Service is sacred. Virgos know this better than all the other signs. —Kauakea Winston

∞ It's best if you refrain from wrestling with problems that resist your solutions. You should be discerning about how you use your superior analytical abilities. Devote yourself solely to manageable dilemmas that are truly responsive to your intelligent probing.

∞ I feel sorry for people who aren't receptive to your input, but you can't force them to give up their ignorance. "Go where you're wanted" is your best policy, along with "Take power where it's offered."

∞ You must enjoy, not apologize for, your precise little obsessions, like how cans and boxes and dishes are organized in the cupboard, and whether the bows in tied shoes are the same size and shape, and which way the toilet paper unscrolls, from the top or bottom.

∞ Risk asking almost too many questions in your drive to know every subtle and nuanced aspect about everything.

∞ As you get older, you become better and better able to help loved ones and allies heal and shrink their insecurities. Don't neglect to apply the same magic to yourself!

∞ Sometimes you create beauty and truth through your savvy skill about what to purge, erase, and shed.

∞ You are authorized to politely request that lovers take showers before and after sex—even during!

LIBRA: Below are hunches and guesses about the topic "How to Be a Libra." One of my readers provided some ideas, which are noted.

∞ Droll Libran pastime: infusing your decision-making with an amused appreciation for how challenging and fun it is to make decisions.

∞ Being an evolved Libra is never knowing what you want once and for all. It's continually debating with yourself about what's the best goal to aim for next.

∞ You need to emotionally feel, not just intellectually conceptualize, the balance, harmony, and justice you seek to create. That's the only way your balance, harmony, and justice can be genuine and robustly impactful.

∞ Grow your roots as big as your branches. —Marilyn Carson

∞ Always keep studying the fine points about how to fall in love with beautiful people, beautiful things, and beautiful speech.

∞ Libra says, "Tell me someone else's relationship problems, and I have them worked out in three minutes. As for my own relationship problems? Might take a good long while longer."

∞ Your ability to see all sides of every story is a gift, though sometimes it may feel like a drawback.

∞ The Libran approach to fighting for what's right doesn't mean getting into loud arguments or trying to manipulate people into seeing things your way. It's your birthright to rely on gentler, smoother styles of persuasion.

Have you developed your innate potential? Have you become skilled at using clear, elegant language to state your truths?

Do you serve the best outcome rather than your ego? Are you willing to understand why others feel the way they do even if you don't agree with their conclusions?

I hope you liberally call on these superpowers. We all need you to express your potency as a role model of integrity and moral rigor.

SCORPIO: Below are hunches and guesses about the topic "How to Be a Scorpio." My readers provided some ideas, which are noted.

∞ Two top Scorpio pastimes are exploring and deploying your intense, fertile creativity; and spiraling gleefully down into a deep dark void in pursuit of deep dark treasures.

Sometimes those two hobbies dovetail quite well. You

can satisfy both pursuits simultaneously: being creative as you fetch treasure from the void.

A favorite variation is when the void you glide into turns out to be a lush wonderland because of your unpredictable creativity.

∞ Scorpio says, "I must regularly empty my metaphorical trash so I always have enough room to gleefully breathe the sweet air and exult in the beauty of the earth."

∞ A Scorpio lover named Elisa Jean says, "We Scorpio allies admire how Scorpios can be so solicitous and welcoming: the best party hosts. They know how to foster social situations that bring out the best in everyone and provide convivial entertainment.

"Yet Scorpios also know everyone's secrets. They are connoisseurs of all the skeletons in the closets.

"And so they have the potential to spawn discordant commotions and wreak havoc on people's reputations. But they rarely do. Instead, they keep the secrets. They far more often use their covert knowledge to weave deep connections."

∞ It's hard to find truly terrible pizza. Likewise, even bad sex is usually a decent diversion.

But many of you Scorpios would rather skip the bad sex so you have more time and energy for the good stuff.

Luckily, you have a built-in Bad Sex Detector that mostly informs you if you're in danger of hooking up with a Bad Sex Practitioner. Lucky you!

∞ Scorpio's friends say, "Eeeee! You scare me! I like it."
—Robie Flannagan

∞ You're wise to periodically summon intense streams

of self-forgiveness for past events that would otherwise haunt you.

∞ You've got to keep poison out of your passion. Got to make sure your zeal heals and never steals others' energy. You can do it!

∞ You can and should be a virtuoso of simmering, ruminating, marinating, steeping, churning, smoldering, fermenting, and effervescing.

SAGITTARIUS: Below are hunches and guesses about the topic "How to Be a Sagittarius."

∞ Always keep your interesting options open. Let your mediocre options shrivel and expire.

∞ Tell everyone that the Emperor is naked, and tell the Emperor, too.

∞ Face stressful situations with supple humor. Regard this practice as an art form or tricky game that you can have actual fun getting skilled at.

∞ Fight for others' rights, even when it doesn't affect you. Make a difference in the lives of those who can't make a difference for themselves, even if they don't thank you.

∞ Wear purple whenever you need to boost your spiritual resilience.

∞ Spend as much time gallivanting outdoors as is humanly possible. Learn the languages of rivers, hills, trees, animals, and clouds.

∞ Refuse to be possessed by others, either demonically or angelically.

∞ Launch your own private revolutions.

∞ Be forever thirsty for knowledge and experiences that feed your joie de vivre.

∞ Get plenty of deep sleep with adventurous dreams.

∞ Blurt out your opinion, then chuckle and yawn.

∞ Make affectionate fun of yourself with kindness and wit.

∞ Dance and sing at unexpected moments.

∞ Use a plethora of exclamation points and fancy, swanky, rococo words!!!!!!

∞ Laugh and smile so much that your cheeks hurt.

∞ Make no apologies and have no regrets about doing what you love.

∞ Find friends who like to argue and not take it personally.

∞ Make sure your interests and passions never reach a limit. Refuse to let the things you already love influence you to close your mind about new things you could love.

∞ Hang out at toy stores and try out the toys.

∞ Don't ever merely run. Gallop. Scamper. Zoom. Dart. Ramble. Lope. Prance. Bound. Bustle.

∞ Cultivate a relationship with at least one animal friend.

∞ Name yourself. Don't allow anyone else to name you. Giving yourself an additional nickname at least once every two years is healthy and wise.

∞ Use your imagination to make routine events seem fascinating and wonderful. Develop a specialty in finding dazzlements.

∞ Be honest to the point of frankness but not to the point of rudeness.

CAPRICORN: Below are hunches and guesses about the topic

"How to Be a Capricorn." One of my readers provided some
ideas, which are noted.

∞ Loosen your firm grasp and steely resolve just enough
so you can allow the world to enjoy you. The peak you
ascended—so carefully, so painfully—gave you wisdom
and compassion. Allow everyone a chance to treasure you
for who you have become. —Solar Lab

∞ The mandate for Capricorn, wrote occultist Aleister
Cowley, is "the complete appreciation of all existing
things ... rejoicing in the rugged and barren no less than
in the smooth and fertile."

∞ Here's another mandate for Capricorns, courtesy of Aleister Crowley: "Refine your rapture."
   And how might you refine your rapture?

• Get more and more skilled at finding out what gives you
pleasure and bringing it into your life.

• Take inventory of your bliss-inducing strategies and
experiment with pushing them further.

• Ask your deep psyche to reveal as-yet undiscovered
secrets about what might give you sublime pleasure.

• Seek new ways to experience euphoria and enchantment, with an emphasis on what also makes you smarter
and healthier.

∞ You almost always know more than you think you realize about teasing out practical solutions that benefit the
most people.

∞ Your serious intensity and earnest focus are strong points.
But you should also be aware that not every decision
you make is momentous and packed with a thousand
implications.

- ∞ Maybe wait until you're 60 years old to dance like a lunatic and play with dolls and study occult magick.
- ∞ When your skills and potencies are fully engaged and serving constructive purposes, you are adeptly expressing your soul's code.

AQUARIUS: Below are hunches and guesses about the topic "How to Be an Aquarius." One of my readers provided some ideas, which are noted.

- ∞ Few people really understand you. So you may need to be your own best friend, the affectionate ally who deeply understands you. But that shouldn't be a problem, since you have many personalities who would love to be each other's best friends.
- ∞ To improve and purify yourself, help others! And do it with flair. As French artist Marcel Duchamp advised, "Do unto others as they wish, but with imagination."
- ∞ Even the finest, most highly evolved Aquarians seem to have never received instructions on how to be an Aquarius. They have been winging it since they were in their cribs. They assume that if they ever received such instructions, the first rule might be, "Ignore these instructions."
- ∞ People love you because you are freaky and eccentric and yet also sincere and kind. You are unconventional, non-conformist, unique, unusual, odd—and also trustworthy, tolerant, non-judgmental, and compassionate.
- ∞ Work 29 hours a day and love it. Play the other 29 hours a day and love it.
- ∞ You know you're an Aquarius when people laugh at some-

thing you said, and you have no idea what it was. You entertain people without trying.

∞ You may have watched and memorized all 139 episodes of *3rd Rock from the Sun*, a TV sitcom about four extra-terrestrials living on Earth and posing as a human family.

∞ Many Aquarians have learned their ideas are ahead of the game. In fact, they realize, the game may not even exist yet. Hence, they learn patience, diligence, and enough resilience to stand alone while waiting for the world to catch up with them. —Marie Poland

PISCES: Below are hunches and guesses about the topic "How to Be a Pisces." My readers provided some ideas, which are noted.

∞ People who don't know much about astrology may say that Pisceans are wishy-washy. That's a lie.

The truth is, Pisceans are not habitually lukewarm about chaotic jumbles of possibilities. They are deeply in love with the world and all its interwoven mysteries. Their tender fervor is often turned up high.

Awash in reverent adoration, they see and feel how all the apparent fragments knit together into a luminous bundle of amazement.

∞ You truly mean these words, originally spoken by Oscar Wilde: "I find the earth as beautiful as the sky and the body as beautiful as the soul."

∞ If possible, have at least one ally who does some of the dreary day-to-day living for you, enabling you to periodically escape to imaginary havens and fantastic sanctuaries.

∞ Forgive everyone—for your sake as much as theirs.

∞ Author Robertson Davies declared, "One learns one's mystery at the price of one's innocence." It sounds poetic, but I don't think it applies to most of you Pisceans.

Here's what I've concluded: The more you learn your mystery, the more innocent you become.

Please note I'm using the word "innocence" in the sense defined by author Clarissa Pinkola Estés. She wrote: "Ignorance is not knowing anything and being attracted to the good. Innocence is knowing everything and still being attracted to the good."

∞ Pisceans are above it all...and beneath it all...while never fully being in it at all. —Elizabeth Kirkpatrick

∞ You have the honor and privilege of understanding and arguing on behalf of all people in all times and places.

∞ You may theorize that you're the only one who has figured out the mysterious riddles of life. You may describe yourself as being lonely in paradise. But the fact is, there are others who know the secret rules you know. Many fellow Pisceans, for example. Go find them.

Element 4

If we don't pursue benevolent trouble and taboo reverence, we may never outgrow our habits, fixations, and stereotypes.

If we pursue benevolent trouble and taboo reverence, we may crack free of our habits, fixations, and stereotypes.

Chapter 11

Your Friendly Stereotype-Busting Mischief
+
My Friendly Stereotype-Busting Mischief
=
Our Friendly Stereotype-Busting Mischief

Holy Attention

Think of mindfulness as a form of "affectionate attention."
        —author and scientist Jon Kabat-Zinn

There is ecstasy in paying attention.
        —author Anne Lamott

Attention is the rarest and purest form of generosity.
        —philosopher and activist Simone Weil

It's almost as if the poets are offering a religion of noticing things,
or a religion of paying attention.
        —poet Ada Limón

Attention is the beginning of devotion.
        —poet Mary Oliver

Sublime Feminine Intelligence

What are the qualities of people who embody sublime feminine intelligence, as I aspire to do?

◈ They are lovers of equality; activists committed to social and economic justice; in service to people who are from disadvantaged backgrounds; excited to protect and preserve the health of the natural world; passionate about diminishing militarism, plutocracy, bigotry, misogyny, and racism.

◈ They believe that no one is free unless we all are free; that the supreme goal is to reduce suffering and increase joy.

◈ They prize their understanding of the interconnectedness of all things.

◈ Listening well is a quality they value.

◈ They are willing to expand and adjust their understandings of the world if they encounter new information that reveals their previous beliefs are obsolete or too narrow.

◈ They consider the needs of as many people as possible, not just the needs of their immediate community and network of allies.

◈ They are emotionally intelligent. They understand it's as crucial to develop a savvy relationship with our feelings as it is to be intellectually smart.

◈ They regard relationship as a crucible for spiritual work.

◈ They are not fundamentalists and authoritarians who believe that only their truths are true. They are willing to consider the value of alternate points of view. They are open to the perspective that everyone has a piece of the truth, but no one has the entire truth.

◈ They regard practical expressions of kindness and compassion and ethical behavior as sacred practices.

◈ They proceed as if loving and caring for animals and plants and the earth are prime tests of our spiritual intentions.

◈ They understand that to accomplish practical changes in service to the greatest good requires hard work in the trenches of political struggle, often having to deal with people who have different beliefs.

◈ They regard play and fun and humor not as diversions from "serious" spiritual work, but rather as being at the center of it.

◈ They are nuanced, not simplistic; respect dialog more than authoritative pronouncements; seek consensus, not doctrinaire obeisance; understand that perfectionism is often the enemy of the good.

◈ They aspire to regard everyone as a potential teacher.

◈ Love is their highest priority, their go-to motivation.

Intimacy with All Things

Enlightenment is intimacy with all things.
—13th-century Buddhist priest and writer Dōgen Zenji

Should we imagine that "enlightenment" is a perfect and permanent realization of ultimate truth?

Is it a possession we can own?

Once we have acquired it, are we forever guaranteed to understand the nature of reality at the deepest levels?

My guess is that there's no such thing as this kind of "enlightenment."

Here's a version of "enlightenment" that appeals to me: a visceral sensation of feeling close to all living things, buoyed by an ever-renewing empathy.

"Holiness is an infinite compassion for others," wrote author and activist Olive Schreiner.

"The soul is awakened through service," said author Erica Jong.

I agree. I say the quest to align one's personal life with the highest good is at least as much about being in service as it is about attaining a transcendent level of awareness or making pious displays of devotion to a deity or ideal.

According to 16th-century Kabbalist, Rabbi Isaac Luria, the idea of "enlightenment" was not some individual personal goal to

escape mortal limitations and gain knowledge, but a group process by humans to assist the Divine in bringing creation into alignment with the original plan—i.e., "on earth as it is in heaven."
     —artist Martha Jablonski Jones

Our happiness, potency, and spiritual skill are impossible and hollow unless we are in service to others. With this in mind, I propose an extension of the Bodhisattva's Vow.

The Bodhisattva Vow: "My own personal quest for illumination is incomplete, and my own personal enlightenment is meaningless, unless I am also devoted to easing the suffering of others."

I suggest we take this vow a step further and say, "My quest for illumination is incomplete, and my enlightenment meaningless, unless I am also devoted to the goals of easing the suffering of others and helping them experience joy and pleasure and liberation and meaningfulness."

A cornerstone of this Extended Version of the Bodhisattva's Vow is that we are committed to providing the fundamental needs of all human beings—their food, shelter, medical care, money—so they have the ability to cultivate joy and pleasure and liberation and abundance.

Proposed bottom-line spiritual philosophy: For any one of us, our life is rooted in the principle that whatever hurts other people hurts us; that injustices experienced by others are also injustices experienced by us.

None of us can truly be free and fulfilled unless we work toward the goal of ensuring everyone is free and fulfilled.

These are not vague abstract ideals. They're the central source of our soul's code and how we organize our beliefs, emotions, and actions.

Perhaps there is a version of "enlightenment" that signifies a transcendent level of awareness: a relaxed and savvy understanding of life as it really is.

If so, here are probable rules about that hypothetical state.

∞ If "enlightenment" doesn't enhance our ability to witness and heal the suffering of our fellow humans, then it's fake enlightenment.

∞ If "enlightenment" encourages us to imagine that expressing our personal freedom excuses us from caring for the health and well-being of our fellow humans, then it's fake enlightenment.

∞ If "enlightenment" allows or encourages us to ignore racism, bigotry, plutocracy, misogyny, and LGBTQIA+-phobia, it's fake enlightenment.

Enlightenment and
Individuation (((◉)))

In most schools of Buddhism, Hinduism, and Jainism, enlightenment is the consummate goal.

In Western esoteric paths, the supreme accomplishment is individuation.

What is enlightenment? What is individuation?

The number of definitions of both may exceed a million.

Here's what Theravadin Buddhist monk and scholar Bhikkhu Bodhi says about enlightenment: "The Buddha describes his attainment as a multifaceted, comprehensive understanding, an act of penetrating the nature of reality—the nature of experience—from multiple angles. It involved understanding the four noble truths from twelve angles, the five aggregates from twenty angles, the links of dependent origination from countless angles."

Bhikkhu Bodhi goes on to explain why he thinks the Buddha's attainment should be rendered by the English term "enlightenment" rather than the currently in-vogue term "awakening." He says, "The word 'enlightenment' better conveys this vast, profound, stable, and comprehensive level of understanding."

Many Buddhists, especially Americans and Westerners, harbor a less technical understanding of the meaning of enlightenment. The variety of definitions is so abundant, it's a challenge to formulate meaningful generalizations.

I like what Zen Buddhist teacher Joan Sutherland testified: "In Buddhist terms, the way things really are is enlightenment, and our experience of the way things really are is also (the same) enlightenment. It is the vast and awe-inspiring nature of the universe itself, and it is the way each of us thinks, feels, and acts when we're aware of and participating in that vast enlightenment manifesting as us."

Sutherland adds, "'Enlightenment' has an absolute quality about it, as though it describes a steady state, something not subject to time and space or the vagaries of human life. We imagine that once over that threshold, there's no going back. But it's far from static."

Here's one more message about enlightenment, from poet Ikkyu: "To all I care about, here's a friendly tip: enlightenment is gaffe upon error upon blooper."

What is individuation? Here are various ways Jungian psychologists and I might define it.

◈ The tender, crafty strategies by which we integrate into our conscious mind the immature powers and dormant gifts of our unconscious mind, thereby becoming a psychologically whole, self-possessed individual.

◈ The shrewd probing and experimentation by which we gain access to the full scope of our soul's code and take all necessary steps to artfully activate our unique genius.

◈ The impossible game we tackle in the hope of releasing ourself from rapt, self-absorbed identification with our conditioned patterns, as well as from the hypnotic spell of our culture's and our clique's dominant paradigms.

◈ The poignant amusement we cultivate as we pay affectionate respect to our ego even as we teach our ego how to be a servant of the Mysterious Sublime Eternal Gorgeous Self that is above and below and beyond and within our conscious awareness.

Can devoted seekers manage a quest for both enlightenment and individuation? I don't see why not. "Go for it!" I say to them.

Individuation is the primary work and play of my own devotional practice. I know I'll never finish doing it. There's no perfect version I will someday embody. It's an endless process I wrestle and wrangle with because it's so fun and interesting.

Bonus! My theory is that to the degree that I individuate, I'm approximating viable versions of enlightenment—of which there are at least a trillion.

Surprise! Individuation can't be accomplished in isolation or on the strength of epic solo struggles. It's the opposite of rugged individualism. It is undermined by selfishness and narcissism, and it doesn't engender selfishness and narcissism.

Individuation requires deep engagement with other creatures. How can we know who we truly are and forge the best versions of ourselves unless we interweave our destinies with those of allies and compatriots—and everyone else, for that matter?

Surprise again! For me, individuation proceeds with greatest alacrity as I seek conscious union with the Divine Intelligence, whose presence permeates every cubic centimeter of the universe.

As I merge my personal awareness with the Supernal Awareness of the Only Being in the Universe, my unique soul's code is activated more and more. My personal genius gets the full-blast nurturing of the Ultimate Genius.

The outrageous paradox, the hilarious and sublime anomaly, is this: As I merge my personal will with the One Will, my personal will thrives.

PS: In the most sublime versions of both enlightenment and individuation, compassionate service to humanity and the earth is an essential element of the quest. I aspire to embody that devotional integrity.

It's a Free Country 🌀

It's a free country. You are free to desecrate nature and have zero concern for our descendants and canonize every borrowed idea that burrowed into your mind when you were coming of age.

You are free to scarf down pesticide-laden junk food and memorize Ford truck jingles and vote for rich old White straight male millionaires.

On the other hand, you are also free to go on jubilant picnics in the wilderness using sustainable dishware and cleaning up after yourself.

You are free to formulate a plan to achieve your precious dreams in ways that also serve our fellow humans and bestow blessings on our descendants.

You are free to regularly revise your philosophy of life to account for the ever-changing contours of your own destiny and the ever-evolving urgencies of our shared culture.

You are free—FREE!!!!—to care dearly about what images and stories and words you allow to flood into your sacred imagination. You are free to regard omnipresent advertising as a form of propagandistic brainwashing. You are free to recognize that other people's freedoms are as important as yours.

Why do I bring these thoughts to your attention? Because I hope that one of your lifelong quests is to develop prowess at not just any old kind of liberation, but rather the savviest, most generous variety.

Empathy Is a Superpower

The ability to imagine and empathize with the lives of others is a superpower.

People who base their political and philosophical opinions solely on their own personal experience are dangerously deficient in their ability to imagine the real lives of others.

They are insulated by privilege. They are unable to conceive that others have different problems that make it difficult to achieve what they themselves have achieved.

They may even hate or distrust the imagination, since its powers provide empathetic insight into people unlike them.

Emotional Intelligence ☍

Those of us who aspire to develop our emotional intelligence often have an intuitive understanding of other people's feelings. That can be a good thing.

But there are less benevolent bearers of emotional intelligence, too: skillful manipulators who read people's feelings with acuity, then expertly coax them to see things their way, sell them things, influence them.

Bah! Humbug! In my view, true emotional intelligence is rooted in kindness, empathy, and sensitivity. It seeks to create connection that's equal in its power dynamic; that is free of manipulative agendas; that cultivates communion and connection for their own sake, as forms of interesting play that generate practical magick.

In this model, emotional intelligence has a moral and ethical intention—a quest not to assert one's own needs as more important than another's, but to recognize the other as a Holy Thou who is as worthy of being treated fairly and kindly as oneself.

Real Compassion ⟳

A reader tried to tell me that we are wise to rise above partisan politics; that we need people who have no ideology fueling their perspective; that it's unspiritual to feed disagreements.

The reader invoked Martin Luther King Jr. as fitting this description. He said that King brought people together as no one has done since.

But the truth is different. Martin Luther King Jr. was fiercely anti-racism, anti-poverty, and anti-militarism. He was uninhibited in his criticisms of the corrupt American system. And he alienated many White people.

In his lifetime and for years after his death, King was a divisive figure. He called for a "radical revolution of values," a relentless devotion to "go out into a sometimes-hostile world, declaring eternal opposition to poverty, racism and militarism."

It's true that he advised us to avoid physical violence. But he was a staunch combatant, a vehement defender of what's right, an uncompromising force advocating a fundamental remaking of American politics and culture.

Can We Love a Nazi?

Some people tell me we should love everyone—even Nazis and White supremacists and misogynists who would deny women power over their own bodies.

What does that mean? How would we "love" someone who perpetrates cruelty and destruction? Of what does the love consist? How is it expressed?

Do we imagine the killers and devastators as they were when they were helpless babies? Is that love? Do we feel sorry for the torments they endured while growing up, which turned them into sick thugs? Is that love?

Do we wonder if someday they may realize their grievous errors and seek atonement? Do we imagine them on their deathbeds, stung with epiphanies about their atrocities? Does our love consist of not wishing for them to get terminal cancer or be struck by a truck?

If those are ways we might "love" Nazis, I am willing to consider such actions. But here's the crucial caveat: None of those expressions of "love" must dilute my determination to fight them, resist them, jail them, and overturn their horrors.

I won't gaze tenderly into their eyes. I won't try to engage them in reasonable conversation. I won't be polite to bystanders who endorse their actions. I won't excuse their violence by citing the traumas they experienced early in their lives. I won't dilute my efforts to convince anyone who listens that they need to be stopped.

Here's my understanding of the strongest, truest version of love: I express it by neutralizing the evildoers who threaten our common good. I fight against them, find ways to counteract them, and work diligently to strip away their power.

Divinatory Homework #111

ARIES: What's the most healing trouble you could whip up?

TAURUS: "Each person is a story that the Soul of the World wants to tell to itself," says storyteller Michael Meade. What does the Soul of the World want to say through you?

GEMINI: Imagine that one of your heroes comes to you and says, "Tell me the most important things you know." What would you say?

CANCERIAN: What's your most interesting problem?

LEO: In author Orhan Pamuk's novel *Snow*, the main character Ka asks a woman named Ipek, "What is the thing you want most from me? What can I do to make you love me?"

Ipek's answer: "Be yourself."

Is there anything you can do to enhance your skill at this art?

VIRGO: Confess your deepest secrets to yourself. Say them aloud when no one is listening except you.

LIBRA: What new name would you choose for yourself if you either shed the name you have now or added to it?

SCORPIO: "A coward is incapable of exhibiting love," said Mahatma Gandhi. "It is the prerogative of the brave."

That's my challenge to you, Scorpio. If you want to press ever onward toward the frontiers of intimacy, stoke your courage.

SAGITTARIUS: What kind of teacher do you need the most right now? What is the ignorance that's causing you to suffer?

CAPRICORN: Spiritual teacher Eckhart Tolle writes, "The most powerful starting point for any endeavor is not the question 'What do I want?', but 'What does Life (God, Consciousness) want from me? How do I serve the whole?'"

Try this, then analyze how it worked.

AQUARIUS: Do you secretly harbor any apocalyptic fantasies? Which part of the world would you like to see come to an end?

PISCES: Imagine you have created a unique religion for your own use. Imagine that your holy books prescribe laughing prayers as a good way to commune with the Divine Source. Speak one of those laughing prayers.

Element 5

If we don't believe the soul always knows how to heal itself, it won't always heal itself.

If we believe the soul always knows how to heal itself, it will always heal itself.

Chapter 12

Your Self-Healing Devotions
+
My Self-Healing Devotions
=
Our Self-Healing Devotions

Love Cues and Clues: Deciphering Love ◎

Love thrives when neither partner takes everything personally, so it's wise for us to cultivate a talent for forgiveness and consistently question our urge to blame.

Love is a game in which the rules keep changing, so it's wise for us to be crafty and improvisational as we stay alert for each unexpected pivot of fate.

Love enmeshes us in our partner's unique set of karmic complications, so it's wise to make sure we're interested in their problems.

Love is a laboratory where we can uncover hidden secrets about ourselves, so it's wise to be experimentally curious.

Love is never an idyllic match of perfectly compatible saints, so it's wise not to let sterile fantasies seduce us away from flawed but fertile realities.

Love is not a low-maintenance machine, so it's wise for us to do regular detailed work on its unpredictable organic wonders.

Love is not a subsidiary of DreamWorks or Disney, so it's wise to keep our romantic stories from being infected by the entertainment industry's simplistic, sentimental myths about intimate relationships.

Loving Our Bodies

Many spiritual teachers make statements like "I am not my body" or "This body is not me."

I revolt and protest. I recoil and denounce. This creepy dismissal is an insult and disparagement. It demeans our bodies' magnificent beauty and besmirches our bodies' sublime role in educating our souls.

I agree that we are not *only* our bodies. I concur that a key part of us is eternal, lives free of earthy limitations, and is spread throughout the interconnected web of life—not just trapped in solitary boundaried form.

But hell yes, I am my body. It's a glorious and intrinsic facet of my identity. It's a miraculous creation that has taken millions of years to evolve into the masterpiece it is now.

So yes, I am my body and yes, this body is me. I adore my body. I am in awe of it. I am delighted to be united with it.

I will also suggest that you are your body, and your body is you. You love your body. You are in awe of it. You are delighted to be united with it.

★

Inflamed by these resplendent facts, I offer the following exhortations:

Let's free our bodies to be as real as anything ever created. Let's be brave and dynamic, graceful and daring, as we sanctify our impossibly marvelous, unfathomably intelligent bodies.

Let's praise our sacred bodies. Thank our blessed bodies. Tell our righteous bodies we revere their uncanny majesty. Say we yearn to learn their heavenly secrets. We promise to treat them as our beloved allies, our sacred treasures, our splendorous possessions.

No shame, no apology: We will be in awe of our body's staggering power to endlessly carry out the millions of chemical reactions that keep us alive and thriving.

How can we not be overwhelmed with veneration for our hungry, resourceful, unpredictable bodies?

Let's study our bodies' abracadabra. Exult in the bounties they stream forth every second. Celebrate their boisterous animal elegance.

Spells for You #8

ARIES: British poet Samuel Taylor Coleridge (1772–1834) had an unusual fetish. He enjoyed eating apples and pears and other fruits while they were still hanging on the tree.

Why? Maybe because the taste was as pure and brisk and naked as it could possibly be—an experience that I imagine would be important to a romantic poet like him.

In accordance with your astrological potentials, I suggest you periodically use Coleridge's quest for ultimate freshness as a driving metaphor. Go to the source to get what you need. Dispense with intermediaries. Be as fresh and raw as the law allows.

★

TAURUS: You Tauruses often have more help than you imagine or call on. But you may not believe that what I just said is true. The enchantments I'm alluding to could even be hidden from you. And if you don't know about them, you won't summon them to serve you.

And indeed, for some Tauruses, the treasures I'm hinting at go forever neglected. Never leveraged.

But let's say that you, Lucky One, recognize and claim your assistance and support. Where do they come from?

Sources you don't expect, perhaps, but also familiar influences that expand beyond their previous dispensations:

∞ Quirky coincidences and amusing interventions.

∞ Opportunities disguised as inconveniences and gifts that don't appear gift-like.

∞ Whether or not you believe in spiritual beings, they, too, may offer help, support, blessings, and resources.

∞ Nodes of dormant genius in your own brain may become available—pockets of grey matter that have been asleep or off-limits, but which could awaken and offer intercessions. Will you inquire into your cache?

GEMINI: Here's my prescription for making best use of your Gemini potentials: Be enchanting, but in understated ways. Be slyly charismatic and respectfully flirtatious and serenely wild. Show how sexy it is to be sublimely relaxed.

Make judicious use of small acts of friendly mischief. Be affectionately unpredictable, always in the service of showing how much you care.

CANCERIAN: Here's an experiment: Keep checking yourself for irrelevant, self-perpetuating negativity and bitterness.

Having a modicum of anger and fear and antipathy is sensible, even necessary. You can't stay healthy without cultivating a medicinal dose of the stuff. It helps you maintain proper boundaries and protect yourself from influences that aren't hospitable.

But it's in your interest to cultivate just the amount you need, no more. It may often be tempting to go too far, but it's crucial that you learn not to.

In my Astrological Book of Life, you Cancerians are destined to learn the art of knowing just how much anger and fear and antipathy you require to thrive.

LEO: Ancient Greek philosopher Plato observed, "Do not train children to learn by force or harshness; but direct them to it by what amuses their minds, so that you may be better able to discover with accuracy the peculiar bent of the genius of each."

The same principle applies to all of us adults who are committed to the goal of lifelong learning. And according to my astrological analysis, it's an especially useful idea for you Leos. Why? Because you are at the top of the list in the zodiac for "Those Most Likely to Retain the Resiliency of Children."

VIRGO: Poet Rainer Maria Rilke felt many people misunderstand the role of love.

"They are inclined to regard love as fun and pleasurable because they imagine that fun and pleasure are more delightful than work," he wrote. "But when done right, work is joyful. And love, which can generate more bliss than any other experience, is most blissful when hard work is in play."

I'm sharing this perspective with you, Virgo, because of all the signs in the zodiac, you're most likely to thrive on it.

Here's how Rilke finished his thought: "Lovers should proceed as if they have magnificent work to achieve."

LIBRA: The Spanish word *delicadeza* can have several meanings in English, including "delicacy" and "finesse."

The Portuguese word *delicadeza* has those meanings, as well as others, including "tenderness," "fineness," "suavity," "respect," and "urbanity."

In accordance with your astrological potentials, let's make it one of your words of power. You can often thrive by expressing an abundance of these qualities. It might be fun to give yourself the nickname Delicadeza.

SCORPIO: I invite you to experiment with the theme "Healthy Obsessions."

Not "Melodramatic Compulsions" or "Exhausting Crazes" or "Manias That Make You Seem Interesting to Casual Bystanders," but "Healthy Obsessions."

To do it as well as you Scorpios were born to do, you must take scrupulous care of yourself as you concentrate on tasks that rouse your zest and zeal.

This may require you to rebel against the influences of role models, both in your actual life and in the movies you've seen, who act as if getting sick and imbalanced is an integral part of being faithful to one's genius.

SAGITTARIUS: What kind of archer do you want to be when you grow up, Sagittarius? Would you like to be:

- ∞ The kind of archer who aims in the general direction of several big targets in the distance
- ∞ The kind who aims at a single medium-sized target in the middle distance
- ∞ The kind who aims at many small targets that aren't too far away
- ∞ The kind who never aims at any target at all, but just enjoys the thrill of shooting lots of arrows everywhere?

I encourage you to settle on one of these four options.

CAPRICORN: Think about your relationship with people who haven't been born yet. This generous foresight is potentially a Capricornian specialty.

What might you create for future humans to use?

How can you make your life a gift to our descendants?

Can you not only help preserve the wonders we live amidst, but enhance them?

Are you willing to embrace Lewis Carroll's admonition, "It's a poor sort of memory that only works backward"?

AQUARIUS: The truths I articulate below comprise essential knowledge for every sign of the zodiac. But you Aquarians may have the greatest potential to fully activate them.

You don't have to be anything you don't want to be.

You don't have to live up to anyone's expectations.

There's no need to strive for a kind of perfection that's not interesting to you.

You don't have to believe in ideas that make you sad or tormented.

You don't have to feel emotions that others try to manipulate you into feeling.

You are free to be who you want to be.

PISCES: "We should not think of our past as definitely settled, for we are not a stone or a tree," wrote poet Czesław Miłosz. "My past changes every minute according to the meaning given it now, in this moment."

So, yes, Pisces, you always have the power to re-vision and reinterpret your past. Keep the following question in mind as you go about this work: "How can I recreate my history so as to make my willpower stronger, my love of life richer, and my future more interesting?"

Your Primal Longings

Your primal longings are the deepest yearnings you have.
- ◈ The essential instructions that brought you here to live in a body on earth
- ◈ Your most crucial goals
- ◈ Your core driving force

Some of your primal longings may still be unknown to your conscious mind. What could be more fun than discovering them in their fullness?

★

First invitation: Weed out wishy-washy wishes and lukewarm longings that distract you from your primal longings.

Second invitation: Be assured that no one knows better than you how to tend to your primal longings and manage them to keep your life energy operating with maximum efficiency and grace.

Third invitation: Say this aloud to see how it feels: "I know exactly what I want. I know exactly what I don't want. I know what I kind of want but I won't waste my time on it because it sidetracks me from what I really want."

Oracular Homework #112

ARIES: Imagine that you get three wishes on one condition: They can't benefit you directly. They have to be wished in behalf of others. What would they be?

TAURUS: In his book *Thus Spake Zarathustra*, philosopher Friedrich Nietzsche said this: "I overcame myself, the sufferer; I carried my own ashes to the mountains; I invented a brighter flame for myself. and behold, then this ghost fled from me."

   Give an example of a time you used this strategy.

GEMINI: To begin the next momentous healing, tell the simple, brave, and humble truth about yourself.

CANCERIAN: Poet William Butler Yeats wrote, "True love is a discipline in which each divines the secret self of the other and refuses to believe in the mere daily self."

   I agree, which is why I advise you to create in your imagination a detailed picture of your loved ones at their best.

   On a regular basis, feel joy and gratitude for their beauty and power—as well as the beauty and power that are still ripening.

   One of your potential strengths as a Cancerian is to be skillful in performing this service.

★

LEO: "You must stay drunk on writing so reality cannot destroy you," said Leo author Ray Bradbury.

What do you get drunk on to avoid being destroyed by reality?

VIRGO: The 14th-century poet Dante was a major influence on 20th-century novelist James Joyce. "I love Dante," wrote the author of the epic novel *Ulysses*. "He is my spiritual food."

And yet Joyce felt he had to absorb Dante in small doses. "Dante tires one quickly," he said. "It is as if one were to look at the sun."

Do you have your own Dante? Who is it?

LIBRA: Renowned Libran cellist Yo-Yo Ma visited the home of computer pioneer Steve Jobs to perform a private concert.

Jobs was deeply touched, and told Ma, "Your playing is the best argument I've ever heard for the existence of God, because I don't really believe a human alone can do this."

What's your best argument for the existence of God?

SCORPIO: "There was another life that I might have had, but I am having this one." So says a character in Scorpio novelist Kazuo Ishiguro's book *The Unconsoled*.

What is another life you might have had?

SAGITTARIUS: It's your birthright as a Sagittarius to create intimate relationships that deepen your understanding of the way the world works. Are you capitalizing on that potential? If not, ruminate on how you could do it better.

CAPRICORN: "A neurosis is a secret that you don't know you are keeping," wrote theater critic Kenneth Tynan.

See if you can figure out what yours might be.

AQUARIUS: Describe the ways in which you believe—secretly or overtly—that everyone should act or think like you.

PISCES: Piscean novelist Jeffrey Eugenides says he doesn't have generic emotions that can be described with one word. "Sadness," "joy," and "regret" don't happen to him.

Instead, he prefers "complicated hybrid emotions, Germanic train-car constructions," like "the disappointment of sleeping with one's fantasy" or "the excitement of getting a hotel room with a mini-bar."

He delights in sensing "intimations of mortality brought on by aging family members" and "sadness inspired by failing restaurants."

Do you have emotions like those? I suspect so. It's a Piscean specialty. If so, name three favorites.

Element 5

If we don't honor the luminous dark joy within us, it will unravel us.

If we honor the luminous dark joy within us, it will weave us a luminous dark joy body.

Chapter 13

Your Secret Sacred Soul Wiles
+
My Secret Sacred Soul Wiles
=
Our Secret Sacred Soul Wiles

Dear Beloved Ego

My friend Dawn Robertson wrote a thank-you note to her ego. I like it! Here's what she said:

> Dear Beloved Ego,
>
> I'm sorry the conscious and spiritual communities have given you such a bad rap.
>
> Thank you for caring how others perceive me.
>
> Thank you for letting me believe I can make a difference in the world—whether true or not.
>
> Thank you for not letting me hide beyond humility to make myself small.
>
> Thank you for the selfies and self-promotion.
>
> Thank you for pushing me to crave validation through my acts of service.
>
> Thank you for allowing me to be a unique human who can be self-interested at times.
>
> Thank you for delightfully reminding me I have a story during the good times and the bad.
>
> Thank you for the drive to be "successful" and allow-

ing that marker to be fluid.

Thank you for pushing me to take myself more seriously.

Thank you for helping guide me to make decisions and reveal my fears.

Thank you for questioning the bullshit around me while others may follow along like sheep.

Thank you for letting me be human and messy.

Dawn Robertson can be found at https://tinyurl.com/Dawn-Robertson, and dawn@cypressrecruiting.com.

Do These Titles Suit You?

Let me know if you deserve and want any of the following titles.
I will alert the proper accreditation committee on your behalf.

- ◈ Empathy Virtuoso
- ◈ Exuberant Compassion Specialist
- ◈ Raucous Wisdom Doctor
- ◈ Pragmatic Idealist with Flexible Strategies
- ◈ Curiosity Genius
- ◈ Intimacy Magician
- ◈ Ticklish Savant of the Soul's Confounding Ploys and Gambits
- ◈ Covert Time Traveler from the Triumphant Future
- ◈ Play Activist
- ◈ Spirit Punk
- ◈ Muse of Social Justice
- ◈ Humble, Kind, Generous Megalomaniac
- ◈ World's Greatest Struggler and Happiest Sufferer
- ◈ Cunning Joy-Summoner and Bliss-Generator
- ◈ Perceiver of Impossible but True Sights
- ◈ Superstar Adept at Conversing with Stones, Wind, Rivers, and Trees
- ◈ Lodestar Inspiratrix of the Quest to Preserve Regenerative Nonsense
- ◈ Trickster Feminist Spell-Caster of Total Life Enjoyment

Decrease Your Connection

I invite you to decrease your connection with anything that:

- ∞ Demeans your spirit
- ∞ Shrinks your lust for life
- ∞ Limits your freedom
- ∞ Compromises your integrity
- ∞ Dishonors your reverence
- ∞ Inhibits your self-expressiveness
- ∞ Alienates you from what you love

I posted the above message on Facebook. In response a reader named Janet said this:

I understand the urge to disconnect from what demeans and diminishes, and have experienced the usefulness of the strategy.

But I think there's also something to be said for just noticing the things that demean, shrink, limit, and compromise, particularly when those things are other people.

I think we can be bridges and pathways for healing when our choices are more than just an either-or disconnecting or not.

Sometimes hanging in there with the discomfort gives me a chance to understand and transform my perception of what I am and what I'm not.

In response to Janet, I wrote the following:

For myself, the world brings such a nonstop flood of things that demean, shrink, and limit, I disconnect from as many of them as possible. But it's not a practical option to disconnect from all of them.

Also: In disconnecting from them, I don't abandon the possibility of learning from them.

As an example, I just ceased any further link with a chronically crabby jerk who happens to be a famous teacher.

In the aftermath, I am mulling what I can keep learning from the crabby jerk (I have already learned a lot!) and from the feelings and thoughts that have arisen in me in response to the crabby jerk's crabby jerkness.

But it would be an act of self-harm for me to continue being linked to this person.

Another reader, Linda Faye Carson, articulated a wonderful amendment to my original statement. She wrote:

> Allow me to put a positive spin on your statement about disconnecting:
> Increase your connection with everything that:
> - Lifts your Spirit
> - Builds your lust for life
> - Expands your freedom
> - Supports your integrity
> - Honors your reverence
> - Expands your self-expressiveness
> - Helps you keep in touch and harmonize with what and whom you love

Salutations ((◊))

What greetings and salutations do you use to bid welcome or say farewell? Here are my favorites:

∞ Ride hard. See deep. Speak true. Live free.

∞ Here's to your amazing health and transformative joy.

∞ May your journey be packed with interesting fun.

∞ The light and dark in me recognizes the light and dark in you.

∞ Sweet songs and wild laughter till we next meet.

∞ May guidance and clarity follow you wherever you roam.

∞ Do no harm but take no shit. Fling no spite and defend your bliss.

∞ What's good?

∞ Boomshakalaka flashbang!

∞ I wish you many beautiful epiphanies.

∞ May your dreams teach you what you need to know.

∞ May you be untamed and deep-sourced and mysterious.

∞ My ancestors honor your ancestors. My descendants bless your descendants.

∞ May evil and boredom never know how to find you.

∞ Nice shoes!

∞ May you have thrilling travels and useful luck and calming thoughts.

∞ Happy permanent eternal world orgasm!

∞ Nice mask!

∞ Marvels and wonders are coming your way.

You Have Educated Me

By publishing a weekly set of astrological love letters in cities all over the world, I have been endowed with an excellent perk: tens of thousands of messages from my readers.

Many convey interesting information about what's going on in their lives, how my oracles impact them, and what I could do to improve my service. Sometimes I respond personally, but the communiqués are too voluminous for me to answer every one. The more likely follow-up is that I incorporate their advisements into future horoscopes.

In the course of our interchange, I have received an extensive education about a wide variety of humans from many diverse cultures.

This marvelous blessing has transformed me into a lover of neurodiversity, cultural diversity, ethnic diversity, biodiversity, and all the other diversities. It's the equivalent of the teachings I might have gotten had I spent years traveling around the world.

In a sense, I *have* voyaged all over the planet, gleaning input not just from newspaper readers in North America, but also in Italy, France, Australia, Japan, the Netherlands, Finland, Hong Kong, Singapore, Cambodia, Venezuela, and Mexico.

And since my column has been on the web since 1995, I have received dispatches from 49 other countries, as well. One of my favorite requests was from a teenage boy in Kazakhstan who wanted to buy my music CD. He knew all the lyrics by heart.

Mine hasn't been a typical tutelage, but it has been thorough and wide ranging. Thanks, everyone!

Oracles for You #9 ☸

ARIES: Below are hunches and guesses about the topic "How to Be an Aries." My readers provided some ideas, which are noted.

- ◈ If you come upon a "square peg, round hole" situation, change the shape of the hole by any legal and ethical means necessary.
- ◈ For Aries, it has to be creative, thought-provoking, and full of movement and color—or why bother? —Shari Ann Lamb
- ◈ "Say to your friend, 'I am an Aries—you know, the best sign.' Your friend replies, 'I didn't think there was a "best" sign.' And you say, 'Now you know.'" —Erin West
- ◈ "Oh goody, a new project! Can I start it with a bang and never worry about finishing it?" —Norma Quesada
- ◈ As you burn your way through a room, step on toes and knock your elbows against others' elbows as gracefully as possible. Be charmingly aggressive.
- ◈ Believe that no one else in the world can be as good at anything as you are. But indulge and even applaud them if they insist on trying.
- ◈ You know you're sexy, and you make sure everyone knows you're sexy. The disarming audacity of your innocent boldness makes it all benign and permissible.
- ◈ Never let someone order you around. When asked, "What do you want to do?", answer with a dignified, "Anything that allows me to be in control of everything."

TAURUS: Below are hunches and guesses about the topic "How to Be a Taurus." My readers provided some ideas, which are noted.

◈ Keep your mind vigorous and your heart brave and your body supple. If you do, your soul will never hunger. —Warren Roffel

◈ Your potent, almost telepathic sense of smell can tell you secrets and give you clues that most people never tune into.

◈ No one can kiss and nuzzle and snuggle and fuck as long and as slow and as deep as you.

◈ You thrive when you are passionately loyal, and others appreciate how passionately loyal you are. —Nosso Lurner

◈ Taurus says, "Come to your senses, people!" —Kim Hammer

◈ Sometimes it is perfectly acceptable, even advisable, to eat an entire extra-large pizza all by oneself. To be fully themselves, many Tauruses need to regularly indulge in non-dangerous excess. —Arden Mailer

◈ Here's one of your potential superpowers, Taurus: You can help people to act in service to the deepest truths and strongest love. You can even teach them how to do it. Have you been ripening this talent? Have you been bringing it more to the forefront of your relationships?

For best results, take a vow that you will nurture in yourself the deepest truths and strongest love in all your thoughts and dealings with others.

GEMINI: Below are hunches and guesses about the topic "How to Be a Gemini." A reader provided an idea, which is noted.

◈ Be witty. You don't have to be intellectual, but you must be clever. If your brain is sluggish, you're not a Gemini.

◈ Like Gemini poet Walt Whitman, you should contain multitudes. And be clear that this is not a pathological condition. The fact that you are a group of different selves should be a triumph and celebration.

◈ Since you have so many sub-personalities, you probably need a wide variety of friends. Different sub-personalities within you may need different friends.

◈ Remember that paradoxes don't need to be paradoctored. Give the universe permission to not make sense. —Lani Joyser

◈ Watch the world go by as you might view a film, observing carefully and thoughtfully, wondering why the director chose to interpret the script as they have, and speculating about the ways you would change the plot and tinker with the attitudes of the actors.

◈ Here's a scenario that could be both an invigorating metaphor and a literal event.

Put on rollerblades. Get out onto a long flat surface. Build up a comfortable speed. Fill your lungs with the elixir of life. Praise the sun and the wind. Sing your favorite songs.

Swing your arms all the way forward and all the way back. Forward: power. Backward: power. Glide and coast and flow with sheer joy. Cruise along with confidence in the instinctive skill of your beautiful body.

Evaporate thoughts. Free yourself of every concern and every idea. Keep rambling until you feel spacious and vast.

◈ Meditate on the question "How many careers can I and should I have in one lifetime?" Impose no limits on your answers.

◈ You have unusual power to find seemingly mutually exclusive things and then trick or compel or charm them to blend their energies.

CANCERIAN: Below are hunches and guesses about the topic "How to Be a Cancerian." My readers provided some ideas, which are noted.

- ◈ Cultivate your natural talent for appreciating the joys of watching and helping things grow: a child, a creative project, a tree, a friendship, your bank account. —Sharon Smith
- ◈ Always exploring what's higher up and further in means you must keep your Cancerian shell expandable. —Anna Trombley
- ◈ A Cancerian says, "How does this place feel? How can I contribute to improving it? Who is feeling joy here? Who is down? How can I help them feel the moods they like?" —Melody Carol
- ◈ Remember that your crab shell and pincers can serve as healthy boundaries or weapons of war. —Jen Bernard
- ◈ Avoid being friends with people who are shallow or callous or way too cool.
- ◈ When you're in a weird mood and say, "It's not you, it's me," it really is you. Help people understand that.
- ◈ You are the leader who knows how to follow.
- ◈ Make sure people respect your psychic privacy. Let them know you will spill your guts only when you are good and ready. —Riley Gamble

LEO: Below are hunches and guesses about the topic "How to Be a Leo." One of my readers provided some ideas, which are noted.

⬖ Leo says, "Thanks for adoring me. Wait! No, not like that! You must follow the proper protocols. Also, if anyone is ever mean to you, my dear, I. Will. Crush. Them!" —Carla Bohon

⬖ Be in charge of how much of your radiance you allow others to see.

⬖ Never allow yourself to be tamed by others. You need to cultivate maximum access to the raw, primal sources of your life energy. Your ability to thrive depends on how well you identify and express the beautiful animal within you.

Here's the only caveat: If you imagine there may be value in being tamed a little, in harnessing your brilliant beast, do the taming yourself. And assign that task to the part of you that possesses the wildest wisdom.

⬖ Your body can be a source of inspirational teaching for your soul. Keep your soul alert for subtle revelations that may arrive via physical sensations and symptoms.

⬖ Scholar Suzanne Juhasz says that Emily Dickinson's eroticism "inflects and charges" her poems. "Erotic desire— sensuous, nuanced, flagrant, extreme, outlandish, and profound—is her way of interacting with the world."

You Leos are wise to experiment with a similar predilection. Enrichments flow your way as you make metaphorical love to the whole world.

The urge to merge should not just be the icing on your cake. It should be the icing, the cake, the plate it's on, your eating of the cake, your feeding of the cake to others, and stories you tell about your encounter with the cake.

VIRGO: Below are hunches and guesses about the topic "How to Be a Virgo." My readers provided some ideas, which are noted.

- ◈ Virgos own the strongest Bullshit Detectors in the zodiac. —Martha Jablonski Jones
- ◈ Your devotion to grasping nuances and details is at the heart of your drive to be whole and complete. Your reverence for the sanctity of minutia is key to grasping the big picture. Your aptitude for analysis is in service to love and understanding. —Tonia Rose
- ◈ The Virgo goal should be synergy, not mere organization. —Pauline Conn
- ◈ Sometimes, you can make things expand by squeezing them. You help things thrive by limiting them. You can encourage things to heal by critiquing them.
- ◈ You are fun to watch while you're working, because you are so imbued with practical idealism. It's inspiring.
- ◈ Makes sure you harbor a hidden wild side that only the best people know about.
- ◈ You are a great protector when you have the confidence to do it.
- ◈ You may be wise to keep a corner of your world just a bit rumpled, thereby avoiding the dangers of excessive perfectionism.

LIBRA: Below are hunches and guesses about the topic "How to Be a Libra." My readers provided some ideas, which are noted.

- ◈ Be proud as you teeter charismatically on the fence. Relish and brandish the power that comes from being in between.

◈ Flatter others sincerely. Use praise as one of your secret healing weapons.

◈ Cultivate a good-natured skepticism that blends discernment with open-mindedness.

◈ Smile and plot in behalf of rapport and goodwill, but never kiss ass.

◈ Libra says, "I form relationships with everyone I encounter, however temporary the exchange might be." —Frankie Lugo

◈ People who fear beauty, as well as those who love it and cannot see it in themselves, may use you Libras as a projection screen. Trust and cultivate your own sense of beauty so you won't absorb others' projections or take them personally. —Brenda Griffin

◈ Libra says, "Oh, I figured out that problem ages ago, fueled by equal parts intuition and reason. I just haven't told you yet what I concluded because you're not ready for the truth. When the time is right, I will share it generously." —Valeri Pfahning

◈ Sometimes you like to make some declaration just so you can change your mind about it.

◈ Avoid restaurants with extensive menus. When the server comes to take your order, tell everyone else to go ahead of you. When it's your turn, close your eyes and point.

SCORPIO: Below are hunches and guesses about the topic "How to Be a Scorpio." My readers provided some ideas, which are noted.

◈ The opportunities to learn and grow never end, and so neither will your sense of purpose. Storyteller Michael

Meade says, "the soul longs for trouble," and I say, "So you might as well look for good, interesting trouble that challenges and fulfills you." —Melissa Grace

◈ Tap into your forbidden thoughts so they might heal you. Discover the secrets you're hiding from yourself so they can guide you. Ask yourself a prying question every day.

◈ Of all the signs in the zodiac, you Scorpios are most likely to regard that old pop tune by the Animals as your theme song. "I'm just a soul whose intentions are good," croons lead singer Eric Burdon, "Oh, Lord, please don't let me be misunderstood."

On the other hand—maybe because you work so hard to compensate for this ache—you may also experience record-breaking levels of being seen and appreciated for who you are.

For best results, do this: Inform your deep psyche that you have no attachment to being misunderstood. And tell your deep psyche that you would very much like to be well understood.

◈ Scorpio says, "I don't tell people that I'm a Scorpio. Don't want or need to fend off their many stereotypes about who we are." —Daniel Solnit

◈ Use sarcasm sparingly. But definitely use it. If wielded with love and wit, it's a fine Scorpionic weapon.

◈ Scorpio, you'll never live any of it down, so don't even try. —Nancy Pace Kossman

◈ Respect everyone who deserves it, but don't take bullshit even from them. —Joy Anderson Gallion

◈ Joy is a luxurious necessity to be pursued, never an afterthought. Be keen to stretch your ability to feel gratified and even jubilant beyond all previous limits.

SAGITTARIUS: Below are hunches and guesses about the topic "How to Be a Sagittarius." My readers provided some ideas, which are noted.

◈ Key to your self-fulfillment: finding joy in continuously learning and expanding your consciousness. —Suzanne Martino

◈ When you give advice to others, be sure to listen to it yourself. —Dan Shoemaker

◈ Be leader of the pack. If you turn around to find no one's following, laugh it off and keep heading toward the future.

◈ Move away from having a rigid conception of yourself and move toward having a fluid fantasy about yourself.

◈ Be the first one to laugh at and correct your own mistakes. It'll give you the credibility to make even more and better mistakes in the future. —Catherine King

◈ Surround yourself with people who respect themselves and claim a role in making the world a better place.

◈ A perk of being a Sagittarius: At least 25 percent of the time you think something is going wrong, a lucky twist happens in your favor.

CAPRICORN: Below are hunches and guesses about the topic "How to Be a Capricorn." My readers provided some ideas, which are noted.

◈ Capricorn says, "I could be wrong, but I doubt it." —Christine Star

◈ You always seem to end up in charge, even when you'd rather not be. Some folks half-consciously resent that, even as they step back and push you forward. —Tim Goncharoff

◈ For Capricorns, it isn't ultimately about the money. It's never just about the money. It's about establishing stability and ensuring future security for you, your family, and your community. —Kia Bordner

◈ Don't take other people's apparent stupidity or rudeness as personal affronts. Try to understand how the suffering they have endured may have led to their unseemly behavior.

◈ Your rate for describing how to be a Capricorn should never be less than $100 per word.

◈ Don't let the people you love ever think you take them for granted.

◈ Be the cautiously optimistic voice of reason. Be the methodical motivator who prods and inspires. Organize as you uplift. Encourage as you build efficiency.

AQUARIUS: Below are hunches and guesses about the topic "How to Be an Aquarius." My readers provided some ideas, which are noted.

◈ Thinking outside the box when you don't even see the box doesn't go far enough. Solution: See and know the box thoroughly, then escape it. —Perig Gouanvic

◈ Over-focused foresight may be an Aquarian problem. The future is your realm, right? Life on earth will improve! Civilization will be amazing! But your forward-looking vision may make you overlook the beauty and glory of the present moment. Take measures to avoid that.

◈ An older Aquarius might say, "When I was young and listened to the song about how 'This is the dawning of the Age of Aquarius,' I felt happy and secure to know I was born in an era that celebrated my astrological sign. Well, it is now many years later. I don't see much evidence that we are in an epoch that admires the best qualities of Aquarians. But I am still an Aquarius who is trying my best to create the Age of Aquarius." —Charmaine Roulos

◈ Aquarians often feel like Aquarian poet Toni Morrison, who said, "I know the world is bruised and bleeding, and though it is important not to ignore its pain, it is also critical to refuse to succumb to its malevolence."

◈ To fully understand an Aquarius may be impossible. One reason is that many of them don't want to be understood. They'd rather keep people guessing.

◈ Add an extra letter or two to your name every year or so—just to keep yourself and everyone else guessing. Or subtract a letter or two from your name. Or adopt a new nickname. Or start spelling your name the reverse of what it is.

◈ Never let your inner dork overwhelm and overtake and overcome you. Except maybe every spring and a few weeks around your birthday and during each full moon and solstice and equinox.

◈ Volunteer to demonstrate how to breakdance at a retirement home holiday party, even if you don't know how to breakdance yourself.

PISCES: Below are hunches and guesses about the topic "How to Be a Pisces." My readers provided some ideas, which are noted.

◈ One of the best ways to build your vibrancy as a Pisces is to use your emotional intelligence to avoid swimming against strong currents for extended periods of time.

Please note that swimming against strong currents is fine, even advisable, for brief phases. Doing so boosts your stamina and fosters your trust in your resilience.

But mostly I recommend you either swim in the same direction as the currents or else swim where the water is calm and currentless. Armed with this intention, you can enjoy vigorous freestyle excursions heading in the same direction as vigorous currents.

◈ Strive to unite with life's most swoonable beauty. —Lorne Murphy

◈ Piscean eyes may simultaneously gaze directly at the object of their attention and also elusively away.

◈ A fun meditation for Pisces: "Am I the dreamer or the dreamed?" —Claudia Palmira

◈ Appreciate why the Jekyll and Hyde story is intriguing, evocative, and mythically beautiful. —Louisa Deasey

◈ Feel all the feelings of everyone ever. But don't get the mistaken idea that they are all yours.

◈ Piscean people carry with them a little of all the signs.

◈ Is any other sign more skilled than you at interweaving the sacred and profane? At simultaneously enjoying and honoring the fantastic and mundane? At benefiting from both the natural and supernatural in the same breath?

No. No other sign can do these things as well as you.

Element 6

If we believe there is no such thing as a coherent, enduring self, we will never create one.

If we believe there is such a thing as a coherent, enduring self, we may create one.

Chapter 14

Your Endless Flow of Initiatory Epiphanies
+
My Endless Flow of Initiatory Epiphanies
=
Our Endless Flow of Initiatory Epiphanies

Retool Your Amazement 🌿

Retool your amazement. Rebirth your achy symbols. Mutate a waning pleasure.

Swagger your lustiest justice. Sing your holiest fury. Mock indulgent cynicism and gratuitous sarcasm.

Sanctify your interesting wounds. Untame your timid healing. Redraw the map of your Dionysian heart.

Trick eternity with your shocking humor. Celebrate your triumphant surrender to forgiveness. Memorize an as-yet undiscovered future of liberated glee.

Astrology Is a Gnostic Art

At its best, astrology stimulates and nurtures our mythopoetic intelligence. It's a psychological improvisation grounded in the language of the soul. Storytelling is its forte, the source of its energy. Those practitioners who understand its true value don't use it in a quest for factual data and crisp answers and logical analysis.

Psychoanalyst Viktor Frankl, a Holocaust survivor, believed the search for meaning and purpose is the supreme goal of most human lives. Astrology provides its best blessings when it is in service to that imperative.

How does the search for meaning and purpose happen? Where does it come from? A key component is the sense that each of our lives—yours, mine, our loved ones', everyone's—is a long, interesting story composed of linked chapters. Most of us want to understand our destiny as an epic myth woven with plot twists and adventures.

There's no one right way to assemble our personal tales, no standardized strategy for creating our one-of-a-kind masterpieces. The process is unruly, accented with surprises, and often nonrational. We want there to be overarching themes that thread their ways from beginning to end, and we also want subplots, mysterious diversions, perplexing cul-de-sacs, and events that don't make total sense but contribute to the artistry of the big picture.

At its best, astrology serves this heroic fun. It's a lyrical tool that helps us craft our epic histories and generate rich troves of meaning.

Doctor Who, the science fiction character who stars in the TV show of the same name, offers sage advice: "We are all stories in the end. Make yours a good one, eh?"

The wise use of astrology can help us do that.

Anthropologist Claude Lévi-Strauss identified an essential quality of living myths. In every culture and time, they are constantly mutating.

In his book, *The Raw and the Cooked*, he analyzed 187 permutations of a particular myth that has circulated among a variety of Indigenous people in South America.

Lévi-Strauss called the version told by the Bororo people "The Bird-Nester's Aria." The hero must visit the dangerous nest of souls and seek the help of a hummingbird to acquire a great dance rattle. If he fails, he might get killed by his father, who has good reason for being angry. (It's complicated.) His quest is fraught with challenges, but he makes all the right moves and obtains the rattle.

Many further adventures follow, some harrowing. At one point, vultures devour the hero's anus and buttocks. Resorting to magic, he creates an artificial ass out of mashed tubers. Hooray! His health is restored. He can once again hold food in his body long enough to extract nourishment from it.

By the end of the tale, the hero is triumphant. All is well. The vengeful father is dead and gone, his lungs floating on the surface of a lake as aqueous plants.

Lévi-Strauss found 186 other versions of this tale in addition to the Bororos'. None were literally true. None could be tested for accuracy and factualness by the scientific method. All provided dream-like stories that were meaningful to the people who valued them. They spoke to the deep psyche, not rational waking awareness. Were they lies? Were they delusions? Were they distortions of reality? Of course not.

The qualities of "The Bird-Nester's Aria" can help us understand the mythic tales that astrology weaves about our personal and collective destinies. They are not precise, objective analyses. Not systematic, methodical depictions of what our experiences mean and how our narratives unfold. They inspire us to be imaginative and creative in our search for meaning and purpose.

"To riff" is a key element in a useful astrological reading. Definition of the verb "riff": "to improvise in the performance and practice of an art, especially by expanding on or making novel use of traditional themes."

Now let's have playful and provocative fun as we riff on the natal horoscope of a seeker named Vandala.

When Vandala was born, Venus was in Taurus in the fifth house and Uranus was in Cancer in the seventh house. They were in a harmonious aspect: sextile, or 60 degrees.

Uranus is the archetype of liberation, disruption, trailblazing, and nonconformity. Venus symbolizes the power of our feelings and the way we evaluate merit, worth, and importance. It also provides information about how love and beauty and pleasure operate in our lives.

In Vandala's life, how does the relationship between Uranus and Venus play out?

With Uranus in the seventh house of close alliances, we might imagine that Vandala has an exciting and unusual relationship

life. She may pair up with unconventional and fascinating part-
ners. Her connections with them may bring constant adventures and surprises. The identity they have as a couple might
have a lively and innovative effect on the spheres through which
they travel.

Venus in Taurus in the fifth house of creativity suggests that
Vandala is extraordinarily fertile, both in earthy and artful ways.
She may have a knack for bearing and raising amazing children,
or for producing useful things that are beautiful and beautiful
things that are useful. Since the fifth house is also the house of
amusement, Vandala could be adept at generating joie de vivre.
She might have an unparalleled lust for life.

With Venus and Uranus in congenial correlation, the two
archetypes are likely to enhance and synergize each other. Maybe
Vandala collaborates with a partner to make movies or write
music. Perhaps they join forces to throw wild parties. Even if
they don't work on projects together, she probably has a talent
for bringing out the winsome qualities in her closest companion—as well as in others whose lives she touches.

As astrologers, we riff on how Venus and Uranus might interact in Vandala's life, what stories their cooperation might suggest. We are improvising. We don't know anything for a fact. We
are dreaming up stories that correspond to the mythic elements
of the horoscope.

If we are conscientious astrologers, we are in dialog with the
person whose chart we are reading. We collaborate with them
to find which stories resonate with them, which of our educated
guesses feel meaningful. The exchange has resemblances to what
happens during psychotherapy.

There are no right answers, no definitive conclusions. The

task is to enjoy imagining the ways the archetypes of Venus and Uranus interact with each other and how their synergy might signify specific adventures and experiences. The qualities of their combined effects may evolve and change, generating different phenomena this year than they did five years ago.

In astrological storytelling, as in dramas about the Bororo hero in quest of the great dancing rattle, there is no final, accurate, permanent rendering that's more definitive than all the others. One hundred eighty-seven astrologers would offer 187 different versions of Vandala's life story, just as 187 groups of Indigenous people produced 187 variations on the tale of "The Bird-Nester's Aria."

If, in addition to Claude Lévi-Strauss, 186 other anthropologists offered their analysis, I imagine the variety of interpretations would be equally legion.

Myths welcome and invite play, experimentation, and improvisation. They call out to be reinvented by those who love them. They are mercurial, always shifting and rearranging.

Let's propose the existence of an astrologer named Job Disney. Maybe he is a close personal imaginary friend of Rob Brezsny. Or perhaps he's an alter ego of Rob who comes alive when Rob slips into an altered state while reading and ruminating on iterations of "The Bird-Nester's Aria."

Now let's imagine that Job Disney hops online via Zoom to discuss Vandala's astrological chart with her. He is delighted when she says she wants him to go light on the literal interpretations of her destiny and instead focus on amusing, dream-like, fairytale yarns about the mythic version of her wild life.

"*Oupá! Manse! Saruunaar! Hoan hô!*" Job says, invoking the Greek, Korean, Mongolian, and Vietnamese terms for "hooray." Vandala has Mercury conjunct the sun and Jupiter in her third house, all trine to Uranus and sextile to Venus. This suggests she adores playful multi-splendored improvisations and experiments with language.

"*Yaşasın! Hurarē! Nsikidzi!*" Job adds, saying "hooray" in Turkish, Bengali, and Chichewa. He's happy. He's bubbly. Conjuring up epic fables and magickal legends are his wheelhouse.

With detailed flourishes (an approach beloved by Vandala, with her Mercury, Sun, and Jupiter in the third house), Job tells Vandala a story about how once upon a time she and her very best friend and freestyle lushbuddy Jammer Go Whammy decide to throw a five-day, five-night party in the Nest of Souls. They raise the money to fund it by creating a series of viral TikTok videos that teach millions of eager learners how to become the gorgeous geniuses they were born to be.

And who do Vandala and Jammer turn to for help and inspiration in creating the Sacred World Party? The god Uranus and the goddess Venus, of course: the best possible co-conspirators for such a jovial jubilee. And those superstar collaborators invite every polyvalent, neurodiverse, multi-ethnic, pluralistic, transnational person on the planet! It's the promiscuous renegade synergy of Venus and Uranus in full bloom! With free magic hummingbird-shaped dance rattles for everyone in attendance!

Vandala gets excited as Job Disney unfolds the tale. Her natural ebullient artistry overflows as she weaves in some of her own true fictions.

"Racy Venus and zany Uranus give us a great sexy spiritual idea," she tells Job. "A do-it-yourself creative exercise that is de rigueur for all revelers. Everyone gets a fresh pair of white cotton underpants along with fabric paints and felt-tip markers. Their assignment: make their own personal Sacred Underwear. Decorated with their favorite holy erotic symbols and inscribed with boomalicious prayers."

"*Ik hou ervan!*" Job exclaims in Dutch. "*Saya suka itu!*" he adds in Indonesian. "*Ahụrụ m ya n'anya!*" he continues in Xhosa. All three phrases mean "I love it!"

"Plus," says Vandala, "everyone is asked to improvise a love song to their future selves—an anthem of praise and gratitude for the gorgeous genius they will someday become. If they ever get stuck or need inspiration, Jammer and I and Venus and Uranus give them prompts to spur their imagination."

For the next 75 minutes, the two storytellers exult in conjuring up wonder tales about Vandala's and Jammer's exploits at the Sacred World Party with their colleagues Venus and Uranus— as well as with honored invitees Neptune, Pluto, Mars, Jupiter, Mercury, Saturn, sun, and moon.

Religious historian Elaine Pagels authored the book, *The Gnostic Gospels*. There, she talks about the open-source, organic tradition of early Gnostic Christianity.

Each Gnostic devotee was regarded as a potential originator of visionary revelation. Each could extend the boundaries and shift the meanings of the evolving body of beliefs and practice.

At its best, astrology is like this: a living, mythic tradition that continually rebels against or outflanks tradition.

Love Cues and Clues: The Guardian Angel of Your Relationship

Imagine that the blend of you and your best ally has created a third essence that hovers near you, protecting and guiding the two of you.

Call this third essence an angel or muse or mentor.

Or call it the soul of your connection or the synergetic force of your relationship.

Or refer to it as the special work the two of you can accomplish together.

Let this magical presence be the third point of your love triangle. Consult it frequently. Ask for love and help. Treat it as the best friend the two of you have.

★

Homework: For all signs: Is there any sense in which your closest alliances are gifts to the world? Do your relationships inspire others?

Do the two of you together serve as activators and energizers, nurturing and exciting the imaginations of those whose lives you touch?

Transparency 🖐

Since I was 23 years old, I have studied the esoteric magickal system known as Hermetic Qabalah. The school where I have matriculated is the Builders of the Adytum.

Other teachings have flowed into the mix, as well, adding idiosyncratic colors and tones. Chaos magick and Goddess worship are key ingredients. Others: astrology, paganism, Tarot, alchemy, depth psychology, Tantra. Taoism, and the Fourth Way.

Blessed by this cavalcade of inspirations, I have established a boisterous and intimate relationship with the Supreme Creator whose name keeps changing. Recent favorites: the Blooming HaHa and the Divine YaYa.

Few people know these facts about me—only a small percentage of my friends and relatives, and an even more minuscule portion of my readers.

I haven't tried to hide my devotional practices. Rather, I am quite sure no one cares much about them. And my love for the work that has afforded me such joyous fulfillment has never spilled over into an urge to proselytize.

There is another reason why I've been ultra-discreet. Many intelligent people are rightly skeptical about the role that religion and spirituality play in our culture. I respect and honor their caution.

The rise of Christian fascism is especially alarming and dangerous to public health. New Age mysticism has become so infected with anti-scientific attitudes and QAnon-style delusions that I swore off all connection with it.

Not all fundamentalists are religious believers, and not all religious believers are fundamentalists. But neither are the percentages miniscule. And I am deeply allergic to fundamentalism in all its forms.

Even Buddhism, whose compassionate rationalism appeals to me more than most mainstream traditions, has succumbed to abusive behavior, with fanatical adherents in Sri Lanka and Myanmar committing atrocities.

In light of these dire considerations, I am scrupulous to avoid promoting or advocating particular religious or spiritual institutions, even as I express enthusiasm for teachings that have been instrumental in my soul's growth.

Here's the solution I came up with for the dilemma: coining a new term to refer to my relationship with the sacred realm. Avoiding "religion" and "spirituality," I call my method *museful numinosity.*

"Museful" means it's infused with an attraction to muse-like sources that inspire me, including humans, animals, and spirits. "Numinosity" is an English word that comes from the ancient Greek νοούμενον (*nooúmenon*), meaning "influence perceptible by the mind but not the senses."

So I am not religious. I don't do spirituality. My practice is museful numinosity.

Among its foundational principles: I'm welcoming toward people who don't have similar inclinations. I'm fine if you have no interest in museful numinosity.

I will offer some nuance.

People often leave comments on my social media in which they grieve about how horrible and awful and malignant and destructive all religion is. They are quite sure that religion is responsible for the majority of the world's problems, that religion is the cause of most wars, and that there is nothing at all redemptive or benevolent about any religion anywhere anytime.

These people often don't seem to recognize that there are types of religious paths other than the destructive fundamentalist varieties of mainstream religions. If they have heard of shamanism and Indigenous spirituality, for example, they seem oddly incapable of seeing those practices as quests for transcendent religious experiences.

They make no acknowledgment of the teeming variety of other organized religious and spiritual practices that comprise the total human experience. Bahá'í, Reform Judaism, Vajrayana Buddhism, Bhakti Hinduism, and mystical Christianity are a few, as well as those that have influenced me, which I named earlier.

I have no urge to convince the religion despisers and staunch atheists that they should change their minds. I am glad they have views that are right for them. I feel the same about people who are apathetic toward religion and deities. Follow your truth!

However, I do wonder if the religion despisers and staunch atheists know that I commune with beings and intelligences who are imperceptible to the human senses. My daily communions and conversations with the Divine YaYa are the highlights of my life. I have prayed and carried out Qabalistic meditations and performed ceremonial magick and done a whole lot of things that religious and spiritual people do. My intimate relationship with what I call The Other Real World is primary. It is at the core of my life and informs everything I do.

Again, I have no desire for anyone to be like me. My hope is for all humans to be themselves, purely and strongly.

But I feel it's important that readers of mine who hate religion and spirituality or feel apathetic about religion and spirituality should know the truth about me.

Whenever you read anything I write, you should know that it originated in my connection with the One Being in the Universe who is the source of us all.

Here's another crucial caveat. There is an important way that I resemble Christians like Cesar Chavez, Martin Luther King Jr., Harriet Tubman, Dorothy Day, Dolores Huerta, Bishop Desmond Tutu, and Sojourner Truth: My passion for social justice is rooted in my intimate relationship with the Creator.

That treasure fuels my quest to undo all that contributes to patriarchy, misogyny, bigotry, racism, oppression of LGBTQIA+ people, the perpetrators of ecocide, militarism, and plutocracy.

A Reader Protests

A reader who calls herself Sally Skeptic wrote me the following email:

> Dear Rob: I sure don't like so much God stuff mixed into your various writings. And Goddess stuff. What a mess! Can you cut it out, please?
>
> I understand it's common for the desperate delusional masses to believe in an Ultra Being, but you? Pul-lease. You're smarter than that.
>
> I just can't abide all the "Divine Wow" and "Cackling Goddess" nonsense you dispense; it doesn't jibe with the practical, sensible, unsuperstitious, non-mushy world that I hold dear—and that I see represented mostly accurately in your work. —Sally Skeptic

Here's my response to Sally Skeptic:

> Dear Sally: I can't accommodate you. You will have to keep dealing with the cognitive dissonance that arises from reading the oracles of a "smart" person who also has an intimate relationship with You-Know-Who.
>
> Just so you're clear about how I perceive the Living Intelligent Consciousness That Pervades Every Cubic Inch of the Universe: It is the interplay of the Supernal NonBinaries: the Divine Wow formerly called "God" and the Blooming HaHa formerly called "Goddess."
>
> More precisely, it is the Torrential and Tortur-

ous Ecstasy spawned anew every nanosecond by the glide of the Divine YaYa's virile eternity against the Blooming HaHa's voluptuous infinity. It is the Cosmic Fuck that recreates the universe again and again in every nanosecond.

And here's my place in that great mystery: I seek the highest possible bond with its stupendous delight; I aspire to locate myself permanently in the crux of the flux of the Cosmic Fuck.

Why Do People Believe in God but Not in Fairies?

A reader asked me, "Why do so many people believe in God but don't believe in fairies?"

Here's one response: Most people in Western culture don't have much of a relationship, let alone an intimate connection, with The Other Real World: the Dreamtime, the astral plane, the realm of the ancestors, the-place-we-all-come-from-and-to-where-we-will-return.

Those who do have such a relationship are far more likely to be on conversational terms with fairies and other denizens of The Other Real World.

Another factor in the absence of communion between humans and fairies is that many humans spend little time in the natural world, where The Other Real World is especially accessible to our waking awareness.

A third factor is the rationalists' inability to apprehend or appreciate the exotic intelligence of nonhuman beings. They don't believe there are other modes of acumen, so beings like fairies who command other modes are invisible.

Here's another reason religious people may believe in God but not in fairies. For many, God is an abstract concept they took on through parental and social conditioning rather than through a visceral connection with the live and in-person Divine Intelligence. Their abstract concept obstructs the visceral connection. They don't know God. They *think* God.

★

I am perplexed by how many politically progressive people are adamantly materialist. They are rigidly and belligerently "skeptical" of The Other Real World, even in the face of the fact that relationship with spirits (including beings like fairies) has been a key element in virtually every Indigenous culture.

I am especially puzzled by the dogmatic materialism that some environmentalists cling to. They don't seem to acknowledge that Indigenous peoples' loving relationship with the earth is inherently spiritual.

Dream author Robert Moss says, "Indigenous and ancestral shamans know that we are all connected to the world of the animal powers, and that by recognizing and nurturing our relation with animal spirits, we find and follow the natural path of our energies.

"Yet many of us have lost this primal connection, or know it only as a superficial wannabe symbolic thing that we look up in books and medicine cards without feeding and living every day."

According to The Pluralism Project in the article "Native American Religious and Cultural Freedom," "the animistic perspective is so widely held and inherent to most Indigenous peoples that they often don't have a word in their languages that corresponds to 'animism'; the term is an anthropological construct."

The animist perspective is that just like humans, everything else is alive and animated by spirit: plants, animals, stones, rivers, clouds, glaciers, thunderstorms, planets. They are all our kin: intelligences that have will and agency. They listen and express themselves and always seek relationship.

If we humans learn their language and commune with them,

we enrich our sense of intimacy with the world and deepen our devotion to preserving nature's health and beauty.

Having relationships with fairy-like beings has been common among Indigenous people.

For example, the *Nunnehi* are a race of immortal spirit creatures for Cherokees, and *Yunwi Tsundi* are small humanoid nature spirits.

Here are names used for the "little people" or "fairies" by some other Native American people:

- *Chaneque* (Aztec)
- *Ircinraq* (Yup'ik)
- *Ishigaq* (Inuit)
- *Jogahoh* (Iroquois)
- *Mannegishi* (Cree)
- *Memegwesi/Memegawensi* (Anishinaabe)
- *Nimerigar* (Shoshone)
- *Nirumbee* or *Awwakkulé* (Crow)
- *Nunnupi* (Comanche)
- *Pukwudgie* (Wampanoag)
- *Yehasuri* (Catawba)
- *Canotila* (Lakota)
- *Popo-li* or *Kowi Anukasha* (Choctaw)
- *Mikumwess* (Wabanaki)

The superstition of materialism is the dominant ideology of a majority of people in the world. It's the specious doctrine that physical matter is the only reality and that nothing can be said to exist unless it's perceivable by a human being's five senses or detected by technologies that humans have created.

Materialism paradoxically preaches the value of being agnostic about all phenomena it does not recognize as real, even as it obsessively evades questions about its own fundamentalist assumptions.

Militant atheists make the claim that religion has always been a primary cause of war. If humans weren't under the sway of "the God delusion," they fume, armed conflicts would be infrequent.

But military historian Eric Bergerud, author of four books about various wars, says that's absurd. He notes that while there have been a few religious wars, "most wars in history have been driven by the lust for power and loot."

In other words, the materialist delusion is far more lethal than the God delusion. People who believe there's nothing of value beyond what the five senses can perceive are often the most dangerous of all.

In its analysis of the causes of war, the *Encyclopedia of Wars* states that only 6.87 percent of all historical conflicts have been motivated by religion.

Indigenous botanist Robin Wall Kimmerer writes: "As a scientist, I have been trained to refer to our relatives, the plants and the animals, the water and the Earth herself, as 'it.'

"In Potawatomi languages, we characterize the world into those who are alive and the things which are not. So we speak a grammar of animacy. And that's because in the beautiful verb-based language, a language based on being and changing and agency, the whole world is alive."

Kimmerer says she was driven to study botany because of the central question in her heart: "Why is the world so beautiful?"

Our original instructions are to listen to the cloud floating by and the wind blowing by. That's poetry and prose in English, but it is *wakahan* in the Lakotan language. It means to consciously apply mystery to everything. Everything is alive and has its own consciousness.

— Lakota elder Tiokasin Ghosthorse

Modern post-industrial societies tend to produce un-sane populations—multitudes of people who are unbalanced in their adaptation to the destructive stress of daily existence. One of the symptoms of this un-sanity is the loss of contact between the waking ego and the depths of the self, a contact that requires involvement in dream experiences and information.

Cultures generally resist change, and modern materialist societies are no different in this respect. Devaluation of dreaming and other spiritually efficacious experiences is part of the foundation of "false consciousness" required by capitalist/materialist political economies.

Materialist cultures require that the focus of awareness be upon the material conditions of life and away from involvement with the inner being which is the only road to spiritual maturation.

— anthropologist Charles D. Laughlin

True Skepticism 🌀

Many rationalists fiercely believe there is no such thing as The Other Real World. Some are my friends! They say it's delusional to converse with dead ancestors, consult with deities, consort with fairies, or mingle with animal and plant spirits.

There's no such thing as an invisible world, they assert, repudiating the convictions of most Indigenous people who have ever lived. Anyone who believes in such nonsense must be unintelligent, the scoffers proclaim—incapable of perceiving the truth about the nature of reality.

Those who regard astrology as unmitigated bullshit are usually members of this club. To them, the subject I specialize in is a blight on culture. It has less than zero value.

A term some of these fanatics use to describe themselves is "skeptic."

But I have found that the majority of those who pride themselves on being skeptics about astrology and The Other Real World are pseudo-skeptics. They are often fundamentalists, as well. Not fundamentalists in the religious sense, of course, but in the sense of believing their way of thinking is absolutely, dogmatically correct, and everyone else who doesn't think like them is wrong and stupid.

What is the difference between authentic skepticism and pseudo-skepticism? Here are my thoughts.

True skepticism does not carry an undertone of anger, ridicule, derision, and pompous conceit. It is even-tempered, clear-minded, and full of equanimity, satisfied with simply showing what is illogical or mistaken in the perspective it critiques.

A true skeptic does not use emotionally charged language in an effort to portray the person whose belief or position she is critiquing as an ignorant fool.

A true skeptic has no attachment to proving that she is smarter than and superior to the person whose argument she is questioning. Rather, she is content to have her argument win on the strength of its adept and elegant reasoning.

A true skeptic is willing to consider the possibility that there may be merit, however small, in the position of the person she is critiquing. She is not afraid that acknowledging this merit will undermine the unconditional truth she purports to possess.

A true skeptic is not consumed with the arrogant certainty that she is always right. In other words, she resists the temptation to be a fundamentalist.

A true skeptic has a respect for the fact that some questions don't have definitive, incontrovertible answers. She recognizes how much about the world is mysterious.

A true skeptic is as likely to be a non-male gender. (Ninety-five percent of the pseudo-skeptics are men.)

A true skeptic shows humility, in the spirit that science popularizer Carl Sagan demonstrated when he said this:

> An atheist is someone who is certain that God does not exist, someone who has compelling evidence against the existence of God. I know of no such compelling evidence.
>
> Because God can be relegated to remote times and places and to ultimate causes, we would have to know a great deal more about the universe than we do now to be sure that no God exists.

To be certain of the existence of God and to be certain of the nonexistence of God seem to me to be the confident extremes in a subject so riddled with doubt and uncertainty as to inspire very little confidence indeed.

A wide range of intermediate positions seems admissible.

Considering the enormous emotional energies with which the subject is invested, a questing, courageous, and open mind is, I think, the essential tool for narrowing the range of our collective ignorance on the subject of the existence of God.

YOUR ENDLESS FLOW OF INITIATORY EPIPHANIES   355

The 80 Percent Rule

Readers of my horoscope column are sometimes surprised when I testify I believe in astrology about 80 percent. "You're a quack?!" they cry.

Not at all, I explain. I have been an ardent student for my entire adult life. About the time my overeducated young brain was on the verge of desertification, unruly wisdom showed up in the guise of astrology, lyricizing my soul just in time.

"But what about the other 20 percent?" they press on. "Are you saying your horoscopes are only partially true?"

I assure them that my doubt proves my love. By cultivating a tender, cheerful skepticism, I inoculate myself against the virus of fanaticism. This ensures that astrology will be a supple tool in my hands, an adaptable art form, and not a rigid, explain-it-all dogma that over-literalizes and distorts the mysteries it seeks to illuminate.

During the question-and-answer segment of one of my performances, an audience member got hostile. "Why do you diss science so much?" he complained.

My accuser had not read much of my work. Otherwise, he'd have gathered abundant clues that belied his theory. In my horoscopes, for instance, I often quote reverently from peer-reviewed scientific journals including *Nature* and *Scientific American* and *Lancet*. And I regularly extol the virtues of the scientific method. "Some of my best friends are scientists," I teased the heckler.

The fact is that I critique science no more than I do all the systems I respect and use. I believe in science about 80 percent—the same as I do in astrology, psychology, feminism, Qabalah, paganism, progressive political philosophy, and 23 others.

I do think science needs extra doses of affectionate critique from people who love it, like me. As one of the dominant ideologies of our age, it has a magisterial reputation comparable to the infallibility accorded to the medieval Church. Some of its devotees promote it as the ultimate arbiter of truth, as an approach to gathering and evaluating information that makes all others unnecessary and irrelevant.

Here's another problem: Though science is an elegant method of understanding the world, not all its practitioners live up to its lofty standards. The field features many men motivated as much by careerism and egotism as by a rigorous quest for excellence. Another worrisome factor is that misogyny pervades every facet of scientific research.

Careerism, egotism, and misogyny are common features in most spheres, of course. But it's a special problem for a field that the intellectual elite touts as the premier purveyor of truth.

There's a further complication: Like the rest of us, scientists may harbor irrational biases and emotional fixations. They purport to do just the opposite, of course. But in fact, they may simply hide their unconscious motivations better, aided by the way the scientific establishment relentlessly promotes the myth that its practitioners are in pure service to objective knowledge.

This discrepancy between the cover story and the actual state of things is, again, a universal tendency, not confined to science. But it's especially unfortunate in a discipline that presents itself as the embodiment of dispassionate investigation.

There are some scientists who, upon reading my words here,

might discharge a blast of nonscientific derision in my direction. Like true believers everywhere, they can't accept what they regard as half-hearted converts. If I won't buy their whole package, then I must be a superstitious, fuzzy-brained goofball.

To which I'd respond: I love the scientific approach to understanding the world. I aspire to appraise everything I experience with the relaxed yet eager curiosity and the skeptical yet open-minded lucidity characteristic of a true scientist.

A fellow astrologer asked me why I care about what science thinks about astrology. Here's what I said:

Because I love science and its methodology and because a lot of people who pay attention to what I write also love science and its methodology.

I want to talk to these smart people about the excesses and distortions of science, in the hope that this will help in a small way to shore up the integrity of science and deepen its capacity to welcome other modes of intelligence as valid.

In the US, science is under threat from theocratic and paranoid and delusional views of the world. We need science to be as strong and vital as possible in the face of that danger.

The scientific method is a fantastic way of learning about the world, and I use it daily. But it's not the only valid way to learn about the world. To dismiss other ways of learning about the world as pseudoscientific is reductionist and fundamentalist. And that damages the credibility of science.

You Must Earn Your Right to
Criticize and Debunk ⟳

Famous scientists like Bill Nye and Neil deGrasse Tyson have tried to debunk astrology without having studied anything more than the most superficial expressions of astrology.

Their efforts are akin to, say, a music critic who summarily belittles all music ever created based on his brief exposure to homeless street musicians he has heard playing in Walmart parking lots.

Let's hope that Tyson and Nye and their fellow skeptical soldiers do a better job if they ever turn their attention to debunking related areas of human inquiry. They might consider, for example, actually reading the books of Carl Jung before debunking Jungian psychology.

Let's hope they will research lucid dream studies before ridiculing them, and that they will gaze at a few of Wassily Kandinsky's paintings before they inevitably trash his art as "unscientific."

The mythological thought of Joseph Campbell would be a fair target for their debunking crusade—as long as they first familiarized themselves with Campbell's books.

Here's a template for how they might proceed—a debunking of the poetry of John Keats, as carried out by an anonymous critic who calls her blog "The Invisible Left Hand of Jesus":

> "Ode on a Grecian Urn," a poem by John Keats, contains many egregious lies, distortions, and inaccuracies. Indeed, it is so replete with statements that are blatantly scientifically inaccurate that its overall verac-

ity is extremely questionable.

Note, for instance, the first two lines, "Thou still unravish'd bride of quietness, Thou foster-child of Silence and slow Time." The term "unravished" is immediately worrisome. One certainly hopes that the urn has not been the victim of forcible sexual intercourse. Taking the effort to deny something so unlikely indicates that such things are, to Keats, within the realm of possibility.

Furthermore, "quietness" is an abstraction related to the relative absence of sound in a place—that is, compression waves traveling through a medium. As a sound wave cannot be married, and therefore cannot logically be called a "bride," it is that much more the case that its absence will never experience matrimony.

The mini-essay above appears at https://tinyurl.com/2p8vhyww.

Carl Sagan and Me and
Ayahuasca ✋

I don't take ayahuasca because I have an aversion to vomiting. But on five occasions, I have taken placebo ayahuasca. (It's disguised as watermelon-flavored Pop Rocks.)

On two of my placebo ayahuasca trips, the spirit of Carl Sagan visited me. He told me that after he died in 1996, he was humbled to find out he had been mistaken about some fundamentalist materialist ideas he had preached.

The existence of spiritual beings was one of the big ones. While alive, he had scoffed at the prospect that there are such things. Now he knows better.

Sagan told me the Ojibwe god Nanabozho himself ushered him to the next world, where he now enjoys studying in an astral ashram with the spirits of Isaac Newton, Johannes Kepler, Galileo, Max Planck, and many other scientists who were close with God even before they departed this realm.

I was gratified, too, that Sagan apologized to me about his summary dismissal of astrology. He now knows that like every other human endeavor, astrology has its mediocre practitioners and its great minds, its weak ideas and its brilliant ideas, and while alive he had focused on mediocre astrologers and weak astrological ideas.

Fairy Tales and Richard Dawkins

Evolutionary biologist Richard Dawkins is an eminent atheist with strong opinions. He says that reading fairy tales to children may harm them by enforcing a false belief in the supernatural. He warns that the "facts" in those old stories are "statistically improbable."

Dawkins would prefer it if children were taught scientific truths rather than fictional fantasies. He says, "It's rather pernicious to inculcate into a child a view of the world" that includes "Santa Claus, wizards, and princesses."

Many psychologists, educators, storytellers, and mythologists would disagree with Dawkins's assessment. In their view, fairy tales are often meaningful stories that speak to the souls of children and adults alike. They have vivid power to illuminate psychological and spiritual themes.

One of my favorite scholars of fairy tales is Jungian psychotherapist Clarissa Pinkola Estés. She writes, "In fairy-tale justice, as in the deep psyche, kindness to that which seems less is rewarded by good, and refusal to do good for one who is not beautiful is reviled and punished.

"When we enlarge ourselves to touch the not-beautiful, we are rewarded. If we spurn the not-beautiful, we are severed from life and left out in the cold."

Dear Beloved Champions, I especially endorse Estés's fairy tale teaching for your use.

Supernatural Communion and
the Scientific Method

I am in intimate communion with supernatural creatures and
nonmaterial beings every day
  and
  I love the scientific method and use it every day.
  Both are true.

★

I study the work of progressive researchers like Howard Zinn,
Naomi Klein, David E. Stannard, and Noam Chomsky to understand how US foreign policy over the last 125 years has consistently decimated political and human rights in Latin America,
Asia, and Africa
  and
  I study Qabalah and Western Hermetic Magick so as to seek
mythopoetic revelations and insights from spiritual intelligences
that aren't fully embodied in the material realm.
  Both are necessary.

★

I aspire to practice the ideals articulated by Andrew Harvey:

> A spirituality that is only private and self-absorbed,
> one devoid of an authentic political and social con-
> sciousness, does little to halt the suicidal jugger-
> naut of history.
>   On the other hand, an activism that is not purified

by profound spiritual and psychological self-awareness will only perpetuate the problem it is trying to solve, however righteous its intentions.

When, however, the deepest and most grounded spiritual vision is married to a practical and pragmatic drive to transform all existing political, economic, and social institutions, a holy force—the power of wisdom and love in action—is born. This force I define as Sacred Activism.

Dreamwork as a Foundation for Activism

Some people imagine I'm a drug-user with a deranged view of reality. I forgive them for their misimpression. The truth is that I'm not in sync or sympathy with deranged aspects of reality, and that makes me seem odd.

I assume they also can't tell the difference between the impact of taking drugs and the influence of doing dreamwork. The latter has been instrumental in shaping my unusual perspectives.

I have remembered and recorded and learned from my dreams since I was 19 years old. They have been creative disruptors and relentless educators. I understand how the freaky beast they have designed and sculpted—me—might appear eccentric to those who have never done such work.

★

I am perplexed by how few people draw on the exotic yet deeply practical revelations bestowed by our dreams.

More and more of us appreciate the value of meditation and mindfulness, but a comparable embrace of dreamwork hasn't happened.

Meditation is a tool for clearing away the monkey mind's and monkey heart's chatter so we might calm down and tune into interesting modes of consciousness beyond our default every-day awareness. Dreamwork can help us do that and much more.

Yes, it's a subtle art that requires a great deal of practice and training. But there is no better way to transmute the unripe and less beautiful aspects of our psyches. Healing pain is never easy, but dreamwork is the closest approximation we have to a miracle cure. It's a matchless method for evoking and crafting our personal genius, and deserves to be at the core of our spiritual work.

This cultural blind spot, the neglect of our dreams' treasure, is an unrecognized form of insanity. Millions of us choose not to use an easily available source of regular insight that can make us smarter about how to redeem our darkness and purge psychic toxins.

I'm convinced that if dreamwork were a regular practice, some of our massive collective problems would diminish. Here's my hypothesis: To the degree that we stop projecting pathology onto others and deal with it in ourselves, we are more likely to act with moral equanimity toward everyone else.

That's why I recommend dreamwork as a foundation for effective activism. Our effort to wrangle compassionately with our shadow self is a potent ground-level technique to purify and strengthen our efforts to redeem the world.

I will reiterate my previous quote from Andrew Harvey: "An activism that is not purified by profound spiritual and psychological self-awareness will only perpetuate the problem it is trying to solve, however righteous its intentions."

Portents for You #10

ARIES: Aries political leader and future president Thomas Jefferson almost pulled off a miracle in 1784.

America was a young country. There were only 13 states and a few unorganized territories. As a representative to the Continental Congress, Jefferson proposed an ordinance that would have prohibited slavery in those territories, including what would later become Tennessee, Mississippi, and Alabama.

By just one vote, alas, the provision failed to pass.

Can you imagine what the United States would have been like if slavery had been partly extinguished decades before the Civil War?

Here's the lesson I draw: At certain turning points, small shifts can have huge long-term consequences—both in the life of an individual and the life of a nation.

You Aries people have substantial potential to identify and initiate key pivots like these as you create your story and contribute to the story of your community. It's one of your birthrights.

TAURUS: The Chukchi people of Siberia are perplexed by the changes in their climate, writes Pulitzer Prize-winning science writer Usha Lee McFarling in the *Seattle Times*.

Thunder and lightning used to be exceptional events, but now they make regular appearances. Bizarre, balmy winds whistle in out of the south.

Elders who were once skilled in the art of reading the sky to foretell the weather are sometimes at a loss. "The Earth is turning faster," said one hunter.

Do you know any local elders who are adept at analyzing the flow of the seasons in your neighborhood? Probably not, unless you hang out with farmers or weather forecasters or climate scientists.

So you may or may not be personally attuned to the shifts in the age-old patterns. Are the daffodils blooming earlier each year? Are the cherry blossoms ahead of schedule? Are the fireflies coming out to play sooner than they used to?

Mostly, yes. But in some years, these phenomena are also later than usual. The nature of the climate emergency is such that mutations in the ancient ways show up erratically.

All that is prologue for my invitation, Taurus: Are you interested in being a wise elder or wise youngster who loves nature so much you crave to learn its rhythms and keep track of its changing patterns?

In all the zodiac, you Tauruses are often best qualified to show the rest of us what it means to be perceptive lovers of the earth.

GEMINI: Can you be a dissatisfied renegade and effervescent lover of life at the same time? Can you identify what's wrong without diluting your amused conviviality?

If anyone can do it with panache, it's you Geminis. Multitasking is potentially one of your superpowers.

You may have few role models to draw from, though, so you will have to trust your intuition and the following advice: Be a generous bitch! A playful protester! A sweet-tempered complainer!

I am especially interested in you applying this dual talent to the work of activism: healing the environment and crusading for justice in behalf of those with lower incomes and fewer privileges.

CANCERIAN: Psychotherapist James Hillman and essayist Michael Ventura wrote the book *We've Had a Hundred Years of Psychotherapy and the World's Getting Worse.* In it, they propose that there are other viable ways to resolve our problems in addition to sitting in a room talking about our deep, private feelings with a trusted counselor.

Another valid approach might be to do work to further social justice, like helping people with low incomes or fighting to preserve the fundamental right to abortion. Taking action to preserve the health and sanctity of the natural world might be another approach.

Hillman's and Ventura's counsel could be an excellent prescription when you are stymied by a personal problem. As you marshal your moral force and collaborate with others motivated by altruism, you may rouse previously untapped insight and power to heal your pain.

One of your potential specialties as a Cancerian is to coordinate your personal concerns with the needs of your community—to serve the greater good by addressing your private good and vice versa.

LEO: My rage against the machine began early. I joined my first anti-war march when I was a sophomore in high school and led a walkout to protest racism when I was a senior. At age 18, I was tear-gassed by the National Guard at a demonstration against America's invasions and occupations of sovereign nations.

In the intervening years, my anger at injustice has broadened and deepened. I've lent my rebel yells and constructive action and poetic expression to many righteous causes. I'm not going to stop.

But a few years ago, I decided to shift my approach. Instead of fighting every abuse that incited my ire, I chose three to concentrate on: the militarism and interventionism of the American government, the extreme financial disparities between the rich and poor, and the environmental degradations caused by corporations and the Pentagon.

Since then, my crusading energy has been more focused and effective.

I invite you to consider a similar focus. Should you give more of your passion to fewer causes? Many Leos thrive by sharpening the scope of their intentions.

VIRGO: The Indian activist Mahatma Gandhi led many peaceful rebellions against oppressive governments, first in South Africa and later in British-controlled India.

At first, he called his strategy "passive resistance," but later disavowed that term because he felt it had negative implications.

He ultimately chose the Sanskrit word *satyagraha*, meaning "love force" or "truth force." "Truth (*satya*) implies love," he said, "and firmness (*agraha*) is a synonym for force. *Satyagraha* is thus the force which is born of truth and love."

According to my reading of your astrological potentials, Virgo, satyagraha should be one of your prime words of power. Your uprising against the forces of darkness—both out in the world and within yourself—must do more than say "no." A refined, exultant YES should be at the heart of your crusade.

LIBRA: In Indonesia, the term *gotong-royong* is defined as the "joint bearing of burdens."

In practice, it means you and I and our allies get together voluntarily to help each other achieve shared goals. It may also be an agreement to provide mutual aid: I help you do what you need to have done, and you help me with my task.

Gotong-royong also implies that we enjoy working together. The emotional tones we cultivate are affection and care. By sharing burdens, we lessen the strain that each of us has to bear.

I bring this to your attention, Libra, because I love to see you be a ringleader who initiates and sustains *gotong-royong*. It's potentially one of your specialties.

SCORPIO: In the history of civilization, there have been few cultures that neglect nightly dreams more than ours. Many eras have paid far more attention to the stories that well up while we're sleeping.

This enervating neglect incurs a personal cost. If you're one of those who rarely recalls your dreams, you suffer a grievous loss of connection with the wisdom of your unconscious mind.

Even if you do stay in touch with your dreams, most of the people around you aren't nourished by theirs. That carelessness isn't totally responsible for the stupendous stupidity and fundamentalist materialism that pervades our culture, but it's a significant factor.

Paying attention to the dream state is an opportunity to gather visceral encounters with the realm where we all originate and still dwell part-time. It provides reminders that we have far more

going on inside us than is apparent to our normal waking awareness. Without regular doses of such healing medicine, we are
prone to devalue everything that doesn't serve our ego drives.

Three astrological signs have a special potential to remedy
the calamitous indifference: Cancerian, Scorpio, and Pisces. Of
the three, I think you Scorpios are best set up to be dreamwork
activists: to embody, exhibit, and express the profoundly practical power of communing with the nightly stories that come from
who-knows-where.

SAGITTARIUS: For over three years, my Sagittarian friend Rosa
risked her sanity and safety in the service of the modern version
of the Underground Railroad. That's how I think of her work
at a sanctuary for women who experienced domestic violence.

The vulnerable souls she counseled were often on the run and
in hiding from their abusers. Most were at the bottom of the scale
of social prestige.

For Rosa, it was an unexpected way to quench her Sagittarian yearning for adventure. On the surface, it seemed wrench-
ing and unglamorous.

Yet she found that assisting scared women to recover their
identity, get jobs, and love life again could be as grippingly gratifying as skydiving or climbing a mountain.

What does adventure consist of for you? Keep an open
mind about it.

CAPRICORN: Let's say you want to buy an 18-karat gold ring.
To get that much gold, miners have to excavate and move six

tons of rock. Then they douse the rock with poisonous cyanide, a chemical necessary to extract the good stuff. In the process, they create toxic waste.

Is the gold ring worth that much trouble and cost? Or might there be other beautiful, valuable things you could obtain without having to use poison and make a noxious mess?

Some people might accuse me of being extra fussy and overly scrupulous in offering these thoughts. Do we have to be so goddamned conscientious about everything we do? Can't we grab a little slack here and there as we seek to enjoy nice, pretty things?

I don't agree with that criticism. In my view, civilization is ultimately destined to develop comprehensive integrity in its approach to extracting and processing the earth's resources. I predict that 200 years from now—hopefully, sooner—almost no one will want to create and own pleasurable and attractive and useful things if they despoil nature and make our environment less hospitable for living creatures.

I believe you Capricorns can and should have a special interest and facility in these themes. What might you personally do to encourage ecologically sustainable approaches to producing beautiful, useful things?

AQUARIUS: Born under the sign of Aquarius, Thomas Paine (1737–1809) was a zealous insurrectionary. He wrote incendiary pamphlets that helped ignite and sustain America's struggle for independence from Great Britain.

Early in his life, however, he worked making women's girdles, which were and are among the most constrictive and oppressive garments.

Do you think there was a connection between his two gigs? Like maybe his later struggle for liberation was an unconscious atonement for his youthful labors?

In the coming years, I invite you to instigate a Thomas Paine-like adjustment. Think of something you did in the past that constricted your spirit or squeezed other people's possibilities.

Use that memory as a launching pad as you unleash your brilliance in the name of abundance and expansiveness.

PISCES: There are more enslaved people in the world right now than at any other time in history: at least 29 million. A disproportionate percentage of them are women and children.

Even more shocking: At least half of all countries have no law against enslavement.

Read more: https://tinyurl.com/LegalEnslavement.

According to my analysis of your astrological potentials, Pisces, you can bestow healing blessings on yourself by responding to this problem in your own unique ways.

To lend your energy to organizations that help free enslaved people. You could start here:

https://tinyurl.com/EndEnslavement, and https://tinyurl.com/LiberateEnslaved.

Here's another suggestion: Use the term "enslaved people" rather than "slaves." This language distinguishes people's identity from their circumstances. It makes clear that an enslaved person is first a human being and second a commodity.

Any effort you devote to slowing and ending the trafficking of vulnerable captives could have beneficial effects on your own life. It may inspire you to:

◈ Express enhanced appreciation for the freedoms you have

◈ Take more thorough advantage of those freedoms

◈ Liberate any part of you that acts or thinks or feels like a person in bondage

◈ Dismantle any tendencies you might have to slip into situations that limit your personal freedom, diminish your willpower, or feel like bondage

Element 6

If we aren't willing to risk stupendous bliss, uncanny splendor, and unpredictable breakthroughs that undermine our belief system, we will stave off bliss, splendor, and breakthroughs.

If we're willing to risk stupendous bliss, uncanny splendor, and unpredictable breakthroughs that undermine our belief system, we will need to develop a resilient knack for adjusting to happy plot twists.

Chapter 15

Your Bold Readiness to Seize
Sublime Buoyancy

+

My Bold Readiness to Seize
Sublime Buoyancy

=

Our Bold Readiness to Seize
Sublime Buoyancy

Is Love Always Courteous?

Is love only love when it's polite and courteous?

Is goodness always the same as niceness?

Do our expressions of compassion need to be unfailingly cordial and tactful?

Must our passion for justice and truth be reined in by tact and gentility?

No. No. No. No.

Sometimes love is unruly, even wild.

Lots of people use their niceness as a cover for being mean and bigoted.

To be effective, compassion may require us to be fierce and relentless.

If we want to create more justice and truth in the world, we might have to act in ways that offend the status quo.

Three Percent Mastery

To achieve "beginner's mind," we dispense with our preconceptions and enter each situation as if seeing it for the first time. "In the beginner's mind there are many possibilities," wrote Zen teacher Shunryu Suzuki, "but in the expert's there are few."

As much as I love beginner's mind, I suggest we also practice beginner's heart. That means approaching every encounter with a fresh wave of innocent, tender, generous curiosity. It's as pure a feeling as if we are invoking it for the first time.

When we cultivate beginner's heart, we do so to enhance our ability to understand reality. It doesn't mean we indiscriminately make ourselves vulnerable to people and situations that might exploit or hurt us.

★

The ever-evolving truth is far too complicated and fluid and slippery and scrambled and gorgeously abundant for one soul to understand—even for genius bodhisattva avatars. (I have heard rumors that there have been a few such characters.)

I am lucky to have bumped up my personal degree of mastery to about 3 percent. That's how much (how little) I understand of the Maddening and Delightful Mystery we are embedded in.

Shocking! I am missing 97 percent of the truth—even though I have always been greedy to learn and experience as much as I can.

Out of necessity, to compensate for my gaping ignorance, I have come up with a strategy to guide me. I formulate amusing, nonbinding hypotheses about what the Great Mystery might be like. Then I collect the experimental data generated as I test my hypotheses. Finally, I observe and analyze the results to deter-mine how well each hypothesis works.

∞ Does it liberate me from suffering, and does it inspire me to help liberate other creatures from their suffering?

∞ Does it make me a smarter and kinder and trickier and humbler fool?

∞ Does it motivate me to embrace what I call the FLUX MOJO? In other words, does it fuel me to overthrow my fixations, cooperate enthusiastically with the never-end-ing change that life asks me to deal with, and continually reinvent my attitudes, perspectives, ideas, and feelings?

∞ Does it engender in me a lust for life and a primal urge to respond creatively to the glorious privilege of being alive and conscious?

∞ Does it fuel my longing to inspire and nurture and play with those who are interested in sharing destiny with me?

The Perfect Sometimes
Undermines the Good

Now and then, I quote or discuss a person who is less than a perfect exemplar of my noble ideals.

Some readers rage at me for doing so. Don't I know, they scold, that so-and-so is a jerk?

I usually do know. And I certainly don't approve of the quoted or discussed person being a creep. I wish they weren't. I'm mad at them for the dreadful things they have done.

On the other hand, if I refused to learn from people unless I agreed with and liked everything they had ever said and done, I would never learn from anyone.

If I condemned to oblivion everyone who didn't reflect all my noble ideals, if I crossed everyone off my list unless they were immaculate angels, I would be bereft of influences except for Mickey, my beloved stuffed bunny from childhood. He is irreproachable.

My general philosophy is that everyone on the planet, including me, is a jerk at least some of the time. In fact, I'm suspicious of people who are apparently so flawlessly well behaved that they are *never* jerks.

Here's the key to making a deeper assessment: How sizable is each person's Jerk Quotient? If it's below 15 percent—maybe even below 20 percent—I'll probably give them a chance to be influences in my life—especially if they're smart and interesting and wild and kind a majority of the time.

I'm not sure there's anyone in public life whose influence hasn't been at least somewhat harmful, even if they have mostly bestowed blessings. A person's noble intentions don't guarantee the intentions are interpreted and used with love and intelligence. Even the Buddha's followers commit crimes against humanity, as we see in Myanmar and Sri Lanka.

What about you? I invite you to cultivate a capacity to derive insight from people who are not untainted saints. Have fun learning from 15 percent jerks or imperfect thinkers you partially disagree with.

★

Here are examples of people from whom I have drawn teachings despite their offenses:

Dr. Seuss had an affair with another woman while his wife was suffering from cancer, and his wife subsequently committed suicide.

Einstein cheated on his wife and treated her horrendously.

William Blake lived in filth.

Gertrude Stein arrogantly declared she was as important a writer as Shakespeare and Homer.

Early feminist author George Sand cheated on her husband.

Edgar Allan Poe married his 13-year-old cousin when he was 26.

Pema Chödrön did nothing about the sexual abuse going on within the leadership of the Shambhala community over the years.

Martin Luther King Jr. plagiarized parts of his PhD dissertation.

The painter Peter Paul Rubens married a 16-year-old female when he was 53.

Walt Whitman had temper tantrums.

Many of the needy causes that Mother Teresa raised money

for never received much help. Just 7 percent of the donations she raised went to the organizations to which they were donated.

In his older age, Gandhi slept with young women in his bed to test his resolve to remain "pure." Among these women was his grandniece.

John Lennon battered women. He was also a cranky guy who was chronically annoyed.

Kurt Vonnegut had a dark, sad, cruel side.

Bob Marley spawned many children and didn't financially support any of them.

Some of my readers even find fault with people I have considered wonderful, like Dolly Parton and Thich Nhat Hanh. I don't have the heart to repeat the claims, but here are links if you want to read:

Dolly: https://tinyurl.com/2r2byedk; Thich Nhat Hanh: https://tinyurl.com/yc6687aj and https://tinyurl.com/2p938bj9.

Two readers challenged me to track down something unseemly about Clarissa Pinkola Estés, who is one of their (and my) favorite authors. In two minutes, I found this: An editor at Ballantine Books, which published *Women Who Run with the Wolves*, says this: "Estés acted like a complete asshole. Her visits to the office were ludicrous; she used to prance around, puffed up like a little marshmallow, waiting for everyone to fall at her feet."

How about me? What's my Jerk Quotient? Here are some awful facts: When I was younger, I broke up with one of my girlfriends in an unconscious and insensitive way, and I still regret it.

Again, when I was younger, an older friend of mine was dying of cancer, and I couldn't bring myself to go see her. This is the most shameful thing I've ever done.

Would you care to confess the sins of any of your heroes, teachers, and role models? Or yourself?

Naturalist Charles Darwin called clergyman Thomas Malthus a "great philosopher." In his magnum opus *The Origin of the Species*, he said his theory of evolution was based on Malthus's ideas.

As Darwin knew well, Malthus advocated genocidal measures to control population growth. In his famous "Essay on the Principle of Population as It Affects the Future Improvement of Society," Malthus proposed killing off underprivileged people.

"Instead of recommending cleanliness to the poor," he wrote, "we should encourage contrary habits. In our towns we should make the streets narrower, crowd more people into houses, and court the return of the plague. In the country, we should build villages near stagnant pools, and encourage settlement in marshy and unwholesome situations.

"But above all," he continued, "we should reprobate specific remedies for ravaging diseases; and those benevolent, but much mistaken men, who have thought they were doing a service to mankind by projecting schemes for the total extirpation of particular disorders."

The evidence is clear that Darwin's theory of evolution had a grotesque pedigree. It was rooted in the work of a would-be mass murderer. Should we therefore dismiss it altogether? Not in my opinion. What's useful is not always derived from what's good.

At the same time, we shouldn't regard this fact as inconsequential. To evaluate all the implicit impacts of Darwinian ideas, we need to know the influences they emerged from. It's crucial to acknowledge the pathology that may color a perspective that's so central to Western culture.

Is there a comparable situation in your own life? Are there essentials you benefit from even though their origins are problematical?

You could be a leader in the effort to be conscientious about investigating the origins of key ideas at the heart of our culture. You could help people you know to become aware of unconscious biases and bigotry they may have absorbed in taking on those ideas as our own.

Perfectionism Sux

Perfectionism is the voice of the oppressor, the enemy of the people. It will keep you cramped and insane.
> —author Anne Lamott

★

Perfection is a stick with which to beat the possible.
> —author Rebecca Solnit

★

The perfect is the enemy of the good.
> —author Voltaire

★

Excellence does not require perfection.
> —author Henry James

★

Perfection is a mean, frozen form of idealism, while messes are the artist's true friend.
> —author Anne Lamott

Maestro of the Obvious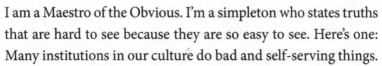

I am a Maestro of the Obvious. I'm a simpleton who states truths that are hard to see because they are so easy to see. Here's one: Many institutions in our culture do bad and self-serving things.

The institutions that do bad and self-serving things are corporations, religions, governments, the media, big science, medicine, the pharmaceutical, academia, publishing, film and art and music industries, the big tech companies, professional sports, and every other system I neglected to name. All of them.

Here's what we maestros of the obvious do: Toward all the bad and self-serving institutions, we develop a discerning skepticism, based on accurate evidence. We criticize them. We do what we can to reform them. And we acknowledge that they may also do some good and helpful things that we are grateful for.

So we go forward, holding in our minds a poised understanding of their contradictions, as intelligent fools do. We cultivate an awareness that everything on earth is flawed and imperfect, and that many imperfect and flawed things (though not all) also have value and beneficence.

We meditate on the psychological concept of co-emergence, which postulates that every beautiful, useful thing is intertwined with some challenging problem; and that many challenging problems have some inspiration and education to offer us.

We meditate on what my daughter said when she was five years old: "There's nothing in the world that is either all good or all bad."

Love Our Imperfections ↻

I propose we set aside a time twice every year when we celebrate our gaffes, flaws, and bloopers.

During this crooked holiday, we aren't bereft with embarrassment about the false moves we have made.

We don't decry our bad judgment or denounce our delusional behavior. Instead, we forgive ourselves for our sins.

We work to understand and feel compassion for the ignorance that led us astray.

Maybe we even find redemptive value in our lapses. We come to see that they saved us from some painful experience or helped us avoid getting a supposed treasure that would have ultimately been a booby prize. At the very least, they taught us how not to act in the future.

We could call it the Love Our Imperfections Celebration.

The Art of Changing Our Minds

Every election campaign season, voters rant about candidates who have been inconsistent. Horrors! How dare they change their minds about the issues?

I don't understand the complaint. In my view, growing riper and wiser requires us to keep changing our minds forever. In 2008, for example, Barack Obama opposed same-sex marriages. In 2012, he reversed his position. A wise decision!

In support of my hypothesis that it's often healthy to evolve our ideas and feelings, I offer quotes on the subject below.

Those who cannot change their minds cannot change anything.
—playwright George Bernard Shaw

The man who never alters his opinion is like standing water, and breeds reptiles of the mind.
—author and artist William Blake

I wanted to be a ballerina. I changed my mind.
—author Beverly Cleary

Like all weak men, he laid an exaggerated stress on not changing one's mind.
—author W. Somerset Maugham

The snake that cannot cast its skin has to die. As well the minds which are prevented from changing their opinions; they cease to be mind.
       —philosopher Friedrich Nietzsche

Only the strongest people have the pluck to change their minds, and say so, if they see they have been wrong in their ideas.
       —author Enid Blyton

A foolish consistency is the hobgoblin of little minds. With consistency a great soul has simply nothing to do.
       —author Ralph Waldo Emerson

Sometimes, being true to yourself means changing your mind. Self changes, and you follow.
       —author Vera Nazarian

The interesting thing is always to see if you can find a fact that will change your mind about something, to test and see if you can.
       —broadcast journalist Diane Sawyer

Almost all of my many passionate interests, and my many changes of mind, came through books.
       —author Annie Dillard

Do I contradict myself? Very well, then, I contradict myself; I am large—I contain multitudes.
   —poet Walt Whitman

The willingness to change one's mind in the light of new evidence is a sign of rationality, not weakness.
   —psychologist Stuart Sutherland

I came from a different mindset growing up, and my mind has changed.
   —singer Katy Perry

Total loyalty is possible only when fidelity is emptied of all concrete content, from which changes of mind might naturally arise.
   —philosopher Hannah Arendt

There is no point in asking me general questions because I am always changing my mind.
   —author Michel Houellebecq

You have the RIGHT to change your mind.
   —talk show host Oprah Winfrey

A person is a fluid process, not a fixed and static entity; a flowing river of change, not a block of solid material; a continually changing constellation of potentialities, not a fixed quantity of traits.
            —psychologist Carl Rogers

We are the sum of our efforts to change who we are. Identity is no museum piece sitting stock-still in a display case, but rather the endlessly astonishing synthesis of the contradictions of everyday life.
            —journalist Eduardo Galeano

PS: Jungian analyst Arnold Mindell explores the relationship between mind and body. He thinks we can achieve optimal physical health if we are devoted to shedding outworn self-images. In his book *The Shaman's Body*, he writes, "You have one central lesson to learn—to continuously drop all your rigid identities. Personal history may be your greatest danger."

Kate Bornstein, author of *Gender Outlaw: On Men, Women and the Rest of Us*, agrees. Raised as a boy, she later became a woman, but ultimately renounced gender altogether. "I love being without an identity," she says. "It gives me a lot of room to play around."

Divinations for You #11

ARIES: How do I love thee, Aries? Let me count the ways.

I treasure your skill at slipping free from unproductive jams.

I admire how you boldly transform yourself into a fresh creation when you've gone as far as you can with the old model.

I applaud the way you rebel against your past and fling yourself open to the unpredictable sweep of the future.

TAURUS: How do I love thee, Taurus? Let me count the ways.

I rejoice that you're a spiritual animal.

I adore how you lose yourself in earthy zeal but never forsake your commitment to the good and the true and the gorgeous.

I'm delighted by your sacred quest for pleasure in all its varieties—from feasting on ice cream and stealing an extra half hour of sleep to noticing beauty in the small details and making love with tender abandon.

More than any other sign of the zodiac, you embody poet Elizabeth Barrett Browning's exultation: "Earth's crammed with heaven." That pleases me!

GEMINI: Why it's always double great to be a Gemini, inspired by my Gemini reader Dominique Q in Toronto:

◈ You're endowed with the ability to have two or more opinions at the same time, sometimes completely contradictory, thereby imitating God's expansive perspective.

◈ You can put yourself into and out of everybody's shoes

with such slippery ease that you never get bored with yourself and also have a knack for avoiding other people's hells.

 You get to enjoy both the odd pleasure of being your
own evil twin and the challenging pleasure of forgiving
your evil twin.

★

CANCERIAN: Artist Richard Kehl tells the story of a teenage
girl who got a chance to ask a question of renowned psychologist Carl Jung.

"Professor, you are so clever. Could you please tell me the
shortest path to my life's goal?"

Jung quickly replied, "The detour!"

Bang! You Cancerians instinctively know that. You are potentially first-class experts at using detours to generate success.

★

LEO: Leo-born poet and journalist Cassiano Ricardo speaks of a
longing "for all that is tall like pine trees, and all that is long like
rivers, and all that is purple like dusk."

Yearnings like those are like tonics for you. They enhance your
intelligence.

★

VIRGO: On my social media, I periodically post "Arguments with
Goddess," which invites people to ask my team of prayer warriors to convey their complaints directly to the Almighty. We are
besieged with heart-rending requests.

"Why can't I cultivate a vision of my life as a path instead of a
battlefield," mourned a Libra.

"Why does God open these wonderful doors," wrote a Leo, "and then, just as I get close, slam them shut!"

We Prayer Warriors treat most pleas reverently, and do our best to reach God's ear. But on one occasion I became mournful when a Virgo wrote. "Could you tell the Creator," she said, "PLEASE make my cat use his litter box!"

No doubt she was trying to be funny, but I thought as I read it, "Here's yet another Virgo who's not asking for what she truly needs the most."

I would love it if you refrained from falling into that error.

LIBRA: How do I love thee, Libra? Let me count the ways.

I'm enchanted when you drum up a "delirium of solutions" (in William Carlos Williams's phrase), and how many of them are elegant.

I rejoice that you're developing an ever-more-finely honed knack for knowing precisely when and how to give your abundant gifts. I'm excited by your growing sense of when to cut back on your giving so as not to overdo it.

I love it when you don't waste time trying to get fixed by influences that can't fix you, and I'm pleased you're learning to recognize the precise soul medicine that can truly heal you.

SCORPIO: Maybe you could benefit from being less sober, solemn, and serious about your intimate relationships. Of course, I don't know for sure. Only you can determine that. But in my experience, some Scorpios can benefit from infusing their intimate connections with more levity.

In case that's true about you, I collected one-liners from Someecards.com for you to use. Consider delivering them to the appropriate allies.

- ◈ "Let's go maniacally obsess about our lives in a soothing environment."
- ◈ "We'll be best friends forever because you already know too much about me."
- ◈ "It would be great if you would schedule your social events around my mood swings."
- ◈ "I'm sorry I drunk-dialed you before realizing you were already in bed with me."
- ◈ "You're one of the few people I would hug right after a Bikram Yoga class."
- ◈ "I wanna do boring things with you."

SAGITTARIUS: Some people put their faith in religion or science or political ideologies. English novelist J. G. Ballard placed his faith elsewhere: in the imagination.

"I believe in the power of the imagination to remake the world," he wrote, "to release the truth within us, to hold back the night, to transcend death, to charm motorways, to ingratiate ourselves with birds, to enlist the confidences of madmen."

I would never assert that one of the astrological signs has greater reservoirs of potent imagination than the other signs. But I don't mind speculating that you Sagittarians are especially blessed in your ability to wield your imagination constructively.

Here's a prime Sagittarian meditation that I hope you carry out regularly: How do you use the power of imagination to remake the world?

CAPRICORN: "Love isn't something you find," said singer Loretta Lynn. "Love is something that finds you."

Singer Kylie Minogue concurs: "You need a lot of luck to find people with whom you want to spend your life. Love is like a lottery."

These perspectives are at best misleading and at worst debilitating. They imply we have no power to shape our relationship with love. My view is different.

I say there's a lot we can do to attract intimate allies who teach us, stimulate us, and fulfill us. Like what?

◈ We clarify the precise qualities we want in a partner, and we make sure those qualities are healthy for us.

◈ We dismantle and dissolve unconscious conditioning that's at odds with our conscious values.

◈ We work to transform ourselves into lovable collaborators who communicate well.

Anything else? What can you do to make sure love isn't a lottery? No one is better than you Capricorns at formulating lucid plans that really work.

AQUARIUS: "We're all a little weird. And life is a little weird. And when we find someone whose weirdness is compatible with ours, we join up with them and fall into mutually satisfying weirdness—and call it love—true love." So declared Robert Fulghum in his book *True Love.*

This observation fits you Aquarians even better than it does the other zodiac signs. In your alliances, you have a profanely sacred duty to embrace the wonders of mutually compatible weirdness.

You need the freedom to share your eccentricities and ally yourself with people whose eccentricities mesh with yours.

PISCES: What do we need to kill off in ourselves to tune in to the beauty that's hidden?

What worn-out shticks blind us to the blessings that life angles to provide us?

Which of our ideas may have been useful and even brilliant in the past, but are now preventing us from perceiving the ever-fresh creation unfolding before us?

It's not enough to shed our stale mental habits just once. The price of admission into lusty living is a commitment to continual dying. We must ask ourselves rude questions and kick our own asses again and again.

Today's versions of beauty, truth, love, goodness, justice, and liberation will pass away.

To keep abreast of the latest developments—to cultivate tomorrow's versions of joie de vivre—we have to immerse ourselves regularly in the waters of chaos.

Our relationship with life's bounties has to be a never-ending improvisation.

There's one sign of the zodiac that has more potential to develop expertise in these arts than all the others. Can you guess which one? It's you Pisceans.

Element 7

If we aren't willing to use "luminous" and "numinous" in the same breath, and if we're not willing to use "vigorous" and "rigorous" in the same sentence, we inhibit the jaunty vitality of our language.

If we are willing to use "luminous" and "numinous" in the same breath, and if are willing to use "vigorous" and "rigorous" in the same breath, we consecrate the jaunty vitality of our language.

Chapter 16

Your Luminous Numinosity
and Vigorous Rigor

+

My Luminous Numinosity
and Vigorous Rigor

=

Our Luminous Numinosity
and Vigorous Rigor

Pick Your Battles

Pick your battles.

But before you finish picking, eliminate some battles you were considering.

Then go ahead and discard a few other battles.

Shed some of the battles you had already chosen.

That's still too many battles.

Maybe not. It's possible you have been shy about waging righteous battles that would be healthy and holy for you.

So let's conclude with this suggestion: Choose just the right amount of battles to energize and heal you, not drain you.

Not Sticking to Astrology

Should poets and philosophers and astrologers—people like me—express critiques of White supremacy, militarism, misogyny, and bigotry toward LGBTQIA+ people, even as they offer poems and oracles and insights for individuals on quests to express their souls' codes?

I say yes.

But some readers inform me that because I am an astrologer, I shouldn't comment on politics. A horoscope writer has no right to talk about politics, they say.

They issue that demand even though I have steadily commented on politics since the beginning of my career. Have they not been paying attention? As just one of countless examples: In all my oracles for the week of November 3, 1988, I endorsed Democratic presidential candidate Michael Dukakis over Republican candidate George Bush.

In my view, everyone has a sacred duty to think about politics and a sacred right to talk about politics.

Novelist and war correspondent Martha Gellhorn observed, "People often say, with pride, 'I'm not interested in politics.' They might as well say, 'I'm not interested in my standard of living, my health, my job, my rights, my freedoms, my future or any future.'"

Gellhorn added, "If we mean to keep control over our world and lives, we must be interested in politics."

Do the people who say that an astrologer shouldn't write about politics mean that only those who have PhDs in political science

should talk about it? That only professional politicians and political pundits should talk about it?

That's a narrow standard I don't subscribe to.

Since I was a teenager, I have been a democratic socialist. In my
early years, I protested and led boycotts and knocked on doors
encouraging people to vote for progressive candidates. I threw
canisters of tear gas back at cops and National Guardsmen who
flung them at me and my friends during our anti-war marches
and occupations.

From the beginning of writing my column, I have infused my
oracles with leftist political commentary. This has been a good fit
for the alternative newsweekly papers that publish me, as most
are also progressive. I syndicate myself now, but in earlier days,
the leftist syndicate AlterNet distributed my column.

The success of my column happened gradually. But there was a
three-month period when it got a big bump in distribution. Many
new newspapers decided they wanted to publish my thoughts.

The occasion was the United States' first military invasion and
occupation of Iraq. In response to this illegal and immoral venture, I filled my horoscopes with condemnation and satire about
the American misdeeds and atrocities. Each one also had references to the personal lives of my readers. My critiques served
as metaphors for psychological factors at work in their destinies or as useful meditations on how the personal and political
were interwoven.

Who would have guessed that would be an excellent marketing strategy? My column's syndication expanded dramatically. Thanks to my responses to Operation Desert Storm, I graduated from dire poverty.

So it's no exaggeration to say that some of my appeal as an astrology columnist has been built on my determination to blend progressive political perspectives with psychological and spiritual insights.

I've been doing that since I started. Anyone who thinks otherwise about my work has missed an essential truth about it.

Wish List ∽

∞ We insist on substantial cuts in US defense spending. Thirty percent is a good start. (Even after such a slash, the US military would still be the world's largest.)

∞ We rise in the morning and look at the world in ways that take nothing for granted. Everything is phenomenal; everything is incredible.

∞ Make abortion safe, legal, normal, and easy to get.

∞ Believe that if there is any such thing as enlightenment, it arises from empathy, sympathy, compassion, tenderness, and a quest to be in intimate connection with and in service to other beings.

∞ Work to substitute renewable energy sources for fossil fuels.

∞ Beginning in elementary school, install the following subjects at the core of the curriculum:
  • How to develop emotional intelligence
  • How to develop one's creativity and imagination
  • How to remember and work with one's nightly dreams
  • How to create interesting and loving relationships
  • How to establish a habit of eating healthy food

∞ End anti-democratic filibuster abuse in the US Senate.

∞ Wrestle and negotiate with our own shadows, making pre-emptive strikes on our personal share of the world's evil, fighting the good fight to keep from spewing our darkness on those around us.

∞ Create a system for universal single-payer health care and health insurance.

∞ Develop a strategy to avoid being enthralled with the hypnotic lure of painful emotions, past events, and worries about the future.

∞ To limit and control corruption in the banking industry, restore Glass–Steagall laws.

∞ Kill off the bad conditioning within us that resonates in pathological harmony with militarism, misogyny, bigotry, and authoritarianism.

∞ Strive to attain freedom from our own unconscious obsessions and conditioned responses.

∞ Overturn the Supreme Court's Citizens United decision. Dissolve and ban laws that regard corporations as people.

∞ Ensure equal opportunity for all genders and people of all sexual orientations.

∞ Dissolve the Electoral College.

∞ Break trances that keep us ignorant of our own magic.

∞ Expand the Supreme Court and impose term limits on its judges.

∞ Cultivate our receptivity to subtle miracles, beguiling ephemera, and marvelous breakthroughs.

∞ Institute a wealth tax on the richest 1 percent of billionaires.

Love Cues and Clues: How to Cultivate a Vibrant Relationship with Me ⊚

Below I offer cues and clues about how to cultivate a vibrant relationship with me.

◈ Disagree with me in respectful ways, using clear language and offering interesting ideas.

◈ Agree with me in respectful ways, using clear language and offering interesting ideas.

◈ Expand my perspective, change my mind, and teach me things I don't know.

◈ Delight me with your unpredictability, your lyrical reverence for the Great Mystery, and your joie de vivre.

◈ Reminisce about the fun times we had together in the past or the fun times we could enjoy in the future.

◈ Turn me on to books, music, websites, movies, videos, TV shows, and people that have animated your sense of wonder and might do the same for me.

◈ Tell me good news that will uplift me.

◈ Describe to me how you celebrate life.

◈ With mercy and patience, suggest to me how I might become a better writer and thinker and feeler. Show me how I might become more of the person I want to be.

◈ Point me in the direction of the beautiful creations you have made or helped to make.

◈ Describe to me how the world would need to change for you to feel it's more like a paradise than it is now.

Auguries for You #12

ARIES: After years of painstaking research, the psychic surgeons at the Beauty and Truth Lab have perfected the art and science of Zodiac Makeovers.

Using a patented technique known as Mythic Gene Engineering, they are able to transplant the planets of your horoscope into different signs and astrological houses from the ones you were born with.

Let's say your natal Jupiter suffers from a supposedly uncongenial aspect with your Moon. Our psychic surgeons cut and splice according to your specifications, enabling you to be re-coded with the destiny you desire.

Unfortunately, everything I just said is a lie. I made it up.

But here's the good news, Aries: At least potentially, you have the power to reconfigure your life's path—and even transform the way specific planets function within you—using your natural intelligence.

Everyone has a massive mother lode of free will, though many of us don't access more than a portion of it. Of all the signs, you Rams are congenitally allotted a promise to harness a vaster-than-typical share of all.

The ancient astrological epigram is "the planets may impel, but they don't compel." And you might be able to tamper with that formula, shifting it in the direction of "I may even dispel the spell of the impellent and excel at foretelling my own propellant."

TAURUS: "Dear Oracle: I've read horoscope columns written by many astrologers, and yours is the only one that's not prejudiced against at least one of the signs.

"You really do treat everyone equally. You play no favorites. But that's exactly the bone I have to pick with you.

"I'm wondering if you've got a passion deficiency or something. It seems abnormal not to display a hint of bias now and then. —Suspicious Taurus."

Dear Suspicious: My birth chart includes important elements of Taurus and Libra. The Taurus part of me has strong feelings and deep passions, while the Libra part of me is fair minded and well balanced.

They've worked out a synergistic arrangement that enables me to maintain equilibrium as I feed my intensity.

GEMINI: Throw a party for all the people you have been and all the different selves who reside within you now. Invite the teenager who once seethed with frustrated potential and the four-year-old who loved to play.

Include the hopeful complainer who stands in the shadows and dares you to ask for more, as well as the brave champion who emerges now and then to attempt heroic feats of happiness.

Don't forget the various personalities who have contributed to making you who you are, even the "bad" ones. Celebrate your internal diversity. Marvel at how good you are at changing.

(For extra credit, you could invite the characters you've been in past incarnations, like the Balinese puppet-maker and the Nigerian herbalist and the Chinese midwife and the African savannah elephant.)

CANCERIAN: I have written over 2,000 weekly astrology columns, as well as 6,000 daily horoscopes. I have also written and recorded over 1,000 audio horoscopes. Some have been better written and more useful than others, but I've given my utmost effort to every one.

My style has mutated over the years; the weekly written horoscopes I penned in, say, 1994, are so unlike those I write now that they seem to be the product of a different author.

But then I myself have transformed radically through the years. It makes sense that my work has, too. In truth, my personal development has been fueled by my growth as a writer.

I invite you to do what I've just done, fellow Cancerian. Take an inventory of the big tasks you've been doing for years. Evaluate the way they've evolved and how they have shaped your destiny. Engage in an expansive look at the labors of love that have made you who you are.

Doing analyses like these is a Cancerian specialty. We have potent potential to be virtuoso historians of our own life stories.

LEO: Nothing feeds me, nothing moves me, nothing changes me so much as writing horoscopes for you, my readers.

You are my inspiration. You keep me delightfully off-balance as I try to figure out what revelations you need next.

My determination to follow you through all your plot twists prevents me from getting set in my ways or predictable in my communiqués. Thank you!

Now I will suggest that you Leos would benefit from composing notes of gratitude like the one I just wrote: a joyous acknowledgement of the people in your life who feed you and move you and change you the best.

I will also let you know that you potentially have an extraordinary knack for feeling and expressing gratitude. Your power to wield transformative cascades of appreciation is among the greatest in all the zodiac.

There's another feeling that synergizes well with gratitude, especially for you Leos: reverence.

When you respectfully and devotionally honor the sacred beauty of a source you admire, you do yourself a favor. It's one of the most healing acts of self-care.

Keep in mind that reverence is not solely the province of religious people. A biologist may venerate the scientific method. A poet may adore the natural world. An atheist might experience a devout sense of awe about geniuses who have bequeathed to us their brilliant ideas.

What about you? What excites your reverence? What rouses your gratitude? And are there experiences that inspire both your gratitude and reverence?

VIRGO: The cereus cactus grows in the deserts of the southwestern US. Most of the time it's scraggly and brittle looking.

But one night of the year, in June or July, it blooms with a fragrant, trumpet-shaped flower. By dawn, the creamy white petals close and start to wither. During that brief celebration, the plant's main pollinator, the sphinx moth, must discover the marvelous event and come to gather the cactus flower's pollen.

This scenario has metaphorical resemblences to a Virgo specialty. I hope you're ever-alert for sudden, epic, and rare eruptions of beauty that you can feed from and propagate.

LIBRA: I recommend you enjoy an animalistic phase every now and then—in the best sense of "animalistic." And yes, you Libras really do need to feed regularly from your primal instincts.

What might that involve?

- ∞ Identify the part of you that's best described as "a beautiful beast." Be curious about it. Commune with it. Nurture it.
- ∞ Another way to imagine how to proceed is to tune into your visceral intelligence. Regard your body as having a genius of its own that your mind may only be partly aware of.
- ∞ Express your beautiful beast in the real world. See how life responds.
- ∞ Be alert for and receptive to the beautiful beast in other people.

SCORPIO: I turn your attention to Cancerian Cory Doctorow's review of Scorpio author Neal Stephenson's three-volume *Baroque Cycle*. Doctorow says Stephenson's books are like good curry.

"They're mild and interesting when you first taste them, but after you've swallowed, they grow on you, spreading a warm fire throughout your digestive system, making beads of sweat appear on your forehead."

That's a common experience to have when non-Scorpios engage Scorpios.

SAGITTARIUS: "It is not lack of love but lack of friendship that makes unhappy marriages," said philosopher Friedrich Nietzsche.

He believed that if you want to join your fortunes with another's, you should ask yourself whether you will enjoy your con-versations with this person in the coming years—because that's what you will be doing much of the time you are together.

How do you measure up to this standard? What role does friendship play in your romantic adventures? For you Sagittari-ans, the percentage should be high.

If there's anything lacking, seek improvements. Start with your-self. How could you infuse more camaraderie into your expres-sions of love? What might you do to upgrade your skills as a listener and conversationalist?

CAPRICORN: "Supplication" is a Capricornian word of power. It refers to the act of earnestly and humbly asking for what you want. Inherent in supplication is a mood of surrender, although the surrender blooms from potency: a strong, clear realization of what's needed.

When practiced with integrity, "supplication" is a sign of sov-ereignty, not weakness. It means you are raptly united with your desire, feel no guilt or shyness about it, and intend to express it with liberated abandon.

Supplication makes you supple, poised to be flexible as you do what's required to get the blessings you yearn for.

Being a supplicant makes you smarter, because it helps you realize you can't get what you want through the force of your willful ego alone. You need grace, luck, and help from sources beyond your ken and control.

AQUARIUS: As a recovering save-the-world addict, I feel compassionate skepticism towards my fellow junkies who are still in the throes of their obsession.

But I've discovered that just as a small minority of alcoholics can safely take a drink now and then, so can a few save-the-world-aholics save the world a little at a time without getting strung out.

With that as a disclaimer, I authorize you to pursue your personal brand of fervent idealism. Few Aquarians can be totally healthy without tapping into at least a modicum of that stuff.

To keep yourself honest, make fun of your own zealotry every now and then.

PISCES: One of my readers, Jay O'Dell, told me this story: "After my cancer surgery, a nurse said to me, 'You may as well try magical thinking. Regular thinking hasn't helped.' I said to the nurse, 'Well, why the hell not?' That was seven years ago."

In bringing O'Dell's testimony to your attention, I don't mean to suggest you will have any health problems that warrant a strong dose of magical thinking.

But now and then, you may get wrapped up in a psychological twist or a spiritual riddle that could benefit from magical thinking.

And what is magical thinking? Here's one definition: The stories that unfold in your imagination may have important effects on what actually happens to you.

In all the zodiac, which sign is the champion at invoking magical thinking to generate practical effects? You Pisceans!

New Language

As a writer who grasps the power of language to shape our experience, I am in favor of questioning words and phrases that might be hurtful and demeaning to some people. I aspire to keep evolving my usage.

For instance, I no longer employ the words "pioneer" and "pioneering," because they are associated with colonialism, with the theft of Indigenous people's land and the destruction of their cultures. Instead, I may call on words like "groundbreaking" or "innovative."

Since I decided to become a professional writer many years ago, my intention has always been to invoke idioms sparingly. In recent years, I've put a special emphasis on avoiding those that suggest or imply violence: "blown away," "killer smile," "take a stab at it," "jumped the gun," "bite the bullet," "locked and loaded," and "twist your arm."

Another personal project is to wean myself from gendered language—words that have a bias towards a particular sex or conventionally understood gender. That includes "actress," "statesman," and "heroine." There are many others. I'm always on the lookout.

And what about deploying "they" as a singular pronoun? Yes, please. Every dictionary I know of asserts it's now official. I'm not sure why there was ever any controversy. The singular "they" has been in play since at least 1375. Among the eminent authors who have used it were Geoffrey Chaucer, William Shakespeare, Jane Austen, Charles Dickens, and W. H. Auden.

★

There are many lists online that discuss terms we should consider avoiding. I question some of their recommendations. "Spirit animal" is one.

I've encountered people who insist this usage is a cultural appropriation of a Native American concept. In my view, such an argument is tenuous. In fact, many cultures in every part of the world in every historical era have posited otherworldly animals that serve as guides and helpers.

For instance, some of my Polish ancestors regarded the cuckoo as being associated with Zywie, the goddess of health, healing, and longevity. She was even thought to periodically transform herself into a cuckoo. That's why my people sought to divine future events as they might be revealed in the birds' calls and behavior.

Some of my Polish forbears also consorted with *płanetnicy*, "shepherds of the clouds." These spirit creatures had the power to manipulate the weather. If my people maintained good relationships with them, the *płanetnicy* would bestow favors in the form of good weather and, when necessary, rains to nourish the crops.

My Polish relatives didn't use the term "spirit animals" to refer to their supernatural benefactors, of course, since they spoke Polish. Similarly, Indigenous people in the Americas use the terms of their own language to refer to such creature allies. "Spirit animal" is an English term.

Nonetheless, to honor the wishes of those Indigenous people who regard "spirit animal" as insulting, I instead employ terms like "power creature," "medicine animal," "medicine creature," "spirit creature," and others.

I feel fine coming up with new ways to say things. Indeed, it's the writer's job to be innovative with language. Since there's virtually an inexhaustible array of expressions to call on, why would

I ever choose one that I knew was hurtful or offensive?

Here's a guide about using alternative language that I find useful: https://tinyurl.com/LanguageRecommendations.

Another list, published by Brandeis University, offered this definition: "Identity-based oppressive language includes a range of words and phrases including potentially lesser-known slurs, unhelpful euphemisms, and exclusionary words and phrases. The appropriateness of some identity-based language varies between insiders and outsiders of a group."

One reader told me she doesn't like the recommendations of these language lists. She complained that she is fatigued by the effort of having to censor herself.

Here's how I replied: I don't regard it as censorship. People who use language consciously are eagerly alert for the opportunity to evolve the way language is used. They enjoy transcending numbing idioms and worn-out figures of speech so as to stimulate fresh thoughts with an invigorating use of words.

Why should we be attached to using terms that are boring, inexact, and excuses for lazy thinking?

Poets and imaginative writers and other expressive people coin new words all the time, in every language. They help us outgrow outmoded ways of thinking and feeling.

One of my favorite sources for the ever-evolving reinvention of the English lanugage is https://Urbandictionary.com.

"Crazy" appears as a taboo word on the Brandeis list. The description of its problematic use reads, "Ableist language can contribute to stigmas about and trivialize the experiences of people living with disabilities, mental health conditions, and more."

For me personally, "crazy" has always been a positive word. "Crazy wisdom" is one of my lifelong studies. The concepts of crazy wisdom and divine madness have appeared for centuries in many spiritual traditions, including Hinduism, Sufism, Christianity, Buddhism, and shamanism.

In the book *Western Dharma: Buddhism Beyond Asia*, Sandra Bell writes that "crazy wisdom" is a translation of the Tibetan word *drubnyon*, which "traditionally combines exceptional insight and impressive magical power with a flamboyant disregard for conventional behavior."

Many people who enjoy my work have used "crazy" and "crazy wisdom" as complimentary terms to refer to the unconventional inspiration I have provided them. I welcome that designation.

Nevertheless! I will consider dropping "crazy" from my vocabulary, since it may be offensive to some people in ways that it's not for me.

New Words ↻

Below are a few novel words I've coined, plus 12 neologisms I've plucked from The Cunnilinguistic Dicktionary.

- **ahahaha,** exclam. Used to express surprised triumph and explosive amusement while in the midst of a great realization.
- **angel-retentive,** adj. In contrast to "anal retentive," angel-retentive refers to a person with a relaxed openness to the possibility of miracles that confound the rational mind.
- **asymectricity,** n. Energy generated by lopsidedness.
- **autodidactickle,** n. Teaching yourself how to tickle yourself.
- **careeenstable,** adj. Anything that maintains its poise and balance during wild, fast movement.
- **chantepleure,** v. To sing and weep simultaneously.
- **chiaroscurofy,** v. To find a comfortable place where you are partially in darkness and partially illuminated, or half in shadow and half in sunlight.
- **demagnostic,** n. A person who provides leadership by rousing people's noblest ambitions and high ideals, not by pandering to their fears and jealousies. Derived from a blend of "demagogue" and "agnostic."
- **dissident bodhisattva,** n. A bodhisattva or aspiring bodhisattva who believes that existing political and cultural institutions must be overthrown or revolutionized and replaced in order to make it more possible for sentient beings to achieve nirvana.
- **enigmagnetic,** adj. A person who is prone to attracting mysteries.

- **epiphony,** n. A fake realization.
- **fauxbia,** n. A fake fear.
- **flossolalia,** n. An improvised prophetic speech performed while flossing one's teeth.
- **Go fuck yourself,** phrase. A sincere wish that people to whom this phrase is addressed will indulge themselves in life-affirming, self-administered pleasure to the point of rapture.
- **golden bough,** n. Alternative term for penis. Other variations: jade stalk, justice root, starry plough, righteous supplicant, swooping dabbler, tender thunderbolt, frisky risker, raunchy weaver, grateful harvester, worshipful pouncer.
- **hypephobic,** adj. Afraid of hype.
- **indumbnitable,** adj. Incapable of being dumbed down.
- **insurrectionary intimacy,** n. A relationship built on the intention to nurture each other's beautiful qualities, while also thriving on the fact that the bond will inevitably draw out and require redemption of both parties' unripe aspects.
- **lapidrowdy,** adj. Performing intricate tasks with a boisterous spirit. Derived from a blend of "rowdy" and "lapidary," the art of cutting, polishing, and engraving gems.
- **lushbuddy,** n. An alternative term for significant other. Additional signifiers: jellyroll, heartbeat, freestyle, greased lightning.
- **melancholicoholic,** adj. Addicted to sadness; when you can't stop listening to Leonard Cohen records.
- **menstruarchy,** n. Rule by menstruating women. In a menstruarchy, menstruating women are thought to have special powers of perception, insight, and wisdom, and are therefore best qualified to make decisions that affect the collec-

tive. A menstrual council may be composed of women whose cycles vary so that at any one time, several council members are menstruating.

- **mutinyversal,** n. A rebellion against the entire universe.

- **narcissucculence,** n. Succulent narcissism; juicy heroic powers of super-narcissism without the negative connotation that narcissism usually suggests; profound self-love on all levels.

- **Oxymoronic Tao,** n. An expansive mutation of the old Chinese concept of Tao. The Oxymoronic Tao is Tao with an attitude. It's not the calm, abstract, world-weary Tao imagined by the ancient sage Lao-Tse, but an uproarious witchy wow-y Tao of now. It's not invoked by sitting cross-legged in cool, poised contemplation of the ultimate unity of the light and the dark, of the wound and the cure, of the back and forth. Rather, it implies an aggressive desire to jam together even the most incongruous juxtapositions in the spirit of tricksterish love, romancing the contradictions into a slathering pulse of ripe kundalini.

- **psychethanatoil,** n. Soul-death from overwork.

- **psychevivatoil,** n. The blooming of the soul through work. The antidote for psychethanatoil.

- **pyrokleptomania,** n. A brave and noble compulsion to steal fire. Derived from the Greek myth of Prometheus, who pilfered a glowing coal from the gods and gave it as a gift to humankind.

- **reverse panhandle,** v. To stand on a street corner or highway exit ramp and give money to passersby while holding a cardboard sign that reads "I love to give; I need to help; please take some money."

- **selfish bodhisattva,** n. 1. A bodhisattva-in-training who gives too much to others, muting their initiative to care for themself. 2. A grandiose humanitarian whose egotistical attachment to the image of themself as a generous spirit taints the gifts they give. 3. A naïve saint who disseminates idiot compassion, which is a short-term fix offered to suffering people to console them, even though it encourages them to keep doing what brought about their pain.

- **sexcommunicate,** v. To banish one's brain into servitude to one's genitals.

- **silk furrow,** n. Alternative term for vagina. Other freshly coined variations: fluttering phoenix, pearly grove, blooming haha, ambrosial thicket, rumble chamber, bombastic lotus, chthonic riddler, rosy manger, honeyed gateway, Quetzalcoatl's gangplank.

- **smadgic,** n. A wizardly transmutation of a mundane or boring situation into a fascinating adventure or exploration. Derived from "magic" and "smidgen," a small portion.

- **storegasm,** n. Orgasm achieved while walking down supermarket aisles crammed with thousands of colorfully packaged products.

- **taurocoprology,** n. First coined by *Harper's* magazine, it means the study of bullshit—how to use it creatively, how to recognize when it's being used, and how to make it work for you instead of against you.

- **whirlygig,** n. A fact-finding mission that mandates people to wander around aimlessly in unfamiliar places to attract information and inspiration they didn't realize they needed to gather.

- **wild-seed ephiphany,** n. In addition to the benefits of a mere epiphany, a wild-seed ephiphany packs a fiery punch, moving a person to laugh maniacally, unleash a wicked joke, or both. In the wake of a wild-seed epiphany, one feels a spectacular decisiveness about what concrete actions must be taken to infuse righteous order into messy and chaotic places.
- **wowallelujah,** exclam. Uttered during a surge of uncanny intuition that comes while waking up from sleep or ignorance.

Bend words. Stretch them, squash them, mash them up, fold them. Turn them over or swing them upside down. Make up new words. Leave a place for the strange and downright impossible ones. Use ancient words. Hold on to the gangly, silly, slippy, truthful, dangerous, out-of-fashion ones.

—author Kyo Maclear

Revelatory Homework #113

ARIES: What is the most important thing you have never done?

TAURUS: Meditate on death not as the end of physical life, but as a metaphor for shedding what's outworn. In that light, what was the best death you've experienced?

GEMINI: Address this topic: "What I Swear I'll Never Do Again as Long as I Live—Unless I Can Get Away with It Next Time."

CANCERIAN: Give your diagnosis of what you consider the world's greatest problem—and how it affects your personal life.

LEO: "You have more freedom than you are using," says artist Dan Attoe.

How might you lay claim to potential spaciousness, indepen-dence, and leeway that are going to waste?

VIRGO: What might you need to kill off in yourself to tune in to beauty that's hidden from you?

★

LIBRA: What's one thing you have never said to your best ally that you really should say?

SCORPIO: What was the pain or suffering that healed you most?

SAGITTARIUS: What trick do you use to liberate yourself from unnecessary suffering? When you're taking yourself too seriously, what joke to you play on yourself? How do you compassionately bust yourself when you realize you've been indulging in hypocritical behavior?

CAPRICORN: What could you do to love your body better?

AQUARIUS: Everyone influences the world. No matter how powerless we feel, we're all creators who continually churn out energy that shapes our world and the people in it.

   What is the signature of your effect? How do you change the environments you pass through? What magic, for good or ill, do you perform in the daily rhythm? Take inventory and fix any discrepancies between the mark you ideally want to make and your actual impact.

PISCES: What's the single most important question you'd like to resolve before you die many years from now?

Element 7

If we don't pledge our magic soul genius to compassionate service, it will foster grandiosity in us.

If we pledge our magic soul genius to compassionate service, it will continually replenish and regenerate us.

Chapter 17

Your Magic Compassion Soul Genius
+
My Magic Compassion Soul Genius
=
Our Magic Compassion Soul Genius

Invitation to Love the Riddles

I invite you to study the brassy contradictions…

and draw inspiration from the poignant incongruities…

and marvel at the enigmatic ambiguities…

and give your compassionate attention to the
slippery paradoxes…

and say ebullient prayers of gratitude for the contradictions,
incongruities, ambiguities, and paradoxes that are making
you so much wiser and deeper and kinder and cuter.

Thanks for Your Hard Work!

Dear Co-Conspirators:

Congratulations on having such ambidextrous brains and hearts!

Due to your ever-growing ability to blend supple rationality with robust intuition and emotional savvy, you are not falling prey to the inane strains of insanity that are circulating.

Instead, you are achieving glorious triumph after magnificent victory over the fearful fantasizing that passes for the typical use of the imagination.

You are also steadily elevating your skill in the art of paradox. More and more, you are attuned to the amusing fact that when the mythic shifts hit the fan, the apparent opposites turn inside-out.

You know that the rot prepares the way for the splendor; that chaos is the wellspring of rejuvenation.

The people who take everything too personally and seriously and literally may not recognize your ingenious work, but we connoisseurs of the liberated imagination do.

Please accept the thunderous applause of my one hand clapping.

Creating a Golden Age 🌀

No one can foretell the future—not psychics, not visionary philosophers, not doomsayers, not intelligent optimists, not Indigenous shamans.

A persuasive case can be made that this is the worst of times, and an equally compelling case that this is the best of times. Maybe everything will collapse into a miserable dystopia, or maybe we are on the verge of a golden age. It's impossible to know objectively.

Anyone who asserts they know is cherry-picking evidence to rationalize their emotional bent. The variables are beyond our ken.

In the meantime, let's create a golden age. How?

∞ Prepare for the unpredictable. Cultivate mental and emotional states that ripen us to be ready for anything.

∞ Don't be forever lost inside our own heads.

∞ Avoid being enthralled with the hypnotic lure of painful emotions, past events, and worries about the future.

∞ Trust empirical evidence over our time-worn beliefs and old habits.

∞ Turn up our curiosity full blast and tune in to the raw truth of each moment with our beginner's mind and beginner's heart.

∞ Be eager to maintain our poise and grace amid the confounding questions that tease and teach us.

These are excellent ways to prime ourselves for an always-on, simmering-at-low-heat brand of ecstasy—abidingly in the Tao, in the groove, in the zone.

Who We Are 🌀

We are dissident bodhisattvas rebelling against potencies that celebrate fear and blaspheme love.

We are spiritual freedom fighters plotting and wrangling to revere nature and incubate the still small voice and foment the wildest peace we can conjure.

We are subversive mystics stoking the cool blue fires of poetry and lobbying for the liberated imagination.

We are militant ecstatics invoking the transformative powers of pleasure to sanctify and beautify our one and only Earth.

We are mutinous purveyors of grace who redistribute the wealth so that all creatures may have the means to thrive.

Your Specific Goals

You may already understand what I'm about to tell you. But in case you don't, I'll say it. Few principles are more important than those immediately below.

Be crisp and clear about naming your concrete intentions. The more specific your goals, the more likely it is you will accomplish them.

You can't create vivid visualizations of abstract, generalized aims. They may appeal to your intellect, but they can't mobilize you all the way down to the roots of your desires. As a result, your motivation to achieve them will be wan and weak.

★

I began to formally study at an occult magick school at age 23.

I was surprised and amused when the first lesson of the first course, "Seven Steps in Practical Occultism," informed me that the most important thing I needed to do as a magician was to know exactly WHAT I WANT.

What specific experience, feeling, or situation do you want the most?

Mission Statement)((ۿ))(

To celebrate my long-running efforts to inspire my readers, I have composed a summary of the ambitions at the core of my personal mission.

- ◈ To be an aspiring Luminary of Curiosity.
- ◈ To know that playing and having fun and experiencing pleasure are consummate spiritual acts.
- ◈ To explore rowdy reverence and boisterous wisdom and unruly holiness.
- ◈ To not suppress and deny and escape desire. Rather, to apotheosize and exult in desire. To ride its primal power as I perpetrate transformative mystery and lyrical justice.
- ◈ To not suppress and deny and escape my ego. Rather, to apotheosize and exult in my ego as a tool to perpetrate smart love.
- ◈ To identify and blend my personal self with the One Self whose intelligence permeates all beings and all things and all places.
- ◈ To infuse my writing with the soul of music. To infuse my music with the soul of writing.
- ◈ To synergize the Christ archetype with the Dionysus archetype.
- ◈ To explore and experiment with and express sacred trickster feminism.
- ◈ To cultivate a masculine version of emotional intelligence. To develop the most beautiful expressions of masculinity I can imagine.

◈ To know on a visceral level that consciousness is every-where, in all things, in all creatures. To learn to com-mune with the myriad kinds of intelligence, not just the human variety.

◈ To regard listening and empathy as superpowers.

◈ To be ethical and do good while inspired by love more than duty.

◈ To know that the divine feminine is always here, has never waned. But to also know that too many humans have lost direct communion with her. And therefore, to explore how to revive her presence in our awareness.

◈ To live as if there is no such thing as permanent enlight-enment. To be devoted to finding the freshest versions of the raw, ever-evolving truth.

◈ To practice sacred activism. Inspired by intimate ecstatic communion with Divine Intelligence, do practical polit-ical work that fosters justice and fairness for all.

◈ To live as if the personal is the political. To understand on a visceral level that every one of our thoughts, feel-ings, and actions has a political impact beyond our indi-vidual lives.

◈ To wield the specific gifts I have been blessed with to help dissolve racism, misogyny, militarism, plutocracy, LGBTQIA+-phobia, ecocide, and all forms of bigotry.

◈ To love and respect and learn from animals. To seek com-munion with their intelligence.

◈ To understand that all people and all creatures are my teachers.

◈ To act as if one of the great gifts I can give to those I

encounter is to transmute and refine my own darkness, ignorance, and woundedness.

◈ To know that there are Other Real Worlds beyond the material realm, and to relish living there as much as I do living in The Overt Real World.

◈ To live as if our nightly dreams are unparalleled sources of wisdom about how to become soulful and real.

◈ To dedicate my creativity to nurturing, inspiring, and liberating those people who are attracted to my work.

◈ To feel my gratitude going on forever.

Romancing the Paradox 🌀

How do we summon a righteous blend of practical love and constructive anger?

How do we refrain from hating people even as we fight against
the hatred and danger they have helped unleash?

How do we cultivate cheerful buoyancy even as we neutralize
the bigoted, autocratic poisons on the loose?

How can we be both wrathful insurrectionaries and exuberant lovers of life?

How do we stay in a good yet unruly mood as we overthrow
the mass hallucinations?

In the face of global peril, how do we remain dedicated to
building beauty and truth and justice and love even as we keep
our imaginations wild and hungry and free?

Can our struggle also be a form of play?

Oracles for You #13 ☽

ARIES: Below are hunches and guesses about the topic "How to Be an Aries." My readers provided some ideas, which are noted.

- ∞ If it isn't challenging, do something else. —Jennifer Blackmon Guevara
- ∞ If it's easy, it's boring. —Beth Prouty
- ∞ Turn on your sense of wonder full blast and chase the white rabbit right down the rabbit hole. —Suzanne Shettles Charleston
- ∞ Every now and then, test the hypothesis that many of the rules just don't work on you or for you.
- ∞ Argue for fun. Be playful and frisky as you banter. Disagree for the sport of it, without feeling attached to being right or needing the last word.
- ∞ You are a great initiator of ideas who's willing to let go of them in their pure and perfect forms so as to help them bloom to fruition.
- ∞ Friends may tell you, "If I ever need a dragon captured or slain, I'll call you."
- ∞ Don't be shy about telling yourself, "I don't have time to do this right now. I need to go drum up an unpredictable escapade and have as much unruly fun as possible." —Kymberlee della Luce

TAURUS: Below are hunches and guesses about the topic "How to Be a Taurus." My readers provided some ideas, which are noted.

- ∞ Work harder, last longer, and finish with more grace than everyone else. —Destiny Cavill

∞ Be in love with beauty. Crave it, surround yourself with it, and create it. Be especially enamored of beautiful things that are also useful. —Wanda Lookser

∞ Be relentlessly practical. Know how to get things done. Pick up a shovel and dig the grooves for the water signs to flow their feelings through. Grab an axe and chop the wood so the fire signs can burn bright. Gather bricks and mortar and build the structures for the air signs to talk about. —Artis Frevoli

∞ As a Taurus, you are always wise to be reverent toward your five senses. They are your glorious treasures. Your marvelous superpowers. Your sublime assets.

As you deploy them with all your amazement and appreciation unfurled, they will boost your intelligence. They will heighten your intuition in ways that guide you to good decisions. You will tune in to interesting truths that would otherwise remain hidden.

Here's the climax of this counsel: You can cultivate your sensory apparatus with such alacrity and daring that they work almost as extrasensory powers. They are so sharp and clear that they virtually make you psychic.

∞ Know how to make impossibly appealing chocolate hazelnut biscotti. —Grace Gamulto

∞ Listen to the moonrise, taste the mist, smell the clouds, kiss the music, woo the earth. —Azariah Edgolas

∞ Taurus artist Joan Miró loved to daub colored paint on canvases. He said he approached his work in the same way he made love: "a total embrace, without caution, prudence thrown to the winds, nothing held back."

To serve your highest potentials, adopt a similar attitude. Summon the ardor and artistry of a creative lover for all your important activities.

GEMINI: Below are hunches and guesses about the topic "How to Be a Gemini." My readers provided some ideas, which are noted.

∞ Relish the fact that your curious mind and mischievous heart and inquisitive soul will ensure you never need to be bored. —Jonquil Remedy

∞ Create big spacious realizations by weaving together several small hunches.

∞ Do not, under any circumstances, grow up to be a serious adult on the inside. Keep the innocent gaze you had when you were five and use it often—even (and especially!) when looking at mundane things. —Kim Breeding-Mercer

∞ Find at least seven best friends because you will need them all in the long run.

∞ Keep a little angel on your right shoulder and a little devil on your left shoulder. Enjoy listening to them argue and don't get attached to anything they say.

∞ Have fun even when you're not.

∞ Remember that your paradoxes are not always obvious to others. Those who met you when you were Amy Schumer may wonder what's wrong with you when you are Tupac Shakur. Be patient with them. Explain that tomorrow you may be Anderson Cooper or Margaret Cho.

∞ Do the unexpected until it becomes expected. Then abandon it and try a new unexpected experiment.

CANCERIAN: Below are hunches and guesses about the topic "How to Be a Cancerian." My readers provided some ideas, which are noted.

∞ Start all your sentences with, "I feel." —Demetrius Orloff

∞ Enjoy hours of entertainment as you explore the unleashed wondrous powers of your imagination. —Deirdre King

∞ Your memory is SUBSTANTIAL. Your sensitivity is MONUMENTAL. Your urge to nurture is DEEP. Your complexity is EPIC. Your feelings are BOTTOMLESS. Your imagination is PRODIGIOUS.

Because of all these aptitudes and capacities, you are TOO MUCH for some people. Not everyone can handle your intricate and sometimes puzzling BEAUTY.

But there are enough folks out there who appreciate and thrive on your gifts. Make it your quest to focus your urge to merge on them.

∞ Either be a literal mother or else be motherly in meta-phorical or spiritual or unexpected ways that make you feel deep and strong.

∞ The health and well-being of your stomach may be a barometer of your emotional state. If it's off-kilter, and you don't know why, check to see if you're hiding a secret from yourself.

∞ You hate it and love it when people seem able to read your mind. You don't want them to know you all the way through, but you do want them to know you all the way through.

LEO: Below are hunches and guesses about the topic "How to Be

a Leo." My readers provided some ideas, which are noted.

∞ Be confident that YOU ARE THE PARTY! Everywhere you go, bring the spirits of fun and revelry. Be educationally entertaining and entertainingly educational. Charm yourself by making life more interesting for everyone.

At the same time, be kind and humble, never arrogant or insensitive. A vital part of your assignment is to nourish and inspire others with your glow and magnetism. That formula will ensure bounty flows your way.

PS: Regularly reward your admirers and followers with your magnanimous Chesire-cat grin. —Lani Decourse

∞ Play at least as hard as you work.

∞ Set your sleeping position next to an east-facing window so the rays of sunrise fall on you as you wake each morning. —Ryan Impalba

∞ Love yourself more and more each day, forever. Have fun doing it. Laugh about how easy and how hard it is to love yourself so well. Make it into a game that brings you an endless stream of amusement. —Larissa Lanes

∞ It's always advisable for you Leos to carry on a close personal relationship with mirrors. This is true both literally and metaphorically. For the sake of your mental health, you need to be knowledgeable about your image and monitor its ever-shifting nuances. You thrive by undertaking introspective explorations and creative self-inquiry.

Please keep it all tender and kind, though. You're not allowed to bad-mouth yourself. Put a special emphasis on identifying aspects of your beauty that have been obscured or neglected.

∞ Always be looking for supporting actors and understudies,

because it can get tiring having to always get the crowd
going all by yourself. —Laurie Brauss Evan

VIRGO: Below are hunches and guesses about the topic "How to
Be a Virgo." My readers provided some ideas, which are noted.

∞ At your best, you are a flexible purist, an adaptable stick-
ler for detail, and a disciplined yet supple thinker. Maybe
more than any other sign of the zodiac, you can be focused
and resilient, intense and agile, attentive and graceful.

Non-Virgos very much appreciate it when you serve as
a role model for these talents.

∞ Your to-do list must always include "Relax!" —Karen
Moshier Mara

∞ It's your birthright as a Virgo to become an expert at
capitalizing on difficulties. You have great potential to
detect opportunities coalescing in the midst of trouble.
You may have a knack for spotting the order that's hiding
in the chaos.

Wield these skills with artistry, my dear—both for your
own benefit and for the betterment of everyone whose
life you touch.

∞ As often as necessary, lie down on the mossy, piney, leafy
forest floor. Breathe in the earth. Sip the mist. Caress the
breeze. —Conna Meader

∞ You understand the intimate, intricate connections
between mind and body. As you get older, you become
better and better able to use this knowledge for the enjoyment of yourself and others.

∞ You may not always get the answer completely right, but

you are skilled at finding the best answer available. You scan for practical, compassionate solutions that address some of everyone's needs. If anyone can be an expert at creative compromise, it's you.

∞ When the party is over and everyone leaves, you know you are going to stay until the kitchen's clean. Be proud of that! It's one of your charms. —Monica Lark

∞ It's impossible to be perfect. It's neither healthy nor productive to obsess on perfectionism.

You know these things. You understand you can't afford to get bogged down in overthinking and overreaching and overpolishing.

And when you are at your best, you sublimate such manic urges. You transform them into the elegant intention to clarify and refine and refresh. With grace and care, you express useful beauty instead of aiming for hyper-immaculate precision.

LIBRA: Below are hunches and guesses about the topic "How to Be a Libra." My readers provided some ideas, which are noted.

∞ Practice, practice, practice the art of moderation. Do so with the intention of making it a flexible, genial skill rather than an unthinking habit.

∞ Everyone knows that "balance" is a keyword for you Librans. However, there are many interpretations of what balance entails. Here are some:

• An openness to consider several different ways to capitalize on an opportunity, but to ultimately choose just one way

- The ability to see and understand all sides of every story, while also knowing that for pragmatism's sake you may ultimately need to endorse a single version of the story
- The capacity to be both constructively critical and supportively sympathetic
- The facility to be welcoming and inviting while still maintaining healthy boundaries

∞ You need the following on a regular basis:
- Rapturous encounters with unexpected grace
- Elegant eruptions of steely willpower
- Encounters with inspiration that propel you to make some practical improvement
- Brave adjustments in your understanding of how the world works
- Sacrifices of OK things, freeing time and energy for you to cultivate really good things

∞ In one sitting, listen to Pavarotti, Van Halen, Bruce Springsteen, Bach, Lenny Kravitz, Ray Charles, and Barry Manilow. Or do the same with Edith Piaf, PJ Harvey, Hildegard von Bingen, Megan Thee Stallion, Joni Mitchell, and Billie Holiday. —Jodie Hoyster

∞ Be beautiful in the smartest ways you can imagine. Be smart in the most beautiful ways you can imagine. —Ariel Hoover

∞ Make sure your cool attention to detail never gets too chilly. Warm it up now and then. Invite your heart to add its counsel to your head's observations. Tenderize your objectivity.

∞ Is it true that relationships are like sharks? If they don't keep moving, they die? Some Libras need to believe that.

—Artie Regolio

∞ Always be willing to be puzzled. Always be entertained and educated by your puzzlement. Remember that nothing ever changes unless somebody is puzzled.

∞ Applying the Goldilocks attitude is essential. Everything must be just right: neither too much nor too little; neither overly grand nor overly modest.

SCORPIO: Below are hunches and guesses about the topic "How to Be a Scorpio."

∞ Self-command should be your blissful quest, your steady source of inspiration, your fascinating struggle. And what is self-command? Your soul's ingenious management of your intense yearnings and fervent feelings.

∞ Molt like a snake at least once a year. Or twice. Even three times wouldn't be too much.

∞ When you are functioning at your best, you Scorpios crave only the finest, top-quality highs. You embrace joys and pleasures that generate epiphanies and vitalizing transformations.

Mediocre varieties of fun don't interest you. You avoid debilitating indulgences that provide brief excitement but spawn long-term problems.

∞ You belong to no one but yourself. No one can possess you.

∞ Many Scorpios imagine sex to be a magnificent devotion, a quintessential mode of worship, an unparalleled celebration of sacred earthiness.

I endorse and admire this perspective. If our culture had more of it, the art and entertainment industries would offer far less of the demeaning, superficial versions of sexuality that are so rampant.

Here's another thing I love about Scorpios: So many of you grasp the value of sublimating lust into other fun and constructive accomplishments. You are skilled at channeling your high-powered libido into practical actions that may have no apparent erotic element.

∞ Remember that levity, liberty, and the pursuit of fun are as crucial as ambition and status and getting big things done.

∞ To be a Scorpio, you must adore the frozen hot water and the calm cool churning molten lava and the fiery liquid ash rising from the nasty sacred roots and the quiet explosions of orgiastic serenity.

∞ You sometimes feel you have to tone down your smoldering intensity, avert your dark-star gazes, conceal your sultry charisma, dumb down your persuasive speech, pretend you don't have so much stamina, disguise your awareness of supernatural connections, act less like a saint and martyr in your zealous devotions, and refrain from revealing your skill at reading between the lines.

But none of that avoidance stuff usually works very well. The Real You leaks out into view.

In the coming decades I hope you won't engage in much of the hiding behavior I described. I'd love to see you freely pour forth your Scorpionic blessings.

SAGITTARIUS: Below are hunches and guesses about the topic "How to Be a Sagittarius." My readers provided some ideas, which are noted.

∞ On a regular basis, ruminate about the meaning of life and why we are here and how you could contribute to creating a paradise on Earth. Find at least three reasons to laugh uproariously each time you do this. —Jasper Jacobs Jarry

∞ Embrace optimism for both its beauty and its tactical advantages.

∞ You are a teacher, and you love to teach. You are a student, and you love to learn.

∞ Be amazingly wise, be impossibly brave, be expansively visionary—and forgive yourself anytime you can't remember where you parked your car.

∞ Give your fears names like "Gaffe" and "Wheezy" and "Lumpy."

∞ Inspire other people to love being themselves and not wanting to be like you. —Ellis Manosian

∞ Begin three new projects that are beyond your capacity and impossible to achieve with your current levels of intelligence, skill, and experience—and then accomplish them anyway.

CAPRICORN: Below are hunches and guesses about the topic "How to Be a Capricorn." My readers provided some ideas, which are noted.

∞ Keep clambering upwards even if you have no competitors and there's no one else at the top. —Adam Roman

∞ Let's imagine you are in your office or on the job or sitting at your kitchen table. With focused diligence, you're working on solving a problem or improving a situation that involves a number of people.

You think to yourself, "No one seems to be aware that I am quietly toiling here behind the scenes to make the magic happen."

A few days or a few weeks later, your efforts have been successful. The problem is resolved, or the situation has improved.

But then you hear the people involved say, "Wow, I wonder what happened? It's like things got fixed all by themselves."

If scenarios like this happen, Capricorn, I urge you to speak up and tell everyone what really occurred.

∞ Always look older than your age until you are about 30, and then always look at least five years younger than your age. —Alexanne Wabry

∞ Do you sometimes fall under the influence of discouraging thoughts and demoralizing feelings? The best way to chase them away is by doing absorbing work and compassionate service.

∞ When you are right, time is generally on your side.

∞ People look to you and regard you as a role model more than you realize. Your statements and actions often have a disproportionately big impact. Your influence ripples out beyond your sphere.

In light of these facts, which may be subtle or barely visible, I encourage you to always be thinking about how you can upgrade your sense of responsibility. Keep checking to make sure your integrity is impeccable.

One other piece of advice, too: Be an example to people without making them feel like they owe you anything.

∞ Get comfortable with your stern, stern ways so you can

be the first to laugh at yourself and let your rules bend.
—Carrie Cleveland

∞ As you take care of everything in your purview and you fix the glitches created by others who have given less than their best, do it in alignment with your own highest standards. Nobody else's standards matter.

AQUARIUS: Below are hunches and guesses about the topic "How to Be an Aquarius." My readers provided some ideas, which are noted.

∞ Aquarius announces to the world, "I go my own way. If you don't comprehend, to hell with you. You'll catch up someday, and when you do, I'll be there with open arms."
—Rebecca Sweet

∞ You are an extra authentic Aquarius if people say that you get yourself into the weirdest, most interesting trouble they've ever seen. You are an ultra-genuine Aquarius if people follow the twists and pivots of your life as they would a soap opera. —Abbie Wisener

∞ Notice shit. Get excited and full of wonder about shit. Talk about shit with others who love to talk about shit. Laugh endlessly about shit. —Washington Ponder

∞ People might say to you, "Just when I thought I had you figured out, you do something unexpected to confound me."

∞ Accept that you don't really have to understand yourself. Be at peace with how you constantly ramble, swerve, and weave to become more of yourself. Appreciate how each electric shift leads to the next electric shift, always changing who you are forever. Within the churning, ever-yearning current, marvel at how you remain eternal, steady, and solid—yet always evolving, always on a higher ground than before. —Georgie Lee

∞ Politely confuse and even unsettle people with your radical social ideals about how compassion, empathy, and emotional intelligence will overthrow predatory capitalism to create a utopia where inner dream space is respected as much as the frenzied marketplace. —Fortune Rebecca Buchholtz

∞ Listen to and secretly enjoy death metal music and rockabilly music, but make your friends think you do so just to flummox and discombobulate and flusterfunk them.

Also, use outlandish words like "flummox" and "discombobulate" and "flusterfunk."

∞ Things you Aquarians might do:

- Be a hopeful cynic and a cheerful skeptic.
- Be able to grasp and articulate complex theories, but sometimes pour salt instead of sugar in your coffee and put your shoes on the wrong feet and get lost as you return home from the grocery store.
- Zig when others zag. Zag when others Zig.
- Rage blithely but fiercely against injustices and cruelty.
- Be owned by a cat. Or by several cats.
- Play with the fantasy that you're an interdimensional being or extraterrestrial who's engaged in an experiment on planet Earth.
- Have pillow fights instead of arguments.
- Fall in love with everything and everyone: a D-List celebrity, an oak tree growing sideways out of a hill, a neon sign with one letter that doesn't light up, a feral cat

with two different color eyes, a slightly chipped mirror in a thrift store, and the newly invented color Neochrome™.

- Pace in your bedroom while listening to slow, mournful music.
- Desperately want to be alone even though you're lonely.
- Just for the hell and the fun of it, walk backward in public places every now and then.
- Hold midnight sex picnics in the park and swing on the swings before the sex starts.
- Fantasize that because you can fly in your dreams, that maybe somehow you really can, but just haven't figured it out yet when you're conscious.

PISCES: Below are hunches and guesses about the topic "How to Be a Pisces." My readers provided some ideas, which are noted.

∞ Pisces says, "I believe in all this excruciating beauty, therefore I am." —Christy Williams Dunton

∞ Now and then, logic may be of only partial use to you. Information acquired through your senses might prove less than fully adequate, as well. On the other hand, your talents for feeling deeply and tapping into your intuition can often provide you with highly accurate intelligence.

∞ Go often to rivers and springs and creeks and streams. Converse with the fairies and undines. Pledge your reverence to the fish and frogs and turtles and beavers. Learn the ways of the crabs and crayfish and eels and water snakes. Sing songs for the dragonflies and whirligig beetles and caddisflies and lacewings.

∞ A mature Pisces says, "It's not personal, it's not personal, it's not personal."

∞ Always be on the lookout for more angles and more feelings and more stories. —Gretchen Knapp

∞ "The psychotic drowns in the same waters in which the mystic swims with delight," wrote mythologist Joseph Campbell. As long as you recognize and appreciate that you are a whoosh of rich contradictions, a vortex of fertile struggles, and a whirl of tantalizing wonders, you will be a mystic swimmer.

∞ Here's the good life, the Piscean way: ever dreaming the impossible dream, ever spinning out fresh fertile fantasies, ever reaching into the depths of your own soul and others' souls. —Jacqueen Willims

∞ When in trouble or in doubt, worship at the altar of creativity. —Kate Bair Lovins

∞ Confuse everyone, but in a friendly way. Keep a sweet, rich air of mystery about you. Somehow, figure out how to use this to your advantage.

Element 8

If we don't worship the blessed abyss, the blessed abyss will hide us from the raw truth.

If we worship the blessed abyss, the blessed abyss will reveal us to the raw truth.

Chapter 18

Your Blessed Raw Truth Abyss
+
My Blessed Raw Truth Abyss
=
Our Blessed Raw Truth Abyss

Long Live You and Me

Long live the beauty that comes down and through and onto all of us.
> —singer-songwriter Laurie Anderson

Long live impudence! It's my guardian angel in this world.
> —physicist Albert Einstein

Long live freedom, and damn the ideologies.
> —poet Robinson Jeffers

Long live the sacred art of believing in nothing and loving everything.
> —the woman on the park bench talking to her cat

Long live also the forward march of the common people in all the lands towards their just and true inheritance, and towards

the broader and fuller age.
            —politician Winston Churchill

Long live all the magic we made.
            —singer-songwriter Taylor Swift

Long live diversity, long live the earth!
            —environmentalist Edward Abbey

Long live the rose that grew from concrete.
            —rapper Tupac Shakur

Long live our memory of the future.
            —my friend Jessamin Werrevo

Long live the pioneers, rebels, and mutineers.
            —rock band X Ambassadors

Long live the weeds.
            —poet Theodore Roethke

Long live your soul, and may I see you do great in life.
            —Hallmark birthday card

Live long and prosper.
—fictional *Star Trek* character Spock

Long live wanting to dwell excitedly in this beautiful garden of mysteries and knowing it as a beginner.
—poet Anah-Karelia Coates

Long live transfinite mountains, the hollow earth, time machines, fractal writing, aliens, dada, telepathy, flying saucers, warped space, teleportation, artificial reality, robots, pod people, hylozoism, endless shrinking, intelligent goo, antigravity, surrealism, software highs, two-dimensional time, gnarly computation, the art of photo composition, pleasure zappers, nanomachines, mind viruses, hyperspace, monsters from the deep and, of course, always and forever, the attack of the giant ants!
—science fiction author Rudy Rucker

Long live everything and everyone I forgot to love.
—my neighbor Alicia Vasquez

Buddhist monk and author Thich Nhat Hanh has the last word:

We are often sad and suffer a lot when things change, but change and impermanence have a positive side. Thanks to impermanence, everything is possible. Life itself is possible.

If a grain of corn is not impermanent, it can never be transformed into a stalk of corn. If the stalk were not impermanent, it could never provide us with the ear of corn we eat.

If your daughter is not impermanent, she cannot grow up to become a woman. Then your grandchildren would never manifest.

So instead of complaining about impermanence, we should say, "Warm welcome and long live impermanence."

Fortunes for You #14

ARIES: "Love is a fire," declared Aries actor Joan Crawford. "But whether it's going to warm your hearth or burn down your house, you can never tell."

I disagree with her conclusion. There are practical steps you can take to ensure that love's fire warms but doesn't burn. I believe it's your sacred duty as an Aries to know about them.

Start with these strategies:

◈ Suffuse your libido with compassion.

◈ Imbue your romantic fervor with empathy.

◈ Instill your animal passions and instinctual longings with affectionate tenderness.

◈ If you notice your sexual urges driving you toward narcissists who are no good for you, use all your Aries-style forceful willpower to redirect those urges toward emotionally intelligent, self-responsible candidates.

★

TAURUS: During regular hikes along my favorite trails, I've gotten to know the local boulders.

Maybe it sounds daft, but I've come to love them. I've even given some names. Slow Blast is one of my confidants. Soul Waker and Tremble Story and Memory Song are old friends. There are many others.

They symbolize stability and constancy to me. When I gaze at them or sit on them, my resolve grows stronger. They teach me about how to be steadfast and unflappable in all kinds of weather. I draw inspiration from the way they are so purely themselves, steadily true to their own nature.

I recommend this practice to you Tauruses. You were born into this life to be a Taurus so you could gain prowess in qualities like these.

GEMINI: *Generation Kill* is an HBO miniseries based on the experiences of a reporter embedded with American Marines fighting in Iraq.

Early on, before the troops have been exposed to any serious combat, they are overflowing with trash talk. A commanding officer scolds them: "Gentlemen, from now on we're going to have to earn our stories."

Although your life is less volatile and risky than theirs, my advice to you is the same: Earn your stories! If you talk big, act big. Make promises and entertain dares and issue challenges only if you're geared up to learn how to be a sovereign of your own destiny.

The good news is that you have substantial potential to do that. It's a Gemini birthright.

CANCERIAN: According to the oracular priestess at the ancient Greek shrine of Delphi, whom I consult in my dreams, "luminous shadow" and "hidden light" are code phrases that are of special use to you Cancerians.

Here are possible interpretations of her message: What dark places in your life may have the potential to shine forth with radiance? How do you help the people you love find redemption in their difficult experiences? What can you do to track down and reveal the secret beauty that aches to be found?

Can you think of any other probing questions?

LEO: A reader scolded me, telling me that none of us should ever answer the question "Who am I?" We should always leave it an open question, he declared, and never speculate on what the definitive answers might be.

I said, "I don't agree. It's fun and useful to come up with provisional answers to the question 'Who am I?', knowing that no answer is the final one."

He said, "Wisdom has nothing to do with fun."

I said, "For me, wisdom and fun are inextricably related and inseparable."

I said, "I get new answers to the question 'Who am I?' all the time, and will continue to do so forever."

I invite you to try my approach, Leo. It's especially propitious for you.

VIRGO: One of your wonderful qualities is your aptitude for helping people. It's also the part of your nature that is most likely to be abused by charming narcissists and charismatic manipulators.

But I predict that in the coming years, you will have a growing knack for freeing yourself from these oppressors. More and more you'll spot potential new ones from a distance, and you'll know how to break the hold that the old ones have on you.

Take this pledge now: "I will serve only the smart, effective people who also serve me."

LIBRA: For a bald eagle in flight, feathers are crucial in maintaining balance. If it inadvertently loses a feather on one wing, it will purposely shed a comparable feather on the other wing.

I think this strategy has metaphorical meaning for you. Do you want to soar with maximum grace and power? Would you like to ascend and dive, explore and scout, with ease and exuberance? Learn from the eagle's instinctual wisdom.

SCORPIO: You can be a connoisseur of temptations if you want to be. It's your birthright to cultivate a knack for attracting and playing with allurements and enticements.

You can also develop a sixth sense about the distinction between good bait and bad bait—between provocative temptations that serve your charmed dreams and debilitating traps that dissipate your integrity.

Here's the payoff: When you focus on the ennobling temptations, they will conspire with you to bloom your soul.

SAGITTARIUS: "The soul should always stand ajar," wrote Sagittarian poet Emily Dickinson. Why? Because "if the heaven inquire, He will not be obliged to wait or shy of troubling her."

My translation: Keep your deep psyche in a constant state of readiness for the possible influx of divine inspiration or unexpected blessings.

Then you're likely to recognize the call when it comes and respond with the alacrity necessary to get the full benefit of its offerings.

This strategy is a key element of the Truth and the Way for

you Sagittarians.

CAPRICORN: "When I look at a sunset, I don't say, 'Soften the orange a little on the right hand corner, and put a bit more purple in the cloud color.'"

Capricorn psychologist Carl Rogers used these words to describe the way he observed the world. "I don't try to control a sunset," he continued. "I watch it with awe."

He had a similar view about people. "One of the most satisfying experiences," he wrote, "is just fully to appreciate an individual in the same way I appreciate a sunset."

I invite you to aspire to cultivate this perspective. It's good medicine for you Capricorns.

AQUARIUS: Some spiritual teachers say you're most likely to succeed at meditation if you sit still in the silence of a sanctuary. They believe you need to retreat from the mundane world to develop compassionate objectivity about life.

The 18th-century Zen Buddhist teacher Hakuin Ekaku had a different view. His motto: "Meditation in the midst of activity is a billion times superior to meditation in stillness."

My opinion: Both approaches can work. Of all the signs in the zodiac, you Aquarians are potentially the most talented at Ekaku's approach.

PISCES: "I have come to be fascinated with the messiness of desire," writes novelist Ashley Warlick, "with the ways people fit themselves together, take themselves apart for each other, for want of each other, for want of some parts of each other."

Your assignment, Pisces, is to celebrate the messiness of desire; to not just grudgingly accept it as an inconvenience you must tolerate, but marvel at it, be amused by it, and appreciate it for the lessons it provides.

Your motto could be, "I bless the messy largesse of my longing." It's potentially a Piscean specialty.

Useful and Soulful Secrets ((ᐊ))

I periodically ask my teammates and beloved champions whether
they have discovered any of the 3,333 Useful and Soulful Secrets
about the Real Reality—as opposed to the 3,333 Obvious and
Sentimental Secrets about the Fake Reality. Below are among
my favorites. I'd love to hear yours.

  ∞ Every conscious act is an act of magick.

  ∞ You will find beauty in everything when you look for it.
    Conversely, you have the power and the right to ignore
    beauty if you want to. But who wants to?

  ∞ In the long run, it's healthiest to side with those who tell
    the most truth.

  ∞ Confucius said, "All wisdom is rooted in learning to call
    things by their right names."

  ∞ Don't stop learning just because you know it all.

  ∞ Truth is sometimes sneaky and mischievous, hiding in
    unexpected places. But that doesn't mean that ALL truth
    is sneaky and mischievous, hiding in unexpected places.

  ∞ Ssshhhh! Communication doesn't solve everything. Do
    your best to communicate, anyway.

  ∞ William James said, "I will act as if what I do makes a
    difference."

  ∞ Don't let yourself be trapped into being who you used to
    be if that's not who you are anymore.

  ∞ Question yourself about your own motivations and possi-
    ble self-deceptions. In so doing, you will develop an acute
    knack about when and how to question others about their

motivations and possible self-deceptions.

∞ No one is ever able to tell the whole truth. That's a bundle of trillions of data points known only to the Eternal Intelligence formerly known as "God."

∞ Be kind to yourself. That is not the same as indulging yourself or spoiling yourself. It means conducting your inner monologue as though you were counseling a friend whom you dearly love.

∞ Look for an oracle that asks you the right questions.

∞ Whatever your problems are, someone has it far worse and someone has it far better.

∞ Applaud creativity, even when its results bother you.

∞ Pretending you don't feel how you feel doesn't make you feel different.

∞ As physicist Richard P. Feynman advised us, the first principle is that you must not fool yourself, and you are the easiest person to fool.

∞ Thoughts are inevitable but believing them is optional.

Love Cues and Clues: Being Only Who You Are ⊚

I will bestow a blessing on you and your closest ally. My hope is that it will help you harness the restlessness that on occasion undermines the dynamic stability of your relationship.

Here's the benediction, inspired by a Robert Bly poem:

As you sit or walk or lie next to each other, share a mood of glad acceptance. Don't be itchy or fidgeting, wondering if there's something better to be or do.

Be united with the unique mood of the moment. Don't wish you were talking about a different subject or feeling a different emotion or living in a different world. Be content to be exactly who you are, exactly where you are.

Divinations for You #15

ARIES: Don't pretend you can't see the messy darkness. Admit to its presence. Accept its reality. But don't get tangled up in it, either.

Gaze into the abyss so as to educate yourself about its nature, but don't become entranced by its hypnotic power.

Scheme to reclaim your power from soul-sucking influences. But don't turn the process into a blood-and-thunder showdown that wreaks epic chaos.

You may be amazed at how much protection and relaxation you can generate for yourself simply by being a poised lover of life who is free of melodramatic reactions.

All the practices I just described are potentially your super-powers, dear Aries.

TAURUS: Some of us may have imagined, from time to time, that we are living in the hippest, coolest, most happening place in the world. New York? London? Berlin? Montreal? Shanghai? Barcelona? I can recall having that delusion while in New York and San Francisco.

But the truth is that everywhere is the center of the world. Of all the signs, you Tauruses understand that best.

Congrats for living there!

GEMINI: I love astrology. It excites my imagination and helps ensure that my relationship with the world isn't overly lit-eral or prosaic. It anchors me in the paradoxical insight that although many things are out of my control, I have huge amounts of free will.

My study of the mysterious meanings of planetary omens provides guidance, keeps me humble, and is a constant reminder that psychology and symbolism and poetic use of language provide an understanding of reality that's as useful as science.

On the other hand, astrology sometimes feels oppressive. I hesitate to be overly reliant on any system, even one as vital and interesting as astrology, which might come between me and the raw truth about reality. I aspire to see the actual people who are in front of me, and not be interpreting everything they do through the lens of their horoscopes.

Now I urge you to do what I've just done: Express your appreciation for something in your life that provides beauty and power, even as you critique its downsides.

This multivalent aptitude is especially available to you Geminis, more so than most of the other zodiac signs.

CANCERIAN: In honor of the fact that you're evolving into a higher-octave version of yourself, I award you the nickname of "Miracle Player," or else "Sleek Cat" or "Giant Step" or "Fate Whisperer." You can have all three, if you like.

You may also use the following titles to refer to yourself: "CEO of My Own Life" or "Self-Teacher of Jubilance and Serenity" or "Fertile Blur of Supple Strength."

Feel free, as well, to anoint your head with organic virgin olive oil, fashion a crown for yourself out of roses, and come up with a wordless sound that is a secret sign you'll give yourself whenever you want to honor the marvelous creature you are on your way to becoming.

The counsel in this oracle stems from my desire to stimulate your imagination as you dream up amusing ways to love yourself. I believe that's a fundamental Cancerian imperative.

LEO: Let's talk about your power to perform magic. I don't mean Houdini-style hocus-pocus, but rather practical wizardry you wield to make your life wonderful.

Here are magical aptitudes that many Leos have substantial potential to draw on:

∞ Identifying situations that empower you to serve both your selfish interests and your unselfish ideals

∞ Radiating your luminous truths in ways that don't intimidate others, but rather inspire them to radiate their luminous truths

∞ Treating your ego as an elegant art project that propels your skill for creating beauty

∞ Taking a vow that what excites you will also make you most useful to others

∞ Developing skill at forming alliances that don't bring out your worst and don't provoke mediocrity, but rather synergize your highest potentials

VIRGO: Visionary Virgo educator Maria Montessori believed that self-discipline motivated by a child's own enthusiasm is far better than discipline imposed on the child by a strong-willed authority.

What is the best way to develop the superior form? She says kids need to understand the difference between good and evil.

Even more importantly, they must not associate good with passive immobility and evil with animated activity.

My translation: To bring the best Virgo-style order, efficiency, and discipline into your rhythm, cultivate an irrepressible desire to perpetrate enjoyable acts of generosity and good will.

LIBRA: "Nothing was ever created by two men," wrote John Steinbeck in his novel *East of Eden*. "There are no good collaborations, whether in music, in art, in poetry, in mathematics, in philosophy. Once the miracle of creation has taken place, the group can build and extend it, but the group never invents anything. The preciousness lies in the lonely mind of a man."

In my view, this statement is delusional nonsense. And it's especially inapt for you. You Libras are potentially adept collaborators: from the seed sprouting all the way to the bloom.

SCORPIO: Love and intimacy come in many forms. There are at least a billion different ways for you to be attracted to another person, and just as many ways to structure your relationship.

Maybe your unique bond involves having sex, or maybe it doesn't. Maybe it's romantic or friendly or holy, or all three of those things.

Do the two of you have something important to create together, or is your connection more about fueling each other's talents?

Your task is to respect and even revere the idiosyncratic ways you weave together, not force yourselves to conform to a prototype. More than most other astrological signs, you Scorpios have the potential to deploy this wisdom wisely.

SAGITTARIUS: It's usually better if you think comprehensively, not defensively; and see futuristically, not didactically; and fantasize fantastically, not diplomatically.

Life responds more warmly to your gambits when you don't get triggered by every little blip that leaps into your field of vision, but rather when you survey the long-term cycles of your life from expansive vistas.

So I suggest you aspire to be a proactive visionary and a high-minded explorer. Weave all the disparate threads into a tapestry that reveals the big picture.

Your ongoing need for new acts of liberation requires you to regularly slough off petty concerns and trivial details.

CAPRICORN: Once I asked my Capricorn readers if they ever obsessed on their longings to such a degree that they missed opportunities to actually satisfy their longings. In response, a reader named John G. sent me the following corrective message:

> We Capricorns comprehend the futility of too much longing. We understand it can be a phantasm that gets in the way of real accomplishment.
>
> It's like a telephone that keeps ringing somewhere but can't be found. We don't waste energy on dreamy feelings that may or may not be satisfied, since that energy is so much better funneled into grasping the details that will bring us useful rewards.

AQUARIUS: From the perspective of most modern conspiracy theorists, the conspiracies they imagine to be loose in the world have been dreamed up and are perpetrated by coordinated groups of malign people.

My benevolent conspiracy theories, on the other hand, are rooted in a hypothesis at the core of Western Hermetic Magick, which is what I have studied with love for years. The hypothesis is that life is divine play—an art project, master game, and sacred ceremony designed by a loving Creator.

This Creator, whose consciousness pervades every cubic centimeter of the universe, provides all necessary help and tools for us to seek liberation from our suffering and realize our essential oneness with all beings in the process of developing, over millennia of incarnations, a unique personal identity.

More than all the other signs, you Aquarians are drawn to conspiracy theories. I invite you to give mine a try—or conjure up your own version of a Benevolent Theory of Everything.

PISCES: Here's a thought from Piscean poet W. H. Auden: "The image of myself which I try to create in my own mind in order that I may love myself is very different from the image which I try to create in the minds of others in order that they may love me."

If what Auden describes is true for you, I suggest you try this experiment. Merge the two images; see if you can make them the same.

And if Auden's description is not true for you, congratulations: You have learned to ripen a chief Piscean potential.

Secret Methods ((ﾐ))

◈ The Prime Codex is hidden in the wall between the Hall of Mists and the Soul Kitchen. When you find it, decorate it with your most lovingly rebellious graffiti.

◈ The Beasts of the Wheels of Time are ticklish. That's a key to reducing their power over you. Another key: Confuse them with your most illuminating gibberish.

◈ It's permissible to permanently borrow the celestial trumpet from the stingy angel if you use it to heal broken souls.

◈ At least once every eclipse, dive into the sleep mirror and cleanse the water you find there.

◈ Use play money to buy two Peaches of Immortality from the Queen of Shapeshifters. One peach will be for you and one for an adversary you care for.

◈ During a full moon, sing your sexy way into the Magic Dumping Ground. Befriend the Holy Squirmer. Ask her to give you the elegant dreamsquawk signs that enable you to find treasures in nightmares.

◈ The Frost Worm will let you pass unscathed through the Forgotten Realm if you prove you have learned to use your third eye to watch TV.

◈ You are the Chosen One, and so is everyone else.

How to Increase Intelligence

How to increase intelligence:

∞ Playful meditation

∞ Creative expressions of practical compassion

∞ Rigorous listening

∞ Learning the language and rhythms of the dreams that visit us as we sleep

∞ Negotiating with the shadowy aspects of our personalities

∞ Reverently communing with the natural world; conversing with creatures and plants

∞ Unruly, affectionate magick that disrupts the numbing status quo

∞ Playdates with ancestors, angels, deities, spirits, elementals, and fairies

∞ Laughter while fucking

∞ Acting with no ulterior motives

∞ Sharpening our perceptions

∞ Disciplined ecstasy and ecstatic discipline

∞ Gazing at the image in the mirror for extended periods

∞ Experiments to expand our self-definition

∞ Liberating ourselves from our suffering

∞ Helping to liberate others from their suffering

∞ Periodically reviewing the history of our lives

Element 8

If we never change ourselves temporarily into unrecognizable miraculous creatures teeming with strange healing magic and incomprehensible beauty, we may never access the full powers of our soul's code.

If we periodically change ourselves into unrecognizable miraculous creatures teeming with strange healing magic and incomprehensible beauty, we will access the full powers of our soul's code.

Chapter 19

Your Freaky Feral Miracle Splendor
+
My Freaky Feral Miracle Splendor
=
Our Freaky Feral Miracle Splendor

Your Prime Objective

Write this declaration on a piece of paper: "I am mobilizing all the energy and ingenuity and connections I have at my disposal... as well as all the additional energy and ingenuity and connections I can call on and will summon... as I accomplish the following intention:"

Then compose a description of the experience or situation or scenario you're most excited to cultivate for yourself in the coming months—the specific circumstances that will be most meaningful and gratifying and interesting to you.

Karmic Credit Card

The KARMIC CREDIT CARD is issued by the SHAMANIC HACKERS OF KARMIC JUSTICE, a division of Rob Brezsny's FREE WILL ASTROLOGY.

★

The KARMIC CREDIT CARD entitles you to enjoy inside connections and special influence with over 1 million deities, angels, demigods, fairy queens, genies, muses, gnomes, sylphs, undines, friendly ghosts, tree spirits, saints both dead and alive, and kinky kind tricksters.

As your spiritual cyberpunks, the SHAMANIC HACKERS OF KARMIC JUSTICE lobby all the Forces of Fate to furnish you with loopholes in cosmic law.

The KARMIC CREDIT CARD may be used to pay off karmic debts incurred by the following:

- ∞ Rash acts committed while being temporarily disloyal to your deep self
- ∞ Unintentional insults
- ∞ Addiction to stress and overwork
- ∞ Decadent excesses committed out of boredom but not malevolence
- ∞ Self-pitying martyrdom
- ∞ Ignoring your heart's desires
- ∞ Being overly nice and polite
- ∞ Boring Goddess or God

∞ Mistakes made because of exorbitant generosity
∞ Impossible choices made at delicate turning points
∞ Messes made while taking the shortcut to paradise that zips across a corner of hell
∞ Using legacies in ways different from how those who bequeathed them desired
∞ Selling yourself out or denying yourself pleasure
∞ Colluding with manipulative jerks who screwed you over
∞ Behavior that stems from you having served as a guinea pig, scapegoat, or dumping ground for the toxic psychic wastes of other people

The KARMIC CREDIT CARD entitles you to FOUR DAYS OUT OF TIME every calendar year.

Each DAY OUT OF TIME is an exemption from cosmic compulsion; a raucous recess; a grace period filled with the uproarious joy that is only possible when your will is absurdly free.

As a further privilege of owning the KARMIC CREDIT CARD, you will be the focus of an annual marathon meditation session by the SHAMANIC HACKERS OF KARMIC JUSTICE, during which time they will perform the following purifications:
∞ Yank the equivalent of three acres of weeds from your psychic landscape
∞ Scrub away grungy buildup on your halo
∞ Haul away emotional baggage cluttering up your free-form destiny
∞ Wash and dry and fold five loads of your metaphorical

dirty laundry

∞ Scour away $50,000 worth of rumpled money karma.

∞ Carry three pickup trucks' worth of garbage out of your nightmares

To enhance the effectiveness of your KARMIC CREDIT CARD, the SHAMANIC HACKERS OF KARMIC JUSTICE suggest you do the following:

∞ Use every resource at your command to blend what you have to do with what you like to do

∞ Make atonement to people you have hurt or acted superior to

∞ Cultivate gratitude for the gifts and teachings your bad karma has provided

∞ Surrender control over anyone you manipulate

∞ Lose your attachment to minor ego gratifications that distract you from your long-term goals

∞ Give other people the exact blessings you would like them to give you

Caveat:

Although special exemptions are possible, the KARMIC CREDIT CARD may not be used to alleviate cosmic payback incurred by the following acts:

∞ Deliberate cruelty

∞ Premeditated evil

∞ Chronic and unrepentant indulgence in "control freak" behavior

∞ Misadventures that stem from an unconscious belief that suffering is glamorous

∞ Wishing for things you don't need and can't use

∞ Wasting your good karma on inferior pleasures and trivial successes

∞ Blaming others for your failings

∞ Taking anger out on the wrong person

∞ Beguiling someone into loving you and then not loving them back

What Color and Smell and Animal Are 'Free Will Astrology'?

What color is "Free Will Astrology"? If "Free Will Astrology" was an animal, which species would it be? What aroma does "Free Will Astrology" emit?

Below are some readers' responses to those questions.

Sue Major: FWA is a goldenrod-and-mustard-colored friendly wolverine wearing a pair of red wax lips and smelling like linden trees in full bloom with a curious bottom-note of starfish and sea urchins and a wafting of warm gingerbread cooling on an open windowsill.

Sarah V.: FWA is raw umber spilled on seaweed. It's a brown bear at dawn. It's variegated English ivy twined around an optical mouse.

It's a wreath of rosemary on a flaking Mexican door. Cherry blossoms on volcanic ash. Persimmon with ginger ketchup. An orangutan at finishing school.

It's the breath of Josephine Baker's cheetah after the banana dance.

Ron Buswa: I think FWA is a duck—an amazingly adaptable creature equally at home on land, in the water, and in the air.

It smells like fresh pepper straight out of the grinder, because Rob gives us the seeds and we have to do our own work, turning the crank, to add them to our plate.

Cattails: FWA smells like the air after a thunderstorm, for its head-clearing and thought-provoking influences.

KiyoteSong: FWA is the color of grass before someone tells you it's green and the sky before someone tells you blue.

FWA is like the dog that taught me to walk. To me, it was a great black beast with four legs and a broad warm back, something that was more present and dependable in my life than any two-legged animal.

I could lie on it or hang on to it for dear life as it walked slowly and carefully by my side, never whimpering or snapping if I pulled too hard.

The smell of FWA: randy and musky like Capricorn's goat; full of life and mischief and tin cans and someone's payroll check; earthy like great expanses of cattle ranch and wheat fields; and transcendental like a freshly opened package of nag champa incense, the one that comes in the blue and white box with spindly, splintery sticks.

Aimee Ryder: FWA is an ultraviolet eagle wafting on the rose-tinged scent of the winds of change.

KG: FWA is striped in three colors. It's too complex to be one color, and stripes are more fun anyway. FWA's stripes are an exotic Prussian blue, a deep, sultry burgundy, and a wild and free hunter green, in decidedly different diagonal directions like a plaid from a parallel universe.

In the animal kingdom, FWA is a beloved housecat—beautiful, warm, soft and furry, always loving and sweet, yet a good mouser, and exceptionally clever.

FWA smells like the pecan shortbread cookies with a whiff of vanilla that my Grandma Elena always made over the winter holidays.

Unlike Grandma Elena's pecan balls, FWA is available year-round and won't make your clothes too tight if you have it every week.

If FWA made a sound (as a musician, I would want to know what it sounds like), it would be like a Gibson Les Paul and Fender Telecaster jamming with a violin, viola, harpsichord, Uilleann pipes, a treble recorder, and tambourine.

Petunia X.: FWA is a translucent angel-monkey smelling of cedar.

Bird in Flight: FWA has an earthy smell, like when you run berserkly through the forest or careen madly down the trails on a mountain bike and then stop somewhere and put your face to the ground and inhale all the life and sexiness of the earth. That smell.

Hummingbear: FWA is an octopus: many-tentacled (the better to engage you with, my dear), able to shift colors according to mood and circumstances.

Theoretically, it should be a dodecapus, with a tentacle for each sign, but that's not exactly an animal. Eight armfuls of loving suction pads will have to be enough.

As for the smell part, I don't know what an octopus smells like. But if I were trying to mix an incense that has the effects the FWA has, I'd use dragon's blood (for other-worldly vision), copal (for sacred euphoria), patchouli (for hipness), and rose (for cosmic love).

And, as an afterthought, essential oil of orange, because it smells nice and helps the florals blend with the resins. But now that I've thought of that, orange is a color, too. Is FWA an orange octopus? Hmmm.

Cynthia M.: FWA is brought to you by the letter O—the circle of life, with no beginning and no end—just perfect suchness in every moment.

FWA is oleander—I don't know the scent, though I imagine hot, humid nights perfumed with the secret songs of the stars.

FWA is orange-orange—bold, brash, vibrant iconoclast that it is—warm, soothing, healing light that it is.

Gena Y.: As for smell, well, FWA is like baking soda toothpaste, the stuff I use to maintain the useful life of my teeth so I can continue to effectively nourish myself for the rest of my days. It's a stimulating, piquant aroma, and it makes me feel awake.

Misha: When I think of FWA, I get a vision of a hyena jumping up and down in a swimming pool making waves and laughing hysterically at a bar of cream-colored soap bobbing in the ripples.

Mermaid: Free Will Astrology is a sleek jaguar with royal purple and deep garnet glowing from its shiny black body. It exudes an exhilaratingly musky freesia/violet scent and rich vanilla/praline taste.

Jaquith: Free Will Astrology's voice is raucous, but not harsh; brash, but not brutish; disciplined in its excesses, not rigid.

Alana K.: FWA smells like sulfur with a hint of orange blossom, beaver, and red-orange banana skin. Or it could be rain-wet gingko trees in Tokyo. Or maybe the color of the sky at 5:22 on summer solstice standing on a red-rock mesa in Arizona.

Pance: If Free Will Astrology were a colorful, scented animal, it would be a glow-in-the-dark, green-colored ferret that smells like smoldering frankincense.

And if it's not that, then it would be a question the color of lugubriousness that smelled of tomorrow.

Cities Where 'Free Will Astrology' and 'Real Astrology' Have Been Published ♦

Albany, New York

Albuquerque, New Mexico

Anchorage, Alaska

Annapolis, Maryland

Arcata, California

Asheville, North Carolina

Ashland, Oregon

Astoria, Oregon

Athens, Ohio

Atlanta, Georgia

Augusta, Georgia

Austin, Texas

Baltimore, Maryland

Bellingham, Washington

Bend, Oregon

Berlin, Maryland

Birmingham, Alabama

Bloomington, Indiana

Boise, Idaho

Boulder, Colorado

Bozeman, Montana

Broward County, Florida

Buffalo, New York

Burlington, Vermont

Cape Cod, Massachusetts

Carson City, Nevada

Champaign, Illinois

Charleston, South Carolina

Charlotte, North Carolina

Charlottesville, Virginia

Chattanooga, Tennessee

Chicago, Illinois

Chico, California

Chilkat Valley, Alaska

Cleveland, Ohio

Coachella Valley, California

Colorado Springs, Colorado

Columbia, South Carolina

Columbus, Ohio

Costa Mesa, California

Crested Butte, Colorado

Dallas, Texas

Davenport, Iowa

Dayton, Ohio

Daytona Beach, Florida

Denver, Colorado

Des Moines, Iowa

Destin, Florida

Detroit, Michigan

Durango, Colorado

Durham, North Carolina
Easthampton, Massachusetts
Encinitas, California
Erie, Colorado
Eugene, Oregon
Eureka, California
Fairfield County, Connecticut
Flint, Michigan
Fort Worth, Texas
Frederick, Maryland
Fredericksburg, Virginia
French Lick, Indiana
Ft. Collins, Colorado
Fullerton, California
Gainesville, Florida
Galesburg, Illinois
Greensboro, North Carolina
Hartford, Connecticut
Hatfield, Massachusetts
Hawaii Big Island
Helena, Montana
Highland Park, New Jersey
Honolulu, Hawaii
Houston, Texas
Hudson Valley, New York
Huntsville, Alabama
Indianapolis, Indiana
Iowa City, Iowa
Ithaca, New York
Jackson Hole, Wyoming

Jackson, Mississippi
Jacksonville, Florida
Kansas City, Missouri
Knoxville, Tennessee
Lakewood, Washington
Lansing, Michigan
Las Vegas, Nevada
Lexington, Kentucky
Little Rock, Arkansas
Livingston, Montana
London, Kentucky
Long Beach, New Jersey
Los Angeles, California
Louisville, Kentucky
Marin County, California
Marquette, Michigan
Memphis, Tennessee
Mendocino, California
Miami, Florida
Milford, New Jersey
Milwaukee, Wisconsin
Minneapolis, Minnesota
Missoula, Montana
Moab, Utah
Molokai, Hawaii
Monterey, California
Myrtle Beach, South Carolina
Naples, Florida
Nashville, Tennessee
New Haven, Connecticut

New York, New York
Newport News, Virginia
Norfolk, Virginia
Norwalk, Connecticut
Oakland, California
Ocean Pines, Maryland
Ojai, California
Oklahoma City, Oklahoma
Omaha, Nebraska
Orange County, California
Orlando, Florida
Palm Springs, California
Pasadena, California
Pensacola, Florida
Philadelphia, Pennsylvania
Phoenix, Arizona
Pittsburgh, Pennsylvania
Port Huron, Michigan
Portland, Maine
Portland, Oregon
Portsmouth, New Hampshire
Prescott, Arizona
Purchase, New York
Raleigh, North Carolina
Red Lodge, Montana
Reno, Nevada
Richmond, Virginia
Sacramento, California
Salem, Oregon
Salt Lake City, Utah

San Antonio, Texas
San Diego, California
San Francisco, California
San Jose, California
San Luis Obispo, California
Santa Barbara, California
Santa Cruz, California
Santa Fe, New Mexico
Santa Rosa, California
Sarasota, Florida
Savannah, Georgia
Scranton, Pennsylvania
Seattle, Washington
Shreveport, Louisiana
Spokane, Washington
Springfield, Connecticut
Springfield, Illinois
Springfield, Massachusetts
St. Louis, Missouri
Statesboro, Georgia
Surf City, New Jersey
Syracuse, New York
Tacoma, Washington
Tampa, Florida
Telluride, Colorado
Traverse City, Michigan
Tucson, Arizona
Tulsa, Oklahoma
Ventura, California
West Barnstable, Massachusetts

Wheeling, West Virginia
Wilmington, North Carolina
Winston-Salem, North Carolina
Woodland Park, Colorado
Campbellford, Ontario
Edmonton, Alberta
Halifax, Nova Scotia
Hamilton, Ontario
Kitchener, Ontario
London, Ontario
Montreal, Quebec
Ottawa, Ontario
Peace County, Alberta
Perth, New Brunswick
Pouch Cove, Newfoundland
and Labrador
Revelstoke, British Columbia
Saint John, New Brunswick
St. Catherine's, Ontario
St. John's, Newfoundland

and Labrador
Toronto, Ontario
Vancouver, British Columbia
Whistler, British Columbia
Wolfville, Nova Scotia
Amsterdam, Netherlands
Baja, Mexico
Bangkok, Thailand
Caracas, Venezuela
Dublin, Ireland
Finland
Hong Kong
Paris, France
Phnom Penh, Cambodia
Rome, Italy
St. Petersburg, Russia
Singapore
Sydney, Australia
Tokyo, Japan

The Entrepreneur and I

During one of the years I attended the Burning Man festival, an entrepreneur approached me with a proposal: "Your work should be getting out to a bigger audience. People are starving for the message you're putting out. That's why you need me. With my marketing machine, your name could become as recognizable as Deepak Chopra's. Let's build an entertainment conglomerate and hawk a hundred Rob Brezsny-style products."

"Nah," I said. "People come to me seeking sanctuary from hype. They know I won't smack them upside the imagination with relentless sales pitches."

I turned him down. He was puzzled.

Meanwhile, for many years I have gotten regular inquiries from marketers who want to pay me money for putting advertisements on my website or advertorials on my social media sites. I always say no. I have turned down well over $500,000 in ad revenue.

I launched my website in 1995 and have never had a paid ad on it. I've offered over 1,400 of my weekly Free Will Astrology columns for free on that site.

I freely give away two hours' worth of my music on Sound-Cloud. I don't make any money from my YouTube videos. I give away large sections of my books *The Televisionary Oracle* and *Pronoia Is the Antidote for Paranoia*.

Have I been naïve? Overly idealistic? Too pure? Self-sabotaging? Woefully unrealistic?

I do earn a decent living. Many newspapers have published my column weekly for years, and the syndication revenues add up.

I also offer my Expanded Audio Horoscopes and Daily Text-Message Horoscopes, which cost money to use. Some people who draw inspiration from my free written horoscopes also choose to pay for my two other services. Hooray!

My weekly newsletter is free to everyone who wants it, but I also encourage affluent readers to contribute a subscription fee if they feel so moved. Many do!

Book sales have been a modest 95,000 copies, but that income has helped.

Do you know about all my FREE STUFF? There's a list starting on the next page.

Further Connections

If you'd like to explore other aspects of my work, here is a list of resources.

- My weekly newsletter:
  https://Newsletter.FreeWillAstrology.com
- My website:
  https://FreeWillAstrology.com
- My Expanded Audio Horoscopes and Daily Text Message Horoscopes:
  https://RealAstrology.com
- Excerpts from my book *Pronoia Is the Antidote for Paranoia*:
  https://tinyurl.com/FreePronoia
- My entire book *The Televisionary Oracle*:
  https://freewillastrology.com/books/oracle
- My music page:
  https://soundcloud.com/sacreduproar
- More free music:
  https://freewillastrology.com/music/listen
- My three Facebook pages:
  https://bit.ly/BrezFB
  and
  https://www.facebook.com/rob.brezsny
  and
  https://www.facebook.com/oroscopobrezsny
- My Instagram page:
  https://www.instagram.com/robbrezsny/
- My Twitter page:
  https://twitter.com/FreeWillAstro

- My YouTube page:
  https://tinyurl.com/BrezsnyYouTube
- Audio and Video Interviews:
  https://tinyurl.com/InterviewRob
  and
  https://tinyurl.com/RobNewDimensions
  and
  https://tinyurl.com/SiriusBrezsny
  and
  https://tinyurl.com/SiriusBrezsny2
- My Tumblr page:
  https://freewillastrology.tumblr.com/archive
- My Amazon Author page:
  https://tinyurl.com/BrezsnyAmazon
- Wikipedia page about my band:
  https://tinyurl.com/WEWwiki
- The homepage for my band:
  https://freewillastrology.com/music
- Want some inspiration as you compose your romantic invitations? Go here: https://bit.ly/LoveAd

Below is a partial list of my audio offerings, including music and spoken word.
- The blasphemously reverent "Prayer for Us" is here:
  https://tinyurl.com/PrayerToUs
- Read the lyrics at:
  https://bit.ly/OurPrayer
- Do you dare gaze into the abyss of happiness?
  Go to https://tinyurl.com/GazeIntoAbyss

- Maybe it's a good time to think about Shadow Blessings: https://tinyurl.com/ShadowBlessings
- All of us are born geniuses, but most of us have been de-geniused by the grind. Want to re-genius yourself? Guidance: https://tinyurl.com/ReGeniusYourself
- Thousands of things go right for you every single day. Listen: https://tinyurl.com/GloryInTheHighest
- Welcome to the Beauty and Truth Lab: https://tinyurl.com/BeautyTruthLab
- You're invited to celebrate Unhappy Hour, a ritual that gives you a license to whine and howl. Go here: https://tinyurl.com/HealingSadness
- How much of the world can you love: https://tinyurl.com/WorldKiss
- Want to get married to yourself? The ritual's here: https://tinyurl.com/YouCanMarryYourself
- Meditate on why this is a perfect moment: https://tinyurl.com/PerfectTrueMoment
- Whenever we say "you asshole" in the future, what we will really mean is "my beautiful friend": https://tinyurl.com/BlessedWithBliss

'Free Will Astrology' in Translation

"Free Will Astrology" has been published in newspapers that have translated it into Italian, French, Dutch, Japanese, and Spanish.

Since 2004, "Free Will Astrology" has been translated into Italian and published in the national Italian publication *Internazionale*. It's at https://www.internazionale.it/oroscopo/.

Since 2015, "Free Will Astrology" has been translated into French and published in the French publication *Courrier International*. It's at https://www.courrierinternational.com/horoscope.

From 2019 to 2023, "Free Will Astrology" was translated into Dutch and published in the Dutch publication *360 Magazine*. Archives are at https://tinyurl.com/BrezsnyDutch.

Since 2018, "Free Will Astrology" has been translated into Japanese and published in the Japanese publication *Courrier Japon*. It's at https://tinyurl.com/BrezsnyJapan.

From 1996 to 2000, "Free Will Astrology"—at that time called "Real Astrology"—was translated into Spanish and published in the Venezuelan publication *Urbe*.

Frequently Asked Questions

Can Rob cast my chart and do a chart interpretation for me?

I love doing personal charts, but I don't have enough time to do such work. I'm busy being a writer and musician.

The astrologer I recommend is my wife, Ro Loughran. Her website is at https://www.roloughran.com. We have studied and discussed astrology together since 1988. We share many perspectives in our understandings about the symbolic meanings of the signs, the houses, and the sun, moon, and planets.

Ro utilizes a blend of well-trained intuition, emotional warmth, and technical proficiency in horoscope interpretation. She is skilled at exploring the mysteries of your life's purpose and nurturing your connection with your inner wisdom.

In addition to decades of astrological experience, Ro has been a licensed psychotherapist since 2000. This enables her to integrate psychological insight with the cosmological perspective that astrology offers.

Ro is based in California, but can do phone consultations and otherwise work with you regardless of geographic boundaries.

Why are the weekly horoscopes updated on Tuesday or Wednesday instead of Monday?

For years I have written my column for alternative newsweeklies, most of which publish on Wednesdays or Thursdays.

The paper that carries your column doesn't advertise your

expanded audio horoscopes. How do I access them?

To hear my Expanded Audio horoscopes, which provide a deeper examination of the cosmic omens shaping your life, sign up and log in at https://RealAstrology.com.

The audio horoscopes are available for $7 apiece, or at a discount for multiple purchases.

The new horoscopes are posted early Tuesday morning.

I also create daily text message horoscopes called Sunbursts. They are available at https://RealAstrology.com.

What are the images that accompany your horoscopes on your website?

Sylvi Alli and Antero Alli created the images featured next to my weekly horoscopes. Find out more about their work at https://tinyurl.com/AnteroAlli.

I was born on a day when the sun changes sign, i.e., on the cusp. Which sun sign am I?

Which sign your sun falls in will depend on your exact time of birth. To cast your personal chart for free and determine the placement of your sun, go to https://tinyurl.com/ChartCast.

Can you recommend books and websites on astrology for beginners?

Experiential Astrology: From the Map to the Territory, by Antero Alli

You're Every Sign: Using Astrology's Keys to Create Success, Love

and Happiness, by Phyllis Firak-Mitz

Intuitive Astrology: Follow Your Best Instincts to Become Who You Always Intended to Be, by Elizabeth Rose Campbell

High School Astrology, by Arisa Victor

How to Read Your Astrological Chart: Aspects of the Cosmic Puzzle, by Donna Cunningham

Soul Centered Astrology: A Key to Your Expanding Self, by Alan Oken

Astrology, Karma & Transformation: The Inner Dimensions of the Birth Chart, by Stephen Arroyo

Astrology of Personality: A Reformulation of Astrological Concepts and Ideals in Terms of Contemporary Psychology and Philosophy, by Dane Rudhyar

The Inner Sky, by Steven Forrest

For lots of useful information about astrology, go to https://tinyurl.com/AstrologyTheory. It's written by L. M. P. McPherson.

Oracular Homework #114

ARIES: Name a good old thing you would need to give up so as to get a great new thing.

TAURUS: Give five reasons why you're a gorgeous creature.

GEMINI: Identify the people in your life who have made you real to yourself.

CANCERIAN: Was there a time you cried because of unreasonable joy? When a cathartic epiphany made you sob? When you wept out of compassion for others' suffering? When you bawled in response to divine intervention?

LEO: What's the best surprise you could give yourself?

VIRGO: "The only thing standing between you and your goal," writes author Jordan Belfort, "is the bullshit story you tell yourself as to why you can't achieve it." What's your bullshit story?

★

LIBRA: You dream of monsters, robot warriors, extraterrestrial ghosts, and zombie vampires. But they're your allies! They protect you and help you defeat your real enemies, who are smiling pretenders wearing white hats. Tell the story of what happens.

SCORPIO: What part of the past are you still in bondage to? What can you do to free yourself?

SAGITTARIUS: Anaïs Nin wrote, "You cannot save people. You can only love them. You can't transform them, you can only console them." Give an example from your own experience.

CAPRICORN: In 1963, the Soviet Union's government decided that feisty, rebellious young poet Joseph Brodsky was not making sufficient contributions to society. He was sentenced to do hard labor at an unheated farmhouse north of the Arctic Circle.

Those 18 months were a turning point in a career that won him a Nobel Prize for Literature. Each night he spent hours reading poetry, learning English, and honing his craft as a writer.

Have you experienced a comparable opportunity? Is there one available now or will there be in the future?

AQUARIUS: What would you be like if you were the opposite of yourself?

PISCES: Finish this sentence "One thing that may interfere with me being fully myself is _____."

If we never feel the intimate rapture that comes from knowing we are made of earth and sun, we blaspheme the earth and sun.

If we ever feel the intimate rapture that comes from knowing we are made of earth and sun, we bless the earth and sun.

Coda

My Sacred Blood and Bones and Nerves
+
Your Sacred Blood and Bones and Nerves
=
Our Sacred Blood and Bones and Nerves

Blurb Jubilee

If novelist Frank McCourt were still alive, I might ask him to provide the same blurb for my book that he gave to three different authors: "You will claw yourself with pleasure while reading this book."

Truthfully, though, I would prefer that my readers caress or hug or kiss themselves while reading this book. Or caress or hug or kiss a person or animal they love while reading this book. I'm all in favor of perpetrating as much joy, pleasure, and sweetness as our beloved earth allows.

Since Frank McCourt has joined our ancestors on the other side of the veil, I have been compelled to seek praise-soaked testimonials from other sources. As I began this quest, a central question was whether I should ask famous people or non-famous people or both.

I decided on both. There are millions of non-famous folks who create their lives as artful masterpieces of service, adventure, and integrity. Just because they aren't celebrities doesn't mean they are less magnificent in my eyes.

Below is an array of souls who have expressed how my horoscopes have affected them. The first few are famous in the usual sense of that word, while the rest are famous primarily to me and the people they help and inspire.

I've been a big fan of Rob Brezsny's work for half my life now, and as an author myself, a little jealous of him, too. That's because he can express in ten words what it takes me a thousand words to say. On top of that, he manages to throw in a comedy act and a Zen meditation session. He's a magician.

Astrology's star has risen dramatically in the past three decades. I'm convinced tht it would not have happened without Rob. With his popular columns, he's reached millions of people and, more importantly, managed to make a connection between two words that were previously never heard together—astrology and intelligence. And while were at it, let's add funny, literate, and profound.

—Steven Forrest, author of *The Inner Sky*

The memoir revelations of elder Poet/Astrologer Rob Brezsny's *Life as an Oracle* is an open door to a Master Class on living life to its fullest. This magical tome invites courageous readers on a deep dive into the esoteric mysteries embedded in daily existence.

The good doctor Brezsny's astrological prescriptions can alleviate the banality so many are burdened by with fresh images and poetics reframing the cosmic within the mundane and the mundane within the cosmic.

I'm wondering if the whole astrology thing is a ruse, an elaborate front, to veil his true identity as the reincarnation of the 13th-century Sufi mystic, Rumi.

—Antero Alli, author of *Experiential Astrology: From the Map to the Territory* and *Sacred Rites: Journal Entries of a Gnostic Heretic*

Astrology is an old means of telling stories about who we are and what might happen and how human life is connected to the cosmos. I find the words that people like Rob Brezsny come up with quite pleasant and sometimes useful. Well, in his case, delightful.

—author Rebecca Solnit, writing on Facebook

I told my therapist how reading the book *Astrology is Real* is affecting me. It's casting a spell, a wisely loving intervention between myself and the way the world looks and behaves. I seem luckier, happier, more at ease with the strange way my life is unfolding.

As I talked, my eyes filled with tears.

"In a year of therapy, I've never seen you so moved," my therapist said. "It sounds like the book is being received by you as what some might call a 'direct transmission.'"

I agreed. "Yes. I've heard it called *shaktipat*—like what I received from Papaji while interviewing him in India in 1993."

—author, photographer, monologist Jeff Greenwald

I'm sending big thanks to Rob Brezsny for the most literary astrology ever!

—poet Jane Hirshfield

Brilliant! Absorbing! Wildly useful! Rob Brezsny gets my nomination for best prophet in a starring role. He's a script doctor for the soul.

—Marisa Tomei, Academy Award-winning actor

I have been a fan of Rob Brezsny for years.

—Marianne Williamson, author, spiritual leader, political activist

I am deeply inspired by the illuminated words of Rob Brezsny. He is a word wizard for the soul. Evidence of the brilliance I find in his astrology column: I consistently read every sign, not just my own.

—SARK, author/artist

Rob Brezsny has transmuted the art for all of us poet astrologers who have come later. He has transformed everyone who has ever read him. He was already changing me from the back pages of the weekly newspapers long before I had a clue what astrology even was.

—Ariana Reines, poet and astrologer

Rob Brezsny's prose is poetic, circular, dancing, combining the narrative voices of Anais Nin, Tom Robbins, and David Ignatow.

—*Rain Taxi*

Brezsny holds his own place next to cultural shamans like Robert Anton Wilson, Timothy Leary, William Burroughs, and Ken Kesey.
    —Popmatters.com
    https://tinyurl.com/BrezsnyPopMatters

Rob Brezsny is a Culture Hero.
    —*Utne* magazine

Rob's oracles are inspiring, thought-provoking, and comforting all at the same time.
    —Suzanne Sifri

I love you, Rob Brezsny's Free Will Astrology! I discovered you back in 2005 while living in Brooklyn. My fiery Puerto Rican neighbor had a best friend—another fiery Puerto Rican. They introduced me to your work, and you captured me instantly. Your upside-down-world thinking made me laugh and also ponder. I was communing with a quirky, wise wizard that tickled my heart.
    —Jamie Okubo

I so appreciate Rob's courageous and playful exploration of our world all while maintaining a soundness of mind and rootedness in truth and equality.
    —Richard Adoradio

Fact, intuition, and myth all have valid roles in our shared reality. Rob's work weaves these three together into a useful map for traversing the terra incognita of our lives. He is a highly skilled Metaphorist.

—Johnny Dwork

I truly think Rob's particular brand of "FIND WHAT WORKS FOR YOU" wisdom has informed me more than any other spiritual leader. I love the depth and breadth of his influences, the sense of delight and whimsy, the care and inclusion and love for his audience. SO glad his mama made him.

—Eleanor Cathleen O'Brien

Even decades into having a public voice, Rob's messaging feels refreshing and vital. I'm so glad I have someone weirder than me to look up to.

I grew up reading his horoscopes, starting back when I was in eighth grade grabbing free copies of the *Stranger* in Seattle. His ideas have shaped and guided my life.

—Vida Rose

Bravo! I thank Rob for sharing his work with us. He inspires us to be fully ourselves and bloom in our own creative way.

—Antola Simonetti

Rob Brezsny is one of the most prolific, far-seeing, artistic writers

of our time. It is a blessing that he shares his gifts with humanity. Bonus! He approaches magnificence while staying humble.
     —Karen Koyne

Rob Brezsny drops wisdom bombs like it's no big deal, thus concealing the enormous power of his insight by laying it out for all to see. Tricky!
     —David Baum

Rob is our modern-day Rumi.
     —Peter Stenshoel

Rob's words and the ideas he shares from other great minds are inspiring. It's alternately comforting and challenging. There's always something that cuts through all the noise and causes me to reflect or re-evaluate just as often as it gives me confirmation and acceptance.
     —John Nelka

It's amazing how Rob speaks to so many people in so many different situations.
     —Sandra Thomas-Comenole

I get Rob Brezsny's weekly newsletter, and I have to make time to read and process it all. I often skip it because it almost ALWAYS makes me cry, connecting at a deep soul level. I have to be ready!

But when I do make the time, and really dig into the magic he shares, I receive amazing gifts and endless support for my continuing evolution.

—Julie Cohen

Rob is on the frontlines of the consciousness wars—a job that would eat me alive. God bless him! Hope he keeps it up.

—David Larstein

Rob Brezsny has been an influence and a spiritual benefactor of mine for years. His writings are profound and funny, and he seems to have a direct channel to the deepest levels of consciousness.

—Bob Chapra

Rob is a fellow spiritual traveler who weekly offers expert, poignant, and generous information, laced together with creativity, wit, and compassion, to everyone who has eyes to see with and ears to hear with.

—Karen Lindsay

Rob has kept me true to my compass when I was surrounded by magnets. All other guides told me my compass must be broken, but he has looked me in the soul and reminded me that it is just right. I cannot tell the world how much I owe this man. I have shared his work with so many, and never have I been met with

less than complete, awe-struck gratitude.
　　—Kanta Bosniak

Rob delivers his message with such amusing eloquence that it
flies under the radar of the conscious mind's defenses against
enlightenment and common sense.

　　As an author and person with a lifetime spiritual practice, I
am awed by his command of his art. As a hypnotherapist, I can
describe his work in the jargon of my trade: it "misdirects attention." What this means is that it directs attention where it belongs,
toward gratitude, by using the distraction of extreme reading
pleasure. The meaning slips in while you're busy smiling.

　　"Freewill Astrology" transcends its genre. Working as a surprisingly on-target astrology forecast, it's also simultaneously
poetry, a self-inquiry tool, and darshan. The latter is a Sanskrit
word that refers to meeting with a spiritual teacher or listening
to him/her speak with a group.
　　—Jessica Coppedge

Rob Brezsny is one of the greatest minds of our time!

　　I don't have a clue how he's able to turn out so much on-target copy week after week in his Free Will Astrology, but I sure
look forward to getting his weekly email of astrological insights.

　　Over the years, his writing has had a profound effect upon me.

　　Probably, the single most important line of his I've repeated
to others countless times is "the importance of avoiding people's
personal hell because it's too expensive for your imagination."

　　I give Rob my highest recommendation for his ability to inspire others with his extraordinarily positive attitude and motivation to make the world a better place!

—Laura Dawson

Rob produces the least self-conscious, most entertaining weekly horoscope available anywhere. He tears away the myths and half-truths to which we have become accustomed, and he replaces these with edgy, incisive new and exciting myths and half-truths. Rob always comes through with the highest level of reality that I can accept.

—Wolf Halton

Rob Brezsny is one the most innovative philosophers of our time.

—Phiam Ash

I love Rob Brezsny's horoscopes. They are subversive and uplifting at once! A balance between what is possible and what is.

—Laurie Burdon

There are some great thinkers sometimes categorized in the "New Age" movement who do not collude with the spiritual bypassing that reinforces economic social stratification. Jeff Brown and Rob Brezsny come to mind.

— Rachael Rice

I want the humble power to make Rob Brezsny know he has made himself immortal with Free Will Astrology. He is one of those geniuses who will be appreciated 100 years from now for having at once both embodied and captured the zeitgeist of our time.

Yeah, I know, his is just an astrology column. And it's not. It's no fucking big deal. He's not saving the world. He's creating the world.

—Sarah Edelman

I've told people that if humankind is still here in the 25th century, it will be because of Rob Brezsny.

—Jim Shea

What a demented, naive, superlatively beautiful soul Rob Brezsny has. I want to thank him for making me feel better than crap with his flowery prosetry.

—Rebecca Miriam Rustin

Thank you to Rob! I have felt the Love he has sent out since my early teens. Great guidance. He introduced me to worlds of self-discovery, feminine wisdom, and the study of psychology and the unconscious.

—Amy Reynolds

I've been reading Rob's work since college days starting around 1989—*Santa Barbara Independent*—and I can say his holy tweak, his lens of the human story, has given me consistent insight and

made me feel less alone for most of my adult life! I'm so grateful!!
—David Simon-Baker

Rob has been rocking my world with his erudite metaphors and analogies since college in the '90s. I love him for his insistent spirit of evolving no matter what.
—Lisa Elin

I thank Rob sincerely for the blessings he has bestowed and for the support he has provided after all these years. Not a week goes by that I am not excited to see his newsletter show up. It has been a long companion along the many roads I have traveled. I thank him with the heights of integrity and with the spirit of the ages. We are all so very grateful for his service.
—Ryan Shortill

I started following Rob when I was 18. I have been reading his horoscopes for 20 years! They have been a constant guidepost in my own evolution. I stop people at work on Tuesdays who happen to be near my cube and read them their horoscope written by him! Thanks so much to Rob for his brilliant writing and cosmic insights.
—Nicole Penick

Rob has revolutionized the genre. I never cease to be delighted when I find out that this or that new acquaintance has been a follower of his column for years or decades. Many are people I would

never expect to be open-minded about astrology or even philosophy and spirituality.
— Dave Ream

Rob is one of the only people that feel as fresh and as current and as relevant as the day I first discovered him on the other side of the country about 15 years ago! Honestly, his longevity is a testament to his authenticity! Soooooo grateful for him!
— Nicola Behrman

Thanks to Rob for sticking with his passion. I've been reading his column for over 20 years. I love the unique and creative way he infuses literature, history, and psychological themes into each horoscope that takes the reader to a whole other dimension.
— Angela Sonia

I've been looking forward to reading Rob's beautifully written horoscopes as soon as they come out every week for years. And I LOVE hearing his warm, wise, humorous voice on the audio horoscopes every week, too. He is a gem. Shine on, Rob!
— Anahita Mosallai

I have been loving Rob's horoscopes for decades. Since 1994 when I first learned of them. Truly amazing that he keeps them so fresh and so accurate and helpful!
— Tauna Houghton

There were only three reasons for me to buy the *Village Voice* for all those years: Michael Musto's gossip, Dan Savage's advice column, and Rob Brezsny's horoscopes. All three were required. The rest was bonus material.

—Lisa A. Claudio

A dear friend turned me on to Rob's horoscopes in an obscure little paper in Montana many years ago. We've raised our children, gone through catastrophes, fought with each other, made up, lived the tough and tender life. And an ongoing thread has been Rob's writings. Thank you, sir.

—Debra Spear

If it wasn't for Rob's guidance, I'd be off into a not-so-healthy direction. Yes, he has helped me cast off the negative interpretations of superstitious astrology.

—Saralinda Spinner

I am completely in love with Rob's mind. My heart flies at the sound of his words. He never fails to remind me of who I am. Thank you, sir, for being a contagious carrier of truth, beauty, and freedom.

—Sunnie Andreu

I giggle out loud and cry silently for the beauty Rob brings out in his words, which evoke healing volcanic eruptions in my soul. He sees the truth of the matter and ejaculates it around like pollen in the wind or the male seahorse as he grunts out thousands of miniature baby seaponies.

I don't want to forget the torrential outpouring of data that I find important enough to take notes on and to use in other situations. I love it. Thank you very much, Rob.

—Dianne Brown

I send links to all my friends and associates who I'm sure will find in Rob's oracles as much inspiration and soulful laughter as I do.

As far as what Rob's writing is like, the two comparable writers that come to mind for me are: Rumi and Mary Daly, the feminist philosopher.

Why Mary Daly? For her ability to really set my mind on fire with her innovative thinking and her word play.

And Rumi, for his authentic and ecstatic expression of the Divine Cosmic Mojo Powers of the Universe running through him.

The blend of these two, mixed with one of the most sacred of healing tools in anyone's medicine bag—humor—is how I would describe Rob's writing.

—Laura Donham

Every week I read Rob's column and my individual horoscope. Every week I want to send him a thank-you note and good vibes to make him happy because he has reconnected my intellect with the immortal parts of me.

—Emily Terrell

Rob is such a lovely soul for encouraging us so dizzily to feast on cosmic candy bars, presenting our challenges and obstacles as charmed events, singing about change as such a blessing to us, and for having such a rip-roaring time with words and sentiments. Rob is honey in the big tea.

—Lara Justine

Rob Brezsny is one of the great universal antennae. Excellent broadcast, the best reception, and I love the message.

—Poetessa61

Rob is a literary hero of mine with his eloquence and his spot-on divinations.

—Momo_dbz_frostafarian

Every Tuesday for years, I read my "Free Will Astrology" horoscopes in the *Village Voice* and was always astounded. Not because they seemed to be a prediction of what my future had in store for me and not because I used them as a guide on how to live my life. In fact, his words seemed more like a confirmation of what was in my heart. A "putting into words" that which I had previously been unable to do.

—Stephanie Argyros

Limitless Gratitude

Astrology Is Real is a collaborative effort. My work to bring it to life has succeeded because of a benevolent conspiracy of helpers and inspirers.

My luminous thanks go out to the multitudes of readers who have taught me how to be the oracle they needed.

My gleeful reverence and rowdy celebration also flow freely to the thousands of magnificent creators throughout history who have educated me about the art of being a soulful human.

Reams of additional assistance have cascaded my way, as well. My friend Paul Hersh has provided exceptional editing and logistical support. With input from me, he also did the interior design of this book. I like to call him a versatile virtuoso. He's at paulhersh9@gmail.com.

Literary consultant and neurodiversity advocate Emily Shurr provided additional editing expertise. She's a Queen of Emotional Intelligence who is also a brilliant thinker.

Graphic artist Sean George has been another key player. He was resourceful and ingenious in helping to create the book cover design. He's at seanrichardgeorge@gmail.com.

The art for both the front and back covers of the book comes from multi-disciplinary creator Elena Ray. Her art and photography stir my soul! They are focused on the holistic arts and the people who practice them. She can be found in Joshua Tree, California, and online at https://elenaray.photoshelter.com/.

I dwell in the Secret Sanctuary of the Most High—and so do you